D0378533

HAVE YOU NO SHAME?

*And Other
Regrettable Stories*

Rachel Shukert

VILLARD ⓥ NEW YORK

For Ben

Contents

One   **Nazis in the Walls** *In which I valiantly defend myself and my loved ones from the brutal cancer bent on the destruction of our people, ruin the wall treatments in my bedroom, and deeply worry my mother.*   3

Two   **The City on the Edge of Whenever** *In which the Shukert family takes a holiday, and an age-old query is answered.*   25

Three   **The Russians Are Coming** *In which I generously place my considerable intellectual and personal resources at the disposal of two Jewish waifs from the newly disbanded Soviet Union, and am rewarded with a glimpse into the passionate Russian soul.*   49

Four   **A Very Goyische Christmas** *In which I reminisce fondly on the heartwarming holiday traditions of my all-American Midwestern childhood in the manner of Jean Shepherd's classic "A Christmas Story," if Ralphie Parker and his family were self-loathing Jews instead of Indiana farm people. Also, I am vomited upon by a very old man.*   73

Five   **Typical Bat Mitzvah Speech, United States, c. 1992–1995** *In which a crack team of Chinese ethnohistorians and paleontologists present their take on this ancient tribal custom, aided by the archeological find of the thirty-first century.*   90

Six   **For the Good and Welfare** *In which I discover and examine
           the peculiar mating rituals of the Jewish youth group and make
           my mother very happy.*   107

Seven   **A Lot of People Are Virgins** *In which I offer and request
           sexual advice from a very high-ranking government official.*   128

Eight   **On the Question of My Obscurity** *In which I recount my
           theatrical triumphs on the stages of Omaha, and meet defeat in
           the dorm rooms of New York.*   142

Nine   **The Anorexic's Cookbook** *In which I offer hard-won tips to
           other aspiring anorexics, ponder the ubiquity of kittens in modern
           health care, and become the unwilling victim of a particularly
           nasty gynecological procedure.*   171

Ten   **A Nice Girl Like You** *In which I venture bravely into
           the job market of a changed and sobered New York City, am
           insulted by querulous gays, asked personal questions by a talking
           sock, and find myself otherwise ill equipped for the world of
           commerce.*   191

Eleven   **Have You No Shame?** *In which a family tragedy brings me
           back to the cattle-strewn bosom of the heartland.*   221

           Acknowledgments   257

Have You No Shame?

One

Nazis in the Walls

I was quite small, perhaps eight, when it occurred to me how deeply I disliked the other children. I mean, it wasn't as if I wanted them dead or anything; it just didn't seem as though we had much to say to one another. I had made an effort when we first moved to the neighborhood, dutifully ringing doorbells and dragging the sprinkler from the garage and setting it up on the lawn, but one can spend only so many afternoons throwing dirt clods at passing cars before the soul cries out for something finer. I'm sure that murdering fireflies and smearing the glowing intestines in a lurid streak across the grass with one's shoe has its own rewards, but none that compare to an evening spent indoors, memorizing the recitative to an obscure Gilbert and Sullivan operetta and congratulating oneself on one's own superiority. Peering out my bedroom window with bemused disdain at the local gang of young ruffians, vulgar Philistines who had probably never heard of Derek Jacobi, as they pelted one another with water balloons or gleefully terrorized some delicate future interior decorator, I invented games of my own. Solitary, secretive games, tailored especially to my peculiar fixations. For example:

PEOPLE WHO WOULD HIDE US FROM THE NAZIS

Naturally, this wasn't my only game. There was "How Many Times," a favorite in which I would select a video—generally something with an epic feel—*Gone with the Wind, The Ten Commandments, Doctor Zhivago*—and, aided by a potent combination of candy corn and DayQuil, see how many times in a row I could watch it before I began to hallucinate. I would read the collected works of Tennessee Williams out loud to an audience of inanimate objects: stuffed animals, Barbies, and my sister, four years younger and as yet unable to protest. Teddy Snowcrop and Marty the Monkey still cite my performance as Blanche DuBois as *the* indelible reading of the decade, and while Mr. Popple called my Amanda Wingfield a "miscast, halfhearted tribute to Laurette Taylor that bears little resemblance to the original," my "electric and electrifying" portrayal of Alma Winemiller in *Summer and Smoke* was, in a word, "definitive." (At press time, my sister could not be reached for comment.)

But far and away my favorite way to spend another long afternoon indoors was to curl up with my blanket, a legal pad, and a two-liter bottle of Diet Coke and make my special lists.

1. The Petersons next door
2. The Begleys across the street (first choice—pinball machine in basement)
3. Mrs. Olsen from school
4. Ms. Koons from school (start coming in with my math homework actually finished, instead of copying answers from board when we check in class)
5. Julie from ice skating (find out last name)

And so on. Sometimes, if she was in the mood, my mother gave me a hand.

"The *Nagels*?" she shrieked. "Are you kidding me? The Nagels would own *slaves* if they could."

"The Nagels give out king-sized Snickers bars on Halloween!"

"The Nagels belong to the NRA and go to that church off Dodge Street where they had Jerry Falwell speak. Cross them off the list."

I crossed the Nagels off the list on account of them being slave-owning, gun-toting Nazis.

My mother began to enjoy herself. "Your little friend Julie? Honey, I know how much you like each other, but that mother of hers would spread her legs for the first SS man that bought her a goddamn beer."

With this I could not argue.

"How about your friend Gretchen's parents? Aren't they Quakers or Mennonites or something? They'd probably do it, if they haven't been rounded up with the Jehovah's Witnesses." She scanned the list again, tapping her teeth together gently. "Hmmm. I don't know if the Petersons are such a good idea."

"You don't think they'd hide us? You gave them the key to our house! *Why would you give our keys to people who want us dead?*"

She sighed. "The Petersons are wonderful neighbors. But they have, what, seventeen, eighteen dogs?"

Another good point. We're not really pet people.

"Five, I think."

"Right. I'll take my chances with Auschwitz."

While my mother busied herself in the kitchen preparing the evening meal of spaghetti, fruit salad, and American-cheese slices fashioned into the shapes of menorahs, shofars, and dreidels with her treasured set of holiday cookie cutters (this is what I ate for eighteen years, and my husband wonders why I'm reluctant to try things like organ meats), I began my next list.

WHAT TO PACK WHEN FLEEING FROM NAZIS

Food, of course: Ziploc bags of Cheerios and Skittles, apple juice boxes, and cans of Diet Coke from the pantry. Family photographs—I'd want images of my annihilated relatives to occupy a place of honor at Yad Vashem.[†] A few suitably depressing items of clothing and, finally, books. The books were the most important. Even an activity as challenging as fleeing the Gestapo was bound to include some downtime, and the titles I packed were chock-full of helpful hints, sure to help me out of any jam or rat-infested crawlspace under an abandoned Warsaw building where I and three others lay hidden, eating rotten potato peels and creeping in the dead of night to relieve ourselves in the frozen sewers. I speak, of course, of the genre known as Young Adult Holocaust literature, a body of work specifically designed to remind Jewish children that no matter how safe they might feel, there will always be those who wish to destroy them. As one perspicacious young reader observed in his "Kid's Review" (in the name of research, I browsed a few such tomes on Amazon recently): "Would you want to be a jew when you are getting ready to be killed by the germans I wouldn't."

There was *Touch Wood: A Girlhood in Occupied France* by

[†] Welcome to the feature of this book entitled "A Note to Our Gentile Friends"! In the spirit of cross-cultural dialogue, this feature, denoted by the symbol of the cross instead of the customary asterisk, will hereafter appear when we deem a reference or joke sufficiently "Jew-y" to require elucidation. Now, Yad Vashem is the Holocaust remembrance museum and memorial in Israel, which houses one of the most extensive collections of Holocaust memorabilia in the world: photographs, Nazi records, and many valuable German collectibles of the time, such as soap made from Jews, lamps with Jew-skin shades, and a large collection of illustrated anti-Semitic propaganda, featuring cartoons of gorgeous blond children in lederhosen and dirndls being menaced by grotesque caricatures of monstrous, threatening Jews, many of whom look disturbingly like Harvey Weinstein. Visiting Yad Vashem is an incredibly affecting, emotional, and often cathartic experience, unless you just don't buy the whole Holocaust thing, in which case it's still worth a visit, just to marvel at the unparalleled scope of Jewish ingenuity. No wonder AIPAC (America's Pro-Israel Lobby) has all those hapless Christian senators under its gnarled, clawlike Jew thumb—am I right?

Renée Roth-Hano, outlining how to pass as a convent-educated Catholic. I learned the appropriate times to cross oneself (out of fear, reverence, or superstition), invoke a saint (for a lost object, a difficult problem, or when beset by a pack of thieves), and that Frenchmen who refer to Jews as "wily Israelites" are less virulently anti-Semitic than those who prefer the more traditional "filthy Christ-killers." *The Island on Bird Street* by Uri Orlev taught me how to burrow under the ghetto wall, how to keep and shoot a gun, and that the only person you can really trust is your pet mouse. And in *Number the Stars* by Lois Lowry, I discovered the importance of being Danish.

Such tales of woe were plentiful, yet unlike their real-life counterparts, these brave, benighted children, these Henryks and Hannahs and Boleks and Shmuliks, rarely wound up in Auschwitz. They might lose all their earthly possessions, be assaulted by classmates and teachers shouting racial epithets, even have parents or younger siblings murdered before them (all events deemed appropriate for young readers and beneficial to the formation of their Jewish identities), but clearly the experience of a death camp, even fictionalized, was just too scary. There was, however, one notable exception: *The Devil's Arithmetic* by Jane Yolen.

It was like a dare, that book. To have read it—not just to have checked it out from the library and stared at the cover, paralyzed with fear for three or four days, but to have actually *read* it—was a kind of status symbol. It marked you as a force to be reckoned with, a deranged loose cannon, the kind of kid who would stick her hand in a tank of piranhas or say "Bloody Mary" three times in the mirror at midnight with a death wish in her eyes. The others would whisper about you in car pool before they picked you up on the first day of school, like you were Dennis Hopper. *Don't mess with her. She's crazy. Loco. Read* The Devil's Arithmetic *cover to cover and ain't been the same since.*

While the film adaptation starring Kirsten Dunst has

somewhat deflated its epic creepiness, *The Devil's Arithmetic* is probably the most frightening book ever written for children. It's certainly the most frightening book I've ever read. The chilling premise is this: Hannah Stern, a modern thirteen-year-old girl, prefers the company of Gentile friends to studying for her Bat Mitzvah and is weary of visiting her elderly grandfather, a semi-catatonic concentration camp survivor who spends his days parked in front of the Hitler—I mean, the History—Channel, weeping uncontrollably. "I'm tired of remembering!" she exclaims. Well, as every Jewish child who has had his Hebrew school class visited by an itinerant representative of the Anti-Defamation League knows, *he who does not remember history is condemned to repeat it.* I think it's printed on the mini-Frisbees they hand out after they've finished terrifying you. For Hannah, with her casual disregard for the suffering of her elders (and at thirteen, she should really know better), this concept will take a particularly vivid form. Upon opening the door for Elijah at her grandparents' Passover seder (to which she has come *grudgingly*—bad girl! *Bad JEWISH GIRL!*), she feels a strange breeze across her face and is mysteriously whisked away to . . . *the magical land of Birkenau!*

The fish-out-of-water/new-kid-in-school scenario is very common to children's literature, playing on a child's fear of strangeness, loneliness, of not belonging. Most of these stories, however, do not feature Josef Mengele as a supporting character. But eventually Hannah, with a little help from her fellow inmates, masters the camp rules for survival—basic bowl-and-potato etiquette, exploiting the lesbian tendencies of the female guards, and of course, "never stand next to someone with a *G* in her number. *G* means *Greek*, and the Greeks don't last long"—only to discover that such rules are merely a superstitious construct devised by the prisoners to delude themselves that they can somehow subvert, or at least delay, the inevitable, and lo, the ungrateful little JAP gets sent to the gas chamber. Ha! That'll learn her!

But lucky for Hannah, instead of paralyzing her central nervous system as she claws futilely at the walls with her fingernails until finally suffocating to death in agony, the gas transports her safely back to her own time like three clicks of a pair of ruby slippers, sadder, wiser, and presumably more willing to call her grandparents once in a while. Maybe even come over, spend a little time, would it kill her? No, it wouldn't. Typhoid, sadistic medical experiments, the hungry Rottweilers when you get off the cattle car, that's what kills you. Bubbe and Zayde only want to see you once in a while, is that such a crime?

The message was hardly lost on me. And as I practiced taking apart the showerhead to check for Zyklon B pellets before I turned it on, I noted to myself that if anyone was going to open the door for Elijah at the seder, it was going to be my sister. She was almost five years younger than me and hadn't even started kindergarten yet; she had a lot less to live for.

This is what we were raised on. These were the stories that filled our heads—I'm speaking in the Rothian "we" now, the "we" that means every Jewish person of my generation anywhere in America. Our parents' generation, the baby boomers, had focused on happy Jewish things like the state of Israel and Sandy Koufax. They seldom spoke of the Holocaust at home or at religious school. It was too recent, too vivid, too painful a reminder of the world's cruel indifference. But we could take on this burden, this legacy of unspeakable pain. Enough time had passed. We wouldn't be crushed under the weight.

I attended a Jewish day school, and my class had an ongoing assignment: once a week we were to find a newspaper article that featured some Jewish content, cut it out, attach it to a sheet of notebook paper with a staple or paper clip (we were not to use Scotch tape, although neat gluing was permissible), and on the notebook paper, *in pen,* inscribe a brief summary of said article. The definition of "Jewish content" was fairly relaxed—a piece concerning a certain Aaron Spelling show might be acceptable, or, depending on our teacher's mood, a review of the new Billy Crystal movie—as was the standard to which our summary was held; a typical sentence might read: "What is Jewish about this article is that it is an article about Israel which is the Jewish country so as you can see this article has something Jewish about it."

It wasn't difficult to find such a story. Jews—not to mention their antagonists—manage to keep themselves in the news. There was always a snippet about Yasser Arafat or Jeffrey Katzenberg somewhere, and in a pinch there was *The Jerusalem Post* my father received in the mail twice a month, in which everything, even the want ads, was Jewish. And it was in this paper, as I struggled to complete my homework in the thirty minutes between *The Golden Girls* and *L.A. Law* one evening, that I discovered the item that would destroy my mind and haunt my soul, that would finally push me from the rocky precipice of sanity into the chasm of Nazi-induced psychosis.

It was here that I first read about the Mengele twins.

Ominously titled "The Girl in the Cage," it was a first-person account from a survivor of the horrifying and perverse medical experiments the Auschwitz camp doctor, nicknamed "the Angel of Death," performed on sets of twin prisoners, mainly children. *Don't*, I told myself, staring wide-eyed at the accompanying ink drawing scratched in a stroke so rough it looked painful. *Stop reading. Find some little piece about Teddy Kollek[†] and call it a day.*

I was nine, but I remember everything in that story like I read it yesterday. How she and her twin sister were discovered hiding under their mother's skirt as they disembarked from the cattle car with cries of *"Zwillinge! Zwillinge!"* ("Twins! Twins!"), and were ripped from her arms as she was sent to her death. How the twin

---

[†] Former mayor of Jerusalem, whom I always pictured as an Ed Koch type in looks and personality, except more butch.

girls were locked naked in a small cage and given injections that gave them seizures. How one day, her sister seized so violently she was taken from the cage and never returned. The unanesthetized, pointless surgeries, the cutting into her leg to scrape at the bone with a scalpel, the chemicals dropped in the eyes to see if they would change color, the chilling times they would sit nude on Mengele's lap, as he petted them fondly, speaking in soft, fatherly tones. And of all the twins kept for torture in the medical block, this girl and her dead sister, four years old when they first arrived, they were the lucky ones. They weren't subject to experimental hysterectomies or sex-change operations. They weren't sewn together back-to-back like the Gypsy twins Mengele had tried to conjoin artificially, who screamed for three days until the gangrene killed them.

Like all children, I was warned from the time I was very small of the peril of talking to strangers. Strangers harbored all manner of unsavory intentions, and a stupid or greedy child taken in by their offers of candies or bicycles was sure to find himself covered with cigarette burns and gagged and bound with electrical tape in a rat-filled subterranean chamber, forced to submit to all kinds of disgusting adult demands involving his private parts. Nearly hysterical one day, I confided my fears to my mother, who consoled me. Most strangers were perfectly nice people, she said, with no intention of hurting children or their private parts. But there were a few bad apples out there, not many, but a few, and it's a shame that they were the ones we heard about, but that's the way it was.

"Don't worry too much, baby," she said, stroking my hair. I buried my small, damp face in the comforting curve of her chest. "You can't go around being afraid all the time. And you know that Daddy and I will protect you, no matter what."

However, the evening I came to her with my Mengele problem, she was in a lighter mood.

"Dr. Mengele, huh? Maybe that's who we'll send you to the

next time you're 'too sick' to go to school." She giggled, greatly amused. "'Oh, a leetle Jewish girl mit a sore thoat? Vell, vee vill RIP her throat out and zen it von't hurt anymore!"

I gazed at her silently, ashen-faced and ill.

"Oh, come on, sweetie. It's a *joke*."

"Jokes are supposed to be funny," I whispered.

She rolled her eyes. "Jesus Christ, will you lighten up? Go finish your damn homework—it's almost time for *L.A. Law*."

She had lied. My mother had lied. Most people were not nice. Most people looked at you and saw a target, a victim, someone to be abused, tortured, exploited for political or professional gain. A helpless plaything upon whom the world's monsters might inflict their own hate-filled perversions, their darkest, basest desires. Such was the nature of being a child. Such was the nature of being a Jew. And by that logic, was not a Jewish child the worst thing to be? They were everywhere, the bad people. They were still out to get us, all of them, biding their time, ready to pounce at the proper moment, when the world was once again susceptible to hatred. Everywhere. The neo-Nazi skinheads who grimaced from the envelopes of Anti-Defamation League fund-raising letters; that girl with the giant pink glasses from preschool who told me that Jews were not God's Children; the mild-mannered mechanic, embedded quietly in some Ukranian community in Michigan, who turns out to be an infamous death-camp guard who made people eat their own ears. My mother said she would protect me from such horrors, that she and my father would keep me safe. Another lie. Where were all those other mothers? Where were the Mengele twins' mothers? Dead. Gassed. Dead, gassed, and useless.

Downstairs, I could hear the first strident bars of the *L.A. Law* theme song.

"Sweetheart?" my mother called up the steps. "Sweetie?"

I took a deep breath. "Yeah?"

She paused, taken aback at the palpable fear in my voice. "Do you want some ice cream?"

Fool. Ignorant of the gathering storm that soon would shatter our comfortable little lives into a million bloody pieces, she dug deeper into her carton of Edy's Grand, dribbling some down the front of her freshly laundered nightgown, while the television— the television! The infernal soundtrack that blocks our ears, our minds, from truth!—flickered across her blank, doomed face. She was watching *L.A. Law;* she couldn't miss *L.A. Law.* But where would she be when they came for Benny, the retarded guy? When they came for the red-haired English lesbian who came on this season? Still watching, still spooning low-fat chocolate chocolate chip into her mouth? *Spoon away, old friend, spoon away.* Because when they come for Douglas Brackman, *when they come for Stuart Markowitz,* it will be too late. Too late for us all.

I didn't sleep that night.

Or the next night.

Or the night after that.

For there in the walls of my bedroom, walls painted in the palest china blue, a color I had chosen myself from the book of paint chips the decorator had brought, creeping so lightly, so stealthily, that senses less acute than mine, brains less agile, might mistake them for the scuttlings of a mouse, there, inside my walls, were the Nazis.

Nazis! Gray eyes glinting in the flickering light, canine ears pressed tightly to the drywall, long-bridged noses, slim and elegant, filled with the scent of the wretched Jew-child. They missed nothing. The moment I closed my eyes would spell my doom, for at this moment they would pounce, and oh! What fresh Hell awaited this helpless Daughter of Israel! But I would not go easily. I would not doom my body to the ash heap. I would not be but another faceless victim, another nameless number, another faggot (in the bundle-of-twigs sense) for their grisly fire! Not I! *Not this night!*

"We need to talk," said my mother. The ballet car pool had just dropped me at home.

I wriggled impatiently, anxious to fix some microwave popcorn and return to my copy of *Nuremberg Diary.* "Um, not now, okay?"

"Yes, now. Sit down."

"I should take a shower . . . I'm sweaty from ballet—"

"Sit down!"

Her vehemence startled me. I sat down. "Am I in trouble?"

"No, honey. You're not in trouble." She blinked hard.

"Mommy! Are you crying? Oh my God! Did someone die?"

"No, sweetheart—"

"Did Grandma die? Did *Daddy*? OH MY GOD! WHAT HAPPENED TO DADDY?"

"Daddy's fine. Everyone's fine."

"So then what do we have to talk about?"

She looked at me for a long moment, eyes hard, pressing her lips into a firm, wry crescent. Lately, I feel the muscles around my mouth taking the same shape. It's an eloquent face, a face that says "*Oy. Oy, vey.* What a sad place the world is, full of fools and monsters." It is my least favorite face.

"What is it? I'M HUNGRY!"

"I got a call today from Mrs. Finkel."

"Mrs. Finkel?"

"The librarian. You know, at the Jewish Community Center. She's friends with Grandma—"

"I *know* who she is. How did she get this number?" I demanded.

"What do you mean, how did she get this number? Probably

she got it out of the Hadassah directory, the same way I would get her number."

Nearly every Jewish woman and girl in the country belongs to Hadassah, the Women's Zionist Organization of America. The local chapter directory is a veritable who's who of area Jewish females. Earlier that week, I had casually mentioned to my mother that we might consider terminating our association with the organization and withdrawing our names from its records, as when They came for us, the Hadassah directory would likely be the first place They'd look.

"Mom!"

"Do you know what Mrs. Finkel told me?"

"Mom, *I* told you—"

"Mrs. Finkel told me that you tried to check out all four tapes of *Shoah* this afternoon."

"So? You're allowed to check out all four tapes! They come as a set! It's like checking out one tape!"

She was still making that damn face. I *hated* that face. "She told me it was the seventh time you've tried to check it out in the past three weeks."

"So what? She kept saying it was reserved."

"It's on the thirteen-and-over list, honey."

"Meaning?"

"Meaning you have to be thirteen or over to check it out. That's the rule."

"That's the first I've heard of any such rule."

"Sweetie, that's the rule."

"IT'S A BULLSHIT RULE!"

My mother's shrill temper flared at last. "And when were you planning to watch all NINE AND A HALF HOURS OF *SHOAH,* HUH? Were you going to take a night off from whatever weird fucking shit you're doing to the walls of your room when the normal people are asleep?"

Never content to let a long period of insomnia pass unproductively, I had kept myself busy in the restless wee hours cutting out pictures of famous Jews from magazines and sticking them on the walls of my bedroom with bits of chewed gum, where they acted as talismans warding off the unspeakable evil that lay in wait. The carefully arranged visages of my kinfolk—Bette Midler, Groucho Marx, Alan Dershowitz—would keep the enemy away, I felt, like a necklace of garlic keeps away vampires. In areas that seemed particularly susceptible to infiltration (above my bed, at the joins) I placed my small collection of posters from Broadway musicals, sure that the mighty phalanx of Jew *and* Gay would prove impermeable for even the most enterprising of the ghostly *Einsatzgruppen* who peopled our drywall. The resemblance to Anne Frank's famous bedroom wall in the Secret Annex, touchingly adorned with colorful postcards and newspaper ads picturing film stars and babies, was not lost on me; however, I reasoned, if poor Anne had only been a bit more judicious, a little more *ethnocentric* in her selections, things might have turned out differently. The Gestapo wasn't going to get me, not with that giant picture of Henry Kissinger on the wall.

"I shudder to think how many times in a row you could watch that goddamn thing," my mother continued, shaking her head. "How many fucking times did you sit through *The Birth of a Nation* last summer? Seventeen? Eighteen? Enough times to make a *sane* person psychotic—God knows what it did to you."

"You think I'm psychotic?"

"Well, you're only eight. We won't know for sure until your late teens/early twenties, when the hallucinations will really start to present," said my mother, the mental-health professional. "Technically it's unethical to diagnose a member of my own family. But since the state of Nebraska certifies that I get to say who's psychotic or not, I'd say you're on that road."

I began to cry.

"Honey, tell me something." She looked thoughtful. "What happens to you when you start to have scary thoughts?"

My cheeks flush. My heartbeat veers wildly out of control. I start to claw at my skin like it's a canvas bag I've been tied in, a canvas bag filled with rats. My stomach churns. I feel like I'm going to pass out, throw up, or, failing those, throw myself out a window, hoping pain or death will distract me. "I don't know," I said.

"Okay." She pursed her lips again. *It's not easy to be the mother of a schizophrenic third-grader, but oy; what are you gonna do?* "Tell me something else. Do you ever think of anything besides the Holocaust?"

The Holocaust. I gasped a little at the sound of it. I had stopped using the word. It hung in my head, unspoken, un-thought-of, like the name of a crush one dares not speak aloud, lest by some Mystical Power of Boy, he should hear it, and abruptly, heart-wrenchingly, withdraw his presence from your lunch table, and if that happened, you might as well not even go back to school. You might as well not even live. You might as well rip the picture of Woody Allen off your wall and let the Nazis come get you.

"Do you ever think of anything besides the Holocaust?" She was waiting for an answer.

"Sometimes. But then—"

"Then what?"

"Well, if I find myself not thinking about . . . it . . . then I make myself think about it. I'll think about something I've read or some picture I saw, and I won't stop thinking about it until I *can't* stop thinking about it."

"Why don't you let yourself not think about it? What do you think is going to happen?"

"Those that do not remember the past are condemned to repeat it," I intoned solemnly. Surely this would end the conversation. I could creep to my room, finish reading Ribbentrop's testimony to the war crimes tribunal, and enjoy the ensuing surge of terror in peace and quiet before dinner.

"Who said that?" my mother asked.

"I don't know. Maybe Elie Wiesel?"

"No! Who said that to you?"

"Oh." I almost laughed. "Everyone."

"Everyone? At school?"

School, Hebrew school, every work of Jewish children's literature I had ever received as a prize or present, every piece of spiky Holocaust memorial sculpture displayed in a Jewish Community Center lobby with a title like *Remember Not to Forget* or *Six Million . . . and Counting.*

It was not yet acceptable for pediatricians to prescribe anti-anxiety medication to small children, nor was she about to launch a verbal attack against a Jewish community and education system that with its overwhelming emphasis on victimhood, its insistence that the youngest and least of its brethren experience the same level of psychic pain as its elders in penance for growing up in a country and time relatively free of hatred or danger, leads to a kind of retroactive survival guilt that would ultimately manifest itself in their unformed psyches in one of two ways. They could subsume their Jewish identities in the culture at large, adolescent bravado masking a furtive shame—"I'm Jewish, but I'm not really *Jewish*" or, even better, the "My family is Jewish, but I'm nothing" school of thought—or they could parlay this inheritance of misery into a Jewish identity that consumed all else, rendering themselves unacceptable to peers, Jew and Gentile alike, their only social outlets the conventions and conclaves of the more observant subsets of Jewish youth movements, where they could excitedly show off the latest fashions in yarmulkes, weep at the beauty of *Shabbos,* and French-braid the hair of the other overweight and homely girls destined to remain virgins until halfway through their master's programs in Jewish education at the University of Wisconsin.

So my mother just said, a little sadly, "Listen to me. The next time you find yourself having those thoughts, I want to you to close your eyes, count to three, and then, as loud as you can, I want you to shout STOP! Okay?"

"STOP!" I shouted.

"No! To yourself!" My mother clutched her ear. "Shout in your head."

I shouted in my head for months. My mother, continuing her good work, banished most of the books from my shelves, replacing them with the Baby-sitters Club and, against her better judgment, Sweet Valley High. "I'd rather have you shallow and sexually precocious then morbidly psychotic," she said. Eventually, the thoughts began to recede. I managed to say the word *Holocaust* aloud. I no longer checked the showerhead for gas or packed small bags full of socks and SnackWell's, and when it was released in theaters a few years later, I managed to see *Schindler's List* with a friend of German-Catholic descent and did not become hysterical—although we had smoked an oddly strong joint in the parking lot before the movie and were forced to discard our popcorn when it began to remind us of a jumbo tub of buttered human teeth, refillable with proof of purchase.

But true salvation would not come until I was in Auschwitz.

I was on a Jewish teen tour, with hundred of other Jewish teenagers from all over the country—somehow it seemed fitting that my first personal encounter with the death camps should also be my first with the Jewish youth of Long Island and New Jersey. The plan was this: a weeklong whirlwind through the best Poland had to offer. We didn't bother to get our feet wet with the more minor camps: Treblinka, Plaszow, the hurriedly abandoned Majdanek, left so intact by the retreating Germans that experts say it could be up and running again at full capacity in forty-eight hours. These would come later.

Instead, we went straight to Auschwitz.

It's the "Space Mountain First" philosophy—don't fuck

around with the Teacups and the Jungle Cruise; go straight for the good stuff and come back if there's time. And after a week spent methodically pulverizing what little faith in humanity we had left, we would spend the second week visiting the glory, wonder, and triumph of the Jewish spirit that is the state of Israel, and in this way would our parents ensure that we would grow up to be the kind of people who would marry other Jews, send our children to religious school, and, after we had built up our medical practices, begin to contribute significant chunks of money to the proper federations and charities.

I was told this experience would change my life.

We spent a bit of time orienting ourselves to our surroundings, recovering from jet lag, surveying the delicate peer dynamic of our new community. Predictably, I had my usual trouble with this last; the social subset that best matched my particular interests—the theater, the sublimity of a well-cut cocktail dress, the life and work of Miss Bette Davis—would not make themselves reliably visible until I reached college, but I persevered, as one must, and soon we were prepared to begin the important business of hysterical weeping.

Which was what I was doing, crumpled against the pillar in the Sorting Room at Auschwitz. We had walked slowly around the cavernous space, examining the enormous mounds of things that had once belonged to people—the mountain of hair, a chamber crammed with children's toys. The faces of even the toughest and angriest among us were streaked with tears, but my wails must have been particularly wrenching (or ostentatious), for almost at once, I felt an arm softly draping my shoulder.

It was Bettina, a tiny blond woman in her seventies. Several Holocaust survivors were traveling with us, but Bettina was by far the best loved—and the least haunted. I turned slightly to look up into her kind face, and she wrapped her arms around me at once, cradling me like a mother.

"Shhh, darling, *sha*. Don't cry like that. Don't cry."

"I can't help it!" I blubbered.

"I know, sweetheart. I know. But not like that. Listen to me, darling. You shouldn't carry our pain," she said, wiping the tears from my face with a folded Kleenex, slightly damp. "Our pain is ours. We don't need you to feel it for us."

"But all the people . . ." I couldn't stop. "All the things."

"They're just things, *bubbeleh*. Just things." She gestured toward a huge case. "And think, maybe some of the people that used those things, they're still alive somewhere!"

I followed her hand to the case full of empty cans of gas pellets.

"Okay," she said. "Not those maybe. But look. Those shoes. Maybe, would you believe it, somewhere in there is a pair of my old shoes? And I'm standing here with you, darling. You see?"

"Isn't it painful here for you?" I asked. "To be here?"

Her eyes darkened. "Painful? Yes, sweetheart, of course. But I'll tell you what. It's a lot better than the last time I'm here."

I laughed out loud, and a girl nearby stopped sobbing for a moment to glare at us. Bettina plunged an arm into her enormous handbag and extracted a wrinkled Halloween-sized packet of M&M's. "Here," she said, patting my cheek. "Take."

I took.

"Eat!"

I ate.

It was as though a giant weight had been lifted from my shoulders. I felt light. I felt free—at least for a couple of days, until the anti-Semitic Polish diet performed its own hate-filled atrocities on my digestive tract and placed me in a situation straight out of a joke book from 1962. "Do you think you might be pregnant?" asked the Polish doctor, responding to my symptoms.

"No," I said. "I have my period."

"So," replied the Polish doctor, "do you think you might be pregnant?" Bah *dum* dum!

But this condition too resolved itself upon our arrival at a kibbutz just outside Tel Aviv, after consuming several quarts of Israeli cucumber salad and roughly a dozen raw tomatoes, and my companions and I, hearts disentangled from the snares of the ghetto, reveled in the birthright of our homeland: its sacred sights, its lack of an enforced drinking age, the overtly suggestive behavior of its young, Uzi-toting security guards.

We also needed to do what any large group of teenagers needs to do when thrown together for a longish period of time in the absence of parental supervision. We needed to do the thing that was, along with the glamour of international travel, the two weeks excused absence from high school, and the distinction of being one of the relatively few of our religious persuasion to see the inside of a gas chamber and live to tell about it, a major selling point of this trip. We needed to get laid; rather, we needed to engage in whatever that defined for us at the time. For me, this consisted of heavy below-the-waist petting, the removal of some (but not all) clothing, and very occasionally, a modicum of light fellatio. Naturally, I was elated at the prospect, yet I felt uncharacteristically calm. I had suffered through days of crippling stomach pain without once believing it was stomach cancer, colorectal cancer, or Crohn's disease. I had flown on an airplane, a Polish airplane, *at night,* and instead of assuming a reflexively fetal position, I spent a very pleasant few hours chatting amiably with some of the British kids, eating boiled sweets, and learning about Manchester United. At Majdanek, my new friend Andrew and I stood oblivious beside a memorial displaying six tons of human ash, and discussed whether the wry Grand Guignol of *Sweeney Todd* or the urbane emotionalism of *Company* was better representative of Sondheim's capabilities as an artist. And so, my question to myself was this: Might I now live a life free from irrational anxiety, unencumbered by guilt and suspicion, able to watch the last scene from *The Sound of Music* without a pillow over my head? Would I stop having that dream, the one where I get into my mother's Honda Civic to discover Hitler at the wheel? Was I fixed?

We were somewhere over the Atlantic on the flight home when a rangy boy slid into the seat beside me. It was the first time I had seen him since three days earlier, when he arrived unexpectedly in my room during a free afternoon and, after a few moments of perfunctory small talk , thrust one hand down my shirt and the other, thrillingly, into my vagina.

"We have to talk," he said.

I figured I'd beat him to the punch. "Look . . . (what was his name? What?), dude, I really like you and everything. But I'm not really looking for anything, like, you know, a *relationship* right now."

He looked a little surprised. *Good.* "Um . . . yeah. I totally feel the same way. I mean, yeah. But that's not what I wanted to talk to you about. I have to ask you something. It's kind of personal."

"Um, okay . . ."

"Okay. Have you ever had an AIDS test?"

What? "Why?"

Accusingly, he held out his middle finger to me.

"Why are you flicking me off?"

"I'm not! But look." He pointed at a hangnail on the offending digit. The skin around it was swollen and slightly rimmed with blood.

"So?"

"So, that's an open wound! And this is the finger that I . . . you know . . . *fingered* you with."

It was slowly coming together for me.

"I've been tested," he continued. "So I know that I didn't give you anything. But if you haven't . . . and you know, you seemed pretty . . . *experienced.*"

How I wish to this day that I had been too proud to contradict him! But instead, pulse rising, I cried, "I'm a virgin!"

A passing El Al flight attendant glanced at us strangely. *Spoiled Americans.*

"Doesn't matter," said the Public Service Announcement I Had Mistakenly Allowed in My Underpants. "You can get it from, like, anything."

"Like, *even blow jobs?*"

"Blow jobs, like, if a guy that . . . *ate you out* . . . had it, you could, like, get it from his tongue, if he had like, bit his tongue . . ." He trailed off, and looked at me with disappointment. "You've really never been tested?"

"No," I whispered.

"Man." He expelled a gust of air, shaking his head angrily. "I did not want to have to go through this again. Fuck. I did *not* want to go through this again."

"I'm sorry," I gasped in weak horror.

"Whatever." He slammed the tray table violently, locking it into an upright position. "I should have asked you before we did anything. Just . . . you should get tested, okay?" He disappeared up the aisle, still shaking his head.

Trembling, I made my way to the lavatory at the back of the plane, where I would remain crouched until the steward announced we would shortly be landing in Houston. I was not fixed. But there were things much scarier in this world than some stupid Nazis.

Two

The City on the Edge of Whenever

My father is not a vain man, but like most people, he is not immune to praise. Should one wish to flatter him, there are a couple of easy ways.

For example, say you are heading down the hallway to the toilet. You approach his home office, a small room littered with the evidence of his many interests—bicycling magazines, novelty yarmulkes, *Star Trek* paraphernalia of varying degrees of ludicrousness—and as if by magic, the door swings open, flooding the hall with whispery folk music evocative of the precise moment fruit starts to rot.

"Cutie, could you come in here and take a look at this?"

"I have to go potty," you say.

"It'll just take a second," he implores.

And so sheets of tracing paper are unrolled and the Magic Markers uncapped, and you are shown how the redevelopment of

Main Street will bring vibrant new life to the town of Social Conservative, Kansas, or Bigot, Oklahoma; how its citizens will turn from the Wal-Mart to the small bookseller, from the Burger King to the artisanal cheese shop; how they will transform from the kind of people who live in rural Oklahoma to the kind of people who live in rural Vermont. And my father is a man full of goodness, and Judy Collins is warbling something about sailors and Maine and the springtime and you are starting to really, really have to pee, so you smile quickly and feign delight at his drawings and diagrams.

"A triumph!" you cry, as a warm bubble of urine surges dangerously close to your inner labia. "Small-town America shall rise again!"

He glows with pleasure like a small boy praised at the blackboard, and the relief of making it to the bathroom on time is made all the sweeter knowing you have made Daddy happy.

Here is the other way to make him happy: mistake him for someone who is not from Nebraska.

"Guess what?" He is beaming, having just returned from a convention somewhere hopelessly cosmopolitan, like Houston or Philadelphia. "Everyone I met there, *everyone,* they all said, 'What? Nebraska? You seem more like you're from someplace like Boston or'" (*wait for it*) "'New York.'"

"They thought I was from New York," he repeats, shaking his head in pleased astonishment. "Isn't that something."

It isn't that he's ashamed of his hometown—far from it. In fact, he has spent the better part of two decades inside and outside City Hall working to make it a better, smarter, more vibrant place. But Omaha proved notoriously resistant to improvement, at least to the kind my father envisioned. I mean, people in Omaha aren't the type who go bragging about their two-digit IQs and total disinterest in anything without an engine, an ammunition belt, or a way to blame it on the gays; but you know, they like a good chain restaurant. They're not about to start commuting by bike. Omaha is Omaha. It shows little inclination to become New York or even Kansas City.[N]

Still, this feeling of vague sheepishness about the hometown is widespread among native Omahans. Run into a few at the mall or at the supermarket, and after conducting a cursory examination of your hair, clothing, and wedding-ring finger, they'll say: "So, you're still out there in New York?"

"Yes."

"You out in, um, Albany . . . or New York City?"

"I live in the city."

"The Big Apple, huh?"

"Yes."

"Isn't it real expensive out there?" This isn't a question, although it is phrased as one. But you can see where this is going.

"Yes, it is."

The interlocutor sighs, wistfully. "It must be nice to live in a big city like that. So much to do all the time; all those different kinds of people. You know, I went to school up in Milwaukee for a couple of years, and I just loved it up there. Guess I always kind of figured I'd end up in some big city too."

[N] Welcome to another helpful feature, called "Great Moments in Nebraska History." This feature will be denoted with N, echoing the initial worn on the helmets of our football team, which some believe stands for "knowledge." If you are one of the seven people who knows our state song, "Beautiful Nebraska," by all means hum along. Standing and the removal of headgear will not be necessary; Nebraskans, unlike some *other* people (*ahem,* Iowa), are a humble people, unnerved by any display of ostentation or pomposity.

And now, Great Moment in Nebraska History: The Lesson of How We Are Perceived by Fellow Midwesterners. I cite an exchange that occurred in Kansas City between my parents and a college boyfriend, who was from there. The four of us were walking to a restaurant on the Plaza (and if you don't know what this is, I direct you to Google, because I am *not* starting a "Welcome to the Kansas City Area" footnote feature), and noticed a couple of pudgy yokels waddling along, consulting a map and staring with awe at the tall buildings and upscale shops as their white, white sneakers gleamed in the night. Gleefully, we mocked them, of course, until my boyfriend said: "No offense, but if my parents were here, they would have said, 'Oh, they're probably from Omaha.'"

This is meant to qualify the speaker as a certain kind of person; a person who reads books, eats Japanese food, and is a Friend to Gays.[N] A person who votes for the candidate, not the party.

"But I guess family is just too important to me," they continue. "I mean, my little nephew/granddaughter/godson, I couldn't leave him for the world." The Omahans smile, as they play their trump card. "You must get lonely up there."

Although I am not currently a childless spinster in my late thirties who has frivoled away her fertile years drinking fanciful cocktails in overpriced shoes, the rebuke is clear. I may have felt compelled earlier to reassure the Omahans that my life is not so fabulous, my employment is at best intermittent, that I rarely put on any piece of clothing with a zipper before 4 P.M. and spend an alarming number of evenings at home watching reality television, but now the temptation has passed. "Oh, no, never!" I chirp. "I'm so busy! Busy, busy, busy! I mean, yeah, I get tired, but it's *so* worth it. I couldn't imagine ever living anywhere else."

"You know, Omaha's not so small anymore," comes the reply. "We just got a J. Crew, so . . ."

Oh, in that case. I mean, now that Omahans have been granted the privilege afforded to the rest of the world's civilized peoples of trying on their barn jackets and pineapple-dotted

---

[N] This is by no means a sure thing. In yet another Great Moment in Nebraska History, we are notable for passing in 2000, with over 70 percent of the popular vote, no less, Initiative 416, or the Defense of Marriage Amendment, soon known as the most restrictive such legislation in the nation. This amendment to previous DOMA legislation not only prohibited same-sex marriage or recognized civil unions but explicitly prohibited such couples from lobbying or petitioning for legislative change and stripped same-sex couples of their common-law relationship rights, effectively reducing the legal status of long-term cohabitating couples to nothing more than roommates. In 2005 the initiative was struck down in U.S. district court as blatantly unconstitutional, to general indifference. Also, a number of gay bars thrive in Omaha, especially the Max, your go-to party spot if you want to pick up shirtless studs in an atmosphere almost undistinguishable from a particularly drunken office Christmas party.

capris before purchase, it's only a matter of time before Gwyneth Paltrow buys a house here.

Still, I know this attitude, at once apologetic and defensive— an inferiority complex tempered by judgmental defiance. It's how I feel when I'm in Europe.

"They thought I was from New York," my father says again, shaking his head in disbelief and pleasure.

Of course they did, and not just because of his Yale diploma, his absence of girth, his fondness for tweed. No, they see the dark complexion, the strong nose, the wild stack of kinky hair, as far from the flat, pale-eyed faces of Slavic peasants who settled the grassy plains of our fair state as the Western Wall is from a Bavarian *biergarten*. My father looks unmistakably like a Jew.

And who, think all those colleagues from Brookline, Bethesda, and Great Neck, *ever heard of a Jew from Nebraska?*

"We weren't supposed to live here," says my mother, peering through the icy windshield at the antiabortion protesters scattering pictures of bloody fetuses on the porch of her obstetrician's house.

"It wasn't supposed to be like this," moans my father, reading the results of a local survey in which an overwhelming majority of re- spondents declare that what Omaha needs most is "more parking."

"What is the matter with this fucking place? Why do you fucking live here?" I scream at both of them after the woman at the liquor store has refused to accept my passport as valid proof of age on account of she's "never seen one of them things before."

"Good for her," cheers my mother. "At least she knows a drunk when she sees one."

I am, of course, a very busy, glamorous, and important person whose opinions are of great significance to the world, so naturally I am asked many questions in my busy, glamorous, and important life. How do you stay so impossibly thin? What is it like being a role model for an entire generation of women? Does this train stop at Thirty-third Street? Did you put on deodorant today? But more than anything else, more than the details of my skin-care regimen or my thoughts on the future of the feminist movement or could I please, please change the fucking cat litter, I am asked: "How did your family wind up in Nebraska?"

Well, I'll tell you. Here is the story, once and for all, of Why My Jewish Parents Live in Nebraska. And when I have finished, if there is time, let us gather around the fire in front of our huts and the elders will tell the story of How the Elephant Got His Trunk.

My father was born and raised in Omaha, a scion, on his father's side, of a family-owned meat market that had made its way across Missouri from Chicago to cater to an untapped market for kosher salami and affordable brisket. My mother was born in South Bend, Indiana, another minor outpost of the Judean Empire of Winnetka, or J.E.W., and moved to Omaha at the age of nine, when her widowed mother married the middle-aged owner of a uniform shop. The Jewish community of the Gate City, Nebraska's largest, was small but stable: there were three synagogues, a Jewish Community Center, and a wide variety of businesses and shops, including two competing kosher butcher shops. One of the butcheries was owned by my family; the other, I was made to understand, was owned by the leaders of a vast and sinister conspiracy aimed at the single-minded ruin of our family. Their network of soldiers and informants, including not just the masterminds but all their former customers, was vast and omnipotent. These people might seem human; they might pat my head at the kiddush[†] after Saturday-morning services or have seemingly pleasant grandchildren, but I should not be fooled. Such people had consumed

[†] The reception held at the synagogue after Saturday morning services, in which the congregants have a little nosh and catch up on the events of the week. Especially popular with the elderly—the men gather in a corner to drink schnapps and kosher plum whiskey, while the woman chew loudly, discuss the relative merits of one another's grandchildren, and attempt to make off with several pounds of rugelach hidden inside their handbags, which are specially lined with tinfoil for the occasion.

Shukert hatred for years along with their all-beef hot dogs and pickled tongue—under no circumstances to be trusted.

"Some people," my grandmother would say, "they act like they're so Jewish, at the synagogue and everything, but I'll tell you something, honey, they're not all so Jewish."

I believe this statement was meant along the lines of Christ's admonition to his disciples in Matthew 6:5–6: "And when thou prayest, thou shalt not be as the hypocrites are; for they love to pray standing in the synagogues . . . that they may be seen of men; and also they that claimest the ground hamburger they sell for sixty-nine cents a pound is as good and holy as that sold for seventy-three cents a pound by those who are beloved of the Lord and blessed in His eyes. . . . verily I say unto thee, they shall reap their just reward." But who can say? My grandmother had her own ideas about things—for example, that shrimp[†] would be kosher "if they were making the laws now" and Easter was "a festival of spring," appropriately commemorated by the presentation to each of her grandchildren of an enormous toy rabbit in a sunbonnet, its belly filled with pastel jelly beans. And Jews dearly love to fight among themselves over petty bullshit. It helps them forget about all the other people out to get them.

So it was from this cozy and resentment-strewn Midwestern shtetl that my parents, brainy overachievers peripherally aware of each other's existence, departed for their brainy overachieving East Coast universities, expecting never to return—except for holidays and school vacations, when my father, despite having gone vegetarian in an act of elegant rebellion that endures to this day,

---

[†] Hello again, dear Gentiles! Obviously, you all know the Jewish religion's feelings on pork, but did you know that shrimp, as well as all other shellfish, is also un-kosher (or *treyf,* as we in the business call it)? Why is this? The answer is: *No one knows.* But I looked it up on Wikipedia, where I do all my research, and gleaned the following: "Shellfish carry hepatitis, which is against Jewish law." So rest easy in your beds, hepatitis carriers! Ye shall not be consumed by the People of Abraham!

would resume his post at the meat grinder. One summer afternoon, my maternal grandmother, in a brief remission from the cancer that would eventually kill her, stopped in to pick up her *Shabbos* brisket and noticed that the young Master Shukert was home from school, as was her younger daughter. My father's parents agreed that this was a very interesting development indeed. Predictably, the young people protested, but the combined willpower of a man who had quit a three-pack-a-day cigarette habit cold turkey, a woman who had spent the previous ten years enduring experimental chemotherapy, and another woman who had kept her children on a *very* strict enema schedule put an end to that. They dated all summer and through the end of college. They got engaged. My maternal grandmother died. They got married and moved straight to Berkeley, where my father was getting his master's in architecture.

It was 1973. My mother grew her hair to her waist and stopped eating meat. My father began to ride a bicycle. Friends and professors came over for dinner. My mother learned to make fondue, which she served on a table made from an orange crate. They had very little money, but they had each other and they lived within walking distance of the house where Patty Hearst was held by the Symbionese Liberation Army.

"Did you know any members of the SLA?" I ask.

"No," says my mother tersely.

"Did you smoke pot?" I ask.

"Go to your room."

Patty Hearst is released, my father finishes his master's, and they move to Austin, where my mother had been accepted into the Ph.D. psychology program at the University of Texas.

"Hook 'em horns!" says my mother.

She begins classes. They have Mexican food and sweet tea in restaurants. My father lands a job at a respected architecture firm and, in the building recession of 1975, loses it. He becomes deeply depressed. They are deeply broke. They stop eating out, and the orange-crate table ceases to be an affectation. My father rides his bicycle with renewed furor, watches *Star Trek* reruns compulsively, and becomes active at the local synagogue. My mother begins to experiment with the contraction *y'all*.

They develop a lasting affinity for the music of Kinky Friedman and the Texas Jewboys.

Finally, after cycling thousands of miles, building several stained-glass light fixtures, and painting a large mural with biblical themes in the foyer of Austin's Conservative synagogue, my father finds a job. A good job, in his field, working in the urban-planning department of a Midwestern city. What's the catch? The city is Omaha.

"I think I can really make a difference there that I couldn't somewhere else at this point in my career," reasons my father.

My mother looks at him. For months he's been anxious, hurt, brooding over the professional successes of less talented classmates and colleagues. But now, at last, the light is back on. "Okay," she says.

"It's only temporary," my father says. "Just for a while. I'll get some good references and some work under my belt, and then we can go anywhere. Boston. New York. Back to Austin, if you want—back to Berkeley, even."

"Berkeley would be good," she says.

So they return. Their families are overjoyed. My father starts his job with the planning department at City Hall, where he interned summers during college. He grows more and more excited about what he might be able to accomplish. My mother begins to write her dissertation and interns at the V.A. hospital, counseling victims of post-traumatic stress disorder who served in Vietnam. She sets her waist-long hair on fire with the *Shabbos* candles and cuts the burnt part off at her shoulders. They make a little money and put a deposit on a house—"a temporary house," says my father. My mother stops saying "y'all" and finishes her dissertation, and suddenly the seventies are over. My father, an intense and charismatic twenty-nine-year-old popular with the local newspaper and television stations, is appointed chief city planning director of the city of Omaha. My mother studies for the Nebraska state licensing exam for psychologists and gets pregnant.

Ladies and gentlemen, that is how people wind up in Nebraska.

Of all the self-affirming inanities that turn up on needlepoint pillows and decorative plaques in hospital gift shops, the most popular are variations of "Live life to the fullest" or, in its more specific and depressing form, "Live every day like it's your last."

The exceeding stupidity of this kind of sentiment is inescapable. If I should live every day like it's my last, why am I having this root canal? Why go to the grocery store, or wait at home for the plumber, or, for that matter, waste precious minutes of our beautiful lives waiting in line for the ladies' room? Let us live life to the fullest. Let us quit our jobs, go in our pants, and jet off to Tahiti, although let us not fly an airline I will refer to as N—west, unless we and our adult diapers wish to live our best lives while stranded in the Detroit airport with no flight information or food vouchers. And let us ignore, for the moment, the likely reality of our last grim day on earth, when we will be semiconscious and surrounded by machinery as our children and grandchildren, nostrils wrinkling at the stench of us, gather around to say good-bye and fret about whether the supplemental insurance will cover the special automatic air-circulating bed they told the nurses to let us have, back when the grief was fresher and they thought we might live.

I don't think my parents are too into maxims, but if they were, theirs would be something like "Fun never paid the cable bill" or my mother's personal favorite, "Don't fuck this up." Caution, responsibility, and moderation are their watchwords. My father pretends not to understand the punch lines to dirty jokes. My mother looks askance at those who hedonistically enjoy a glass or two of wine with a meal—for example, the country of France. But for one week every summer, my father and mother would throw off the duty-bound shackles of the Cornhusker State and give themselves over to the glory of our family vacation; a chance to spread their wings, let their hair down, get drunk.

Not drunk on *alcohol,* of course. My father fears its calories, and my mother, as I believe I have made clear, views the imbibing of it as an indication of some kind of larger emotional problem such as being a goy. They get drunk on Culture, inebriated by Knowledge. They run wild at the sudden abundance of vegetarian restaurants. Euphoric with the dizzying idea that for one splendid week, they might be once again Actual City People in an Actual City. A city where people are not comfortably willing to wait forty-five minutes for a table at the Olive Garden, that does not gauge its worth on which major retailer has recently condescended to bestow it with a franchise. A city with a light-rail system and more than one museum and a slate of decently funded Democratic candidates for office.

A city like where they were *supposed* to live. Where they did live, all those years ago, before politics and the economy and the biological urge to procreate fucked everything up for them. A city where they could feel normal.

"Where would you like to go on vacation this year?" my mother asks my sister and me over dinner one night.

"Disney World!" sings my sister. I roll my eyes. At nine, I am far too worldly for such corporate inanity; still, for just a moment, deep inside, I hope.

"Oh come on," my father says with a sneer. "Let's aim a little higher than that."

She deliberates, thoughtfully dangling her little legs from the dining room chair. "Um. . . . Japan Disney!"

My mother, like many of her race, is gifted with a sigh of supreme eloquence.

My father turns to me. "Rachy? How about you?"

I have recently read and reread a Baby-sitters Club Super Special in which *all* the Baby-sitters, due to some kind of babysitting emergency, went on a Caribbean cruise. Three of them found exciting Caribbean love (not, obviously, with native Caribs), two solved an exciting Caribbean mystery, and all enjoyed what sounded like some pretty exciting Caribbean shopping.

"You want to be stuck on a boat and forced to eat six meals a day with some insurance salesman from Ohio, fine," says my father. "If you ask me, the only good thing about being on a cruise ship is you can throw yourself overboard."

A few days after these early deliberations, after the glossy AAA brochures have arrived and scattered themselves around the house, my sister and I are summoned to receive the exciting news: *Congratulations! You have won an all-expenses paid one-week trip to . . . beautiful downtown [*insert name of major American metropolis here*]!*

We look at each other. My sister's lower lip trembles.

"I really thought we might get to go to Disney World this time," she whispers. A tear is forming in the corner of her eye.

"Me too," I whisper back.

"No Mickey this year," she adds mournfully.

"No Mickey ever," I say.

Our father rouses us around 3 A.M., already outfitted in his traveling costume of button-down oxford, striped tie, and khaki trousers, which differs from his usual raiment only in its lone concession to comfort—the replacement of his more formal penny loafers with a pair of well-worn Weejuns. He has also selected a fresh shirt unmarred by noticeable ink stains at the pocket; after all, this *is* the day he and his family will certainly plunge from the sky to their deaths, and naturally he wants to look his best. Our flight isn't for another five hours or so, but my father likes to get over to Omaha's Eppley Airfield with plenty of time to spare. One never knows what kind of delays or confusion might beset one at an enormous ten-gate airport like Eppley. Besides, he's been up all night thinking of possible disaster scenarios: ice on the wings, a fire in the galley, Libyan terrorists with undetectable plastic explosives (remember when the Libyans were the terrorists? The good old days) and how best to handle them—why shouldn't we be up to keep him company? There will be plenty of time for sleep very soon, when we were dead.

But in general, our plane did not crash into the sea, explode in midair, or burst into flames at the end of a too short runway; nor were we hijacked by masked gunmen and rerouted to Luanda to await execution pending an eleventh-hour rescue operation by the Israeli Special Forces, and after my father has engaged in his customary histrionics at the baggage claim, we pile into a cab. Peering out the windows at the unfamiliar landscape—the tall buildings, the purposeful pedestrians, the pigeons—my mother marvels: "Isn't it amazing? Just seven hours ago we were in Omaha, and now we're in a whole other city. A whole other state!"

Seven hours? Is that all? With the predawn wake-up call, the dragging of overpacked suitcases for miles through crowded airport terminals, and the afternoon spent strapped to a chair next to a man convulsing and spewing mouth froth all over his nice Davenport College necktie (that would be Daddy), the past seven hours have seemed like enough time to enrich uranium.

"Yes, amazing," I say.

"Almost like magic," my sister adds helpfully. "Ow! Stop touching me!"

Arriving at whatever midrange chain hotel reasonably close to the city center is having a special this week, my father enjoys his final seizure of the day at the check-in desk. If we are not sent out, luggage in hand, to sleep in the streets, we are permitted to proceed to the elevator. My sister and I, completely batshit crazy at this point, take the opportunity to be incredibly obnoxious.

"Mommy! Rachel keeps knocking on my head really hard. With knuckles!"

"Well, I just want to see if anything's in there."

"THERE'S NOTHING IN THERE!"

"Really? Nothing? You don't have any brains?"

"Shut up! You're stupid."

"I'm stupid? You're the one who just said there's nothing in your head!"

"Is so!"

"Poop, maybe. Runny diarrhea poop."

"Your face is diarrhea poop!"

The elevator door opens. The air fills with the intoxicating perfume of chlorine, the aroma of laughter, of summer, of all that is Fun and Good and Urine-Resistant about childhood, and two little girls appear, their sleek hair freshly damp, enormous towels wrapped tightly around their shoulders. My sister and I stare at them longingly as my parents exchange a smug glance. *Who brings their children to a bustling, culturally rich metropolis,* they think, *and lets them waste the whole afternoon swimming? What kind of parents are these?* The girls' teeth chatter and their lips are blue, but their faces are filled with delight, delight in the knowledge that they might swim again tomorrow, and again the day after that, accompanied by other children they have met, new friends from Cincinnati or Dallas. They will gorge on Snickers bars from the vending machine and play endless games of Marco Polo and Categories—with really good categories, like European Capitals and Prime Numbers—and lounge in the Jacuzzi until they almost get encephalitis, which my mother says can happen if you stay in there too long, but they won't have encephalitis. They'll have fun.

Fun, fun, fun. And what will we have?

Allow me to walk you through a typical day of a Shukert Family Vacation.

6:30 A.M.: My father wakes up and begins preparations for his morning run/reconnaissance mission, during which he will survey the lay of the land and the most time-efficient routes to various tourist attractions, shopping, et cetera. We are not expected to be awake as he prepares; however, my mother is.

> DADDY: (*full voice*) Aveva, where in the . . . *goddamn it* . . . is my athlete's foot gel?
>
> MOMMY: (*seething*) I packed it.
>
> DADDY: Well, I can't *goddamn* find it—
>
> MOMMY: (*full voice*) What do you want from me, Marty? I *packed* it. Look in the pocket of the big suitcase—
>
> DADDY: I already *looked* there, it wasn't—(*shouting*) FUCK!
>
> MOMMY: (*also shouting*) What? What happened?
>
> DADDY: I stubbed my fucking *toe* on the fucking . . .
>
> thing . . . (Frustrated, he kicks the "thing" again, hard.)
> FUCK!
>
> MOMMY: Marty! Shhh! The girls are still sleeping.
>
> Oh, the girls are awake.

6:45: My father leaves. My mother, sister, and I try to fall back asleep on the lumpy, unfamiliar hotel bed (or, in my case, as they didn't have any more double rooms available, the roll-away army cot.)

7:05: I fall back asleep.

7:06: My mother shakes me awake. "Honey, if you want to take a bath or anything, you better do it now because Daddy's going to need to shower when he gets back."

7:10: My sister turns on the TV. *Cartoons!* I drop all pretense of slumber.

7:30: "Where the hell is your father?" wonders my mother.

8:00: "Where the hell is your goddamn father?" wonders my mother.

8:30: My father, drenched in sweat, enters the room, drinking a can of Diet Coke. Rapturously, he launches into a monologue extolling the virtues of urban street life, of the success of recent metropolitan beautification efforts and the sublime beauty of rapid transit, until he pauses, noticing the TV. "Why are none of you dressed? And why are you watching this shit?"

8:34: After the abrupt termination of her program, the last of my sister's wails subside. Father showers, as the womenfolk dress, hastily.

8:50: We eat breakfast in a small bagel shop down the street from the hotel. It is rush hour. My sister and I are the only children; all the other patrons appear to be grabbing a quick coffee before heading to their jobs in executive sales. My sister tastes the orange juice, pronounces it too orangey, and says her stomach hurts. My mother takes her to the bathroom.

9:12: My mother and sister emerge from the bathroom. "Did she go?" asks my father. My mother shakes her head.

"Shut up!" says my sister. She eats a package of ketchup as my mother mops her damp little brow with a wet wipe.

9:15: We set out on an invigorating, culturally stimulating walk to a major international modern art museum, where we will spend the first half of the morning. "Is it far from here?" I ask my father.

"No," he says, "not very far."

9:45: In order to pass the time, my father is delighting me with a lecture on turn-of-the-century urban development and architecture. "You'll notice that the elaborate façade on the courthouse there is perfectly symmetrical . . . the intricate colonnade, which belies a Viennese influence . . . extremely typical of the neoclassical period . . . Of course, I'm really a modernist at heart, so this isn't really my thing, but on the way to the science museum we'll see some excellent examples of . . ." My sister begins to emit the low grunting sounds that indicate another search for a toilet is close at hand.

10:15: A full hour after embarking on our forced march— I mean, our invigorating, culturally stimulating walking tour— we arrive at the major international modern art museum, having covered roughly 5.4 miles on foot. "The bus would have taken twice as long," my father says with confidence. "And a cab, forget about it."

"The closest ladies' room is on the third floor," the woman at the counter tells my mother, handing her four buttons of thin, sharp-edged metal. She and my sister disappear. I cut my finger on the edge of my button and blink back tears.

10:17: Monet.

10:19: Seurat.

10:21: Renoir, Pissarro, Gauguin, Cézanne, Rousseau.

10:25: Vuillard. Bonnard. Toulouse-Lautrec. "Are all those ladies prostitutes?" I ask my father, having recently learned the word.

"Where the hell is your mother?" he sputters in reply.

10:35: Modigliani. Giacometti. Braque. Gris.

10:45: Picasso. My mother and sister return.

11:00: Matisse. "What is the matter with her?" my father asks, noticing my sister's tear-stained face as she sits on a bench in the middle of the room, kicking her stubby feet in their pink plastic sandals.

"She pushed too hard, and when she wiped there was blood and she got scared, okay? Is that all right with you?" my mother asks testily.

11:15: Assorted cubists.

11:30: Assorted surrealists. "Like it," intones my sister, pointing at an eerily still De Chirico.

11:45: German expressionists. I like these, as they foreshadow with brutal eloquence the impending Nazi threat, a subject particularly dear to my heart.

12:00: Abstract expressionists, and one of their many subsets (Morris Louis, Helen Frankenthaler), whom I like to think of as "Depressed Jews." These artists, aptly, were a particular favorite of my mother's. "Look," she sighs rapturously, holding my hand as we gaze at a gorgeously bleak Rothko. "What does that make you think about?"

"Death," I say.

"Good," she says.

Nearby, a couple in their thirties, outfitted in his 'n' hers football sweatshirts, stand before an enormous Pollock that, despite its almost childish exuberance, holds a note of melancholy in its intricate webbing and looping, a hint of the ineffable and the desperately sad, the enigmatic vindictiveness of life and the impermanence of the universe.

"Oh, come on," the man booms, startling the well-dressed Europeans whispering in front of a de Kooning. "What a crock of shit. *I* could have done that."

Well prepared for such situations, my sister speaks up. "Yeah, but you *didn't.*"

My mother beams.

12:30: Andy Warhol, and then, just as Andy would have wanted it, GIFT SHOP!!!!!!

12:32: My father disappears into the architecture section. "You can have *one* thing," my mother warns.

12:40: My mother is leaning toward a book as my one thing— *Picasso for Kids, In the Studio with Matisse,* or *Modernism and Me: How to Make Your Child Even Further Unable to Relate to Her Peers.* I am leaning toward a brightly colored plastic box filled with beads and strings bearing the irresistible legend Make Your Own Ballerina Jewelry!

12:42: My mother buys all of the above. "What do you want, sweetie?" she asks my sister.

"To poop!" is the plaintive reply.

1:00: My father, laden with carrier bags, emerges from the architecture section. "Science museum?" he asks.

1:45: My father, under duress, consents to our eating lunch. My sister, after consuming a carton of applesauce, a large bowl of lettuce, a hard-boiled egg covered with French dressing, and a Hershey bar dipped in ketchup, has managed to expel a few pebbles of something unpleasant from her tiny bowels. Exhausted by the effort, she sleeps in my mother's arms as we make our way on foot to our next destination, the world-renowned science museum. "So, string theory," my father begins, falling in step beside me. "Well, its basic purpose is to explain the fundamental constituents of reality as . . ."

2:30: Arrive, on foot, at world-renowned science museum. Mother and Father may or may not be speaking.

2:45: I suffer panic attack inside giant model of human heart.

2:50: Mother suffers panic attack upon weighing self in food and nutrition exhibit.

2:55: Father suffers panic attack when suddenly I go missing. Mother is again in toilet, with sister.

3:00: Alone at last, I bliss out in Hall of Congenital Deformities.

3:10: Deformed limbs!

3:15: Deformed livers!

3:20: IN UTERO SIAMESE TWINS JOINED AT THE HEAD!

3:30: BLESSED ART THOU, O LORD OUR GOD, KING OF THE UNIVERSE, WHO VARIEST THE FORMS OF THY CREATURES!

4:00: A mighty crackle echoes through the Hall of Congenital Deformities as the museum's loudspeaker rouses itself. I tear my gaze from a little-visited exhibition detailing the relationship between congenital syphilis and hydrocephaly and raise my eyes to the heavens, as though God himself is about to speak.

"Rachel Shukert. Please report to the visitors' desk. Rachel Shukert."

Has it really been over an hour since I last saw my parents? Time flies when you're having fun.

4:05: Father is most displeased.

"What the *fuck* is the matter with you?" he asks, nostrils flaring. His voice has achieved the high-pitched, strangulated quality it has during periods of high emotional distress. He speaks this way often to his computer, before he punishes it by coloring on its keyboard with orange permanent marker, in what he imagines to be a kind of ritual shaming. "*Where the fuck have you been?*"

"Sir, there's really no need for that sort of language," chimes in the guy at the desk, pursing his lips with righteous disapproval.

I sense an ally. "Don't yell at me, Daddy," I say in my smallest voice. "You *scare* me when you yell at me."

My mother yanks me ever so gently away from the watchful eye of the desk guy. "We were very, very worried about you. Do you understand? *Very,* very worried."

"Yes."

"Now, where were you?"

I don't want to tell her. The last thing I need is a repeat of the *Shoah* incident.

"Walking around," I say. "Looking at the animal stuff."

Unlike most children, I have never shown even the slightest interest in the animal kingdom. My mother raises an eyebrow.

"Looking for *you*!" I add.

"Listen to me," says my mother. "You must never wander off like that again. Ever. Do you promise?"

I promise. Another lie. I will probably wander off and require paging over the loudspeaker the next time we go to Target, let alone somewhere with displayed models of diseased reproductive organs.

"Can we go to the gift shop now?"

"No gift shop."

"Not even for astronaut ice cream?"

"Not even for astronaut ice cream."

"Keem!" shouts my sister. "WANT ASTWONAUT KEEM!"

We go to the gift shop.

4:45: We emerge from the gift shop. My sister, clutching a bar of dehydrated ice cream in one hand and a large plush hand puppet in the shape of a grasshopper in the other, demands to be taken to the bathroom.

"No," says my mother.

"So, Rachy," my father begins, "it's a shame you were gone, because you missed a really *fascinating* exhibit about the speed of sound and its relation to—"

"Marty," my mother interrupts. "I would really, really like to go to Lord & Taylor. Could I do that?"

"I thought we were going to go to the Jewish museum now," my father says, looking hurt, "and then go look at that synagogue that was built during the Revolutionary War. You'll like that," he adds, nodding toward me. "It's beautiful."

"Marty," my mother repeats. "I would really, really like to go to Lord & Taylor."

"Fine," says my father. "Fine. What about you, Rachy?" He looks at me, his face full of hope.

My sister's allegiance was unquestioned. She was my mother's daughter through and through, and besides, my father would be unwilling and unable to accommodate her prodigious intestinal needs. But I could go either way. I weighed my options. I could go with my father, and spend the next seven million hours watching him take photographs of baseboards and ceiling details while lecturing me about the Moorish influence in eighteenth-century Sephardic architecture, or I could go with my mother to a midrange department store, where any initial expectation would be cut down with a sharp "No, we are not going to the Rachel Department. *This time is for Mommy and we are going to the Mommy Department,"* and spend the next seven million hours watching her try on nineteen different pairs of dress slacks, none of which she will buy.

On the other hand, my mother would probably take us in a taxi.

6:15: The set time for my rebuffed and hurt father to meet us at the Lancôme counter at Lord & Taylor.

7:00: The time my rebuffed and hurt father actually appears at the Lancôme counter at Lord & Taylor.

7:20: It is almost time for dinner. If we are in New York City, we eat a slice of pizza or French fries at the McDonald's in Times Square where my mother was once, thrillingly, mugged by a roving troupe of gangland mimes, before racing to the Broadway show my father had bought tickets for in the TKTS line next to the army recruiting station. If elsewhere, we repair to our hotel room for a short break before the evening meal.

"Can we go swimming now?" I ask.

"SWIMMING!" my sister bellows. For such a tiny person, barely four years old, she has an unusually deep and resonant baritone voice. It is striking enough in her adult self, but when she was very small it was even odder that she sounded possessed by Ted Koppel.

But there will be no swimming. Instead, we are washed and groomed, dressed in our finest casual separates, and taken to a decent restaurant of my parents' choosing. At home we might eat at Subway several times a week, or consume pudding and packets of salad dressing standing up in front of the television, but on vacation we were expected to go somewhere that requires a modicum of proper table conduct, sit there like ladies, and *behave.*

"You're a very lucky girl, you know," my grandmother once informed me. It was a rare trip on which she and my grandfather had accompanied us, and I had complained too long and too loudly in an art museum. I was hungry; I wanted pizza. I was thirsty; I wanted a soda. My feet hurt, I was tired, why couldn't we go back to the hotel and watch pay-per-view like normal people? My grandfather, if I remember correctly, voiced similar complaints, though he seemed strangely exempt from admonishment. "Someday, you'll be so grateful that you had parents who would take you to these places so you could get some culture."

My grandmother told a lot of lies. Shrimp was kosher. Ice cream makes you thin. The warm can of Sprite she was serving you had *not* been purchased during the Ford administration. And my personal favorite: "Don't be angry with Mother. Your mother is your best friend."

Clearly, my grandmother's mother had never ransacked her room in a frenzy searching for contraband marijuana.

The waiter arrives to take our order, and I decide to forgo my usual plain pasta with a hint of olive oil and order something worthy of the occasion—something sophisticated and bold, something that is actually on the menu. This will prove difficult. I do not eat green vegetables. I do not eat yellow vegetables. I will eat nothing with a creamy texture or garnished with a dressing or sauce of a creamy texture. Obviously, I eat no meat.

It is my turn. He is stylishly dressed, our waiter, with a deep suntan and a silver bracelet on one wrist. I think he is the most handsome man I have ever seen. He smiles at me. "And what would you like, ma'am?"

Shyly, I point at a dish I have selected—something with rice and fresh tomatoes. "Does it have meat in it?" I ask.

He frowns regretfully. It does.

Taking a deep breath, I ask the question I have heard my mother and father ask a thousand times. "Would it be possible to have it without the meat?"

"I'm so sorry, sweetheart. It's premade with a beef stock."

I cast my eyes downward. *Stupid! Of course it's not possible.* But "sweetheart"! There is hope!

He kneels before me gracefully, peering into my face, and asks gently, "Are you a vegetarian, honey?"

"You're a vegetarian because you're a Jewish person," a girl whose name I cannot remember once informed me imperiously. She paused to fill her tongue with a dollop of bright pink frosting, her enormous fish eyes staring blank and unblinking from behind huge lavender glasses. A preschool classmate had brought cupcakes to share, cupcakes, my teacher informed me, containing lard. She had thoughtfully provided me with a prewrapped granola bar kept for these occasions. Thanks.

"Only Jewish people are vegetarians," the girl continues. As usual, I am the only one of either persuasion. "Because Jewish people are weird. And vegetarians are weird. You're both, so you're extra, extra weird." The frosting coats her mouth thickly as though it were built up with a palette knife, like a messy de Kooning. Not that she would know who that is.

"I'm a vegetarian too," says the waiter. "Here, let's take a look at the menu together and find something delicious for you. You like tomatoes, don't you?"

I love tomatoes, but not as much as I love him. He crouches beside me, frosted tips bent over the menu in my shaking hands, and I want to marry him, or someone just like him. And I want to stay in this city forever, a city where the waiters are also vegetarians, where museums are filled with art and deformities, the shops are filled with dress slacks and perfume, and the streets are filled with Jews and blacks and vegetarians and kind young men, and none of them care if the pool is already closed when they get back to the hotel because swimming is for people without dreams.

Three

The Russians Are Coming

We watched the end of the Soviet Union on television, just as we had watched the *Challenger* explosion five years before, the little ones seated Indian-style on the rough blue carpet of the assembly room, we big kids at the back of the room against the cupboards, at last permitted the dignity of a chair from which to witness the Events That Shape Our World.

I suppose it was a happy day. Millions would at last shake off the oppressive yoke of communism and enjoy the freedoms we took for granted in Nebraska: the freedom to hoard canned goods, to purchase stonewashed jeans with zippers at the ankle, to wipe with velvety name-brand toilet paper. Surely this was a good thing for humanity. Also, we were for the time being safe from imminent nuclear annihilation, another good thing. Omaha, we were often told, was certain to be a target on account of the Strategic Air Command headquarters just outside the city limits. This very base was the birthplace of the *Enola Gay*, and our assured destruction would have a neat karmic symmetry to it. As I was already the sort of child who carefully checked my body for tumors each evening before bed, this unexpected reprieve from compulsive morbidity was delightful. I looked forward to falling asleep that night unfettered by visions of mushroom clouds, melted skin, and ghoulish sufferers of radiation sickness prowling the ruined streets like crazed packs of extras from *Dawn of the Dead*.

But endings are often bittersweet, and this was no exception. The cold-war era was a very special time to be a child. We were appreciated. World leaders hell-bent on universal destruction might be crazily accumulating nuclear armaments like the lucky winners of a Nickelodeon-sponsored Toys "R" Us shopping spree, but even the homeliest child could send a hand-lettered plea for peace or a winsome crayon drawing where Children of Many Colors held hands around a giant dove to the proper political personage, and land herself a spot on the evening news. She would be profiled in *Scholastic* magazine, given a hometown parade and a press conference with the mayor. She might get to meet the pope, or Michael J. Fox, and if cute, ethnically "diverse," in a wheelchair, or heir to major donors to the Republican Party, she might even be paraded (or wheeled) through the White House Rose Garden to receive a grandfatherly hug from President Reagan himself, before he delivered a humble, awestruck speech in her honor, full of phrases like "out of the mouths of babes" and "and lo! A little child shall lead us."

But Reagan was out of office now, and in his place was President Bush, a gaunt, lipless man with a bizarre, electronic cadence to his voice, like the pixilated monster congratulating you for correctly answering a math problem on your PC Junior.

"Do you think George Bush likes kids?" I asked my father, fingering the faded Dukakis button stuck to his bulletin board.

"No," he replied. "I think he likes Saudis."

And now the Soviet Union was gone too. There would be no more market for adorable letters for peace addressed to feckless dignitaries. No more tragic Soviet "twins"[†] to cast a mournful pall over safari-themed Bar Mitzvahs. The Jews would be free now. Free to work. Free to worship. And, most important, free to *leave*.

"Does anyone have any questions?" asked Mrs. Nussbaum, our principal. She turned down the volume on the TV and gazed at us with concern.

Noah Levine raised his hand. "Can we watch *DuckTales*?"

"No. Anyone else? Yes, Joshua?"

"What about *Darkwing Duck*?"

She sighed. "All right."

As we knew, Mrs. Nussbaum continued, things had been bad for the Jews in the former Soviet Union for some time. However, since its dissolution, many Jewish families who had previously been refused exit visas—mockingly termed "refuseniks" by the Communist government—were flooding out of the broken country in torrents. Most were settling in (or for) the state of Israel, but the lucky ones managed to gain entry to the United States. She lowered her voice dramatically, beaming at us. "And some of those families are going to live right here in Omaha!"

They were coming here, she continued, because of a massive effort by the Jewish Federation to bring new families to our community. Hundreds of cities were jockeying for them, like first-round NBA draft picks, but little old Omaha had won. Wasn't that exciting?

Danny Edelstein raised his hand from the front row. He was a thin boy, the skin around his mouth perpetually red and chapped from constant licking, giving him the look of a diseased clown.

[†] Howdy, Gentiles! Now, a "twin" or "twinning" in this context refers to the practice, popular in the 1980s, of symbolically sharing one's Bar or Bat Mitzvah with an oppressed Jewish teen in the Soviet Union. Barred from having a celebration by the institutionalized anti-Semitism of the Communist regime, the fortunate little comrade could take consolation in the fact that his or her name would be engraved for posterity on a small plaque in the Bernard and Ida Weinstein Memorial Walkway at Temple B'nai Shalom of Grosse Pointe, Michigan.

"Yes, Danny?"

"MY CAT HAD FIVE KITTENS!" Danny shouted, jumping to his feet.

"Danny, you are being disruptive," Mrs. Nussbaum said firmly. "Please sit down."

Danny remained standing.

"Danny, SIT DOWN!"

Danny giggled wildly, licking his lips.

"Danny, I'm counting! One . . . two . . ."

Danny sat down.

She continued. "Now, of course, some of these families have children. And we are very lucky, because next week two new children, from the former Soviet Union, are going to be students at our school. It will be a great privilege to have them here, and we're all going to make them feel very welcome. They've been through a great deal."

Melissa Gitnik waved her arm wildly. "Can we ask questions now?"

Mrs. Nussbaum sighed. "Yes, you *may* ask questions now."

A flurry of sticky hands flew up in the air.

"Are they boys or girls?" called Jacob Feinberg.

"What are their names?" asked Leah Rosen.

"Do they speak English?" wondered Jeremy Paskowitz.

"MY CAT'S KITTENS CAME OUT HER VAGINA!" yelled Danny Edelstein. He was marched immediately into the hallway, cackling and licking all the way.

Mrs. Nussbaum waved her arms for silence. "It's a boy and a girl. I don't know their names yet, but I do know they won't speak any English. So we are all going to be very kind and patient, and on our very best behavior."

We had a couple of Russian kids at our school already. They had come to the States as toddlers, and apart from a few differences (the heavy accents of their parents, the toothless, chain-smoking grandmothers, the gelatinous beet-based items they brought for lunch in Tupperware containers), they were indistinguishable from the rest of us. Omaha was a soft landing for a Soviet immigrant: safe, cheap, with a close-knit, supportive Jewish community. Even at a low-paying job, if you worked hard, saved a bit of money, and learned the language, in a few years you could buy a shitty car, a small house, a life.

"Do you know the ages of the refugee children, Mrs. Nussbaum?" Nathan Finkel enunciated crisply in his nasal drawl, looking primly down over the rims of his aviator bifocals like a disapproving spinster. Nathan Finkel was one of those deeply nerdy children who, despite their obsequious efforts to win over powerful adults, are neither bright nor precocious enough to be of interest for long.

His cousin Bitterman, the other Nathan, was at his side, like him in every way but for the wide band of elastic strapping his little bifocals to his head. Nathan Bitterman had a habit of walking into things—walls, jungle gyms, panes of glass—face first, often hitting his head so hard he would be knocked out cold. Unfortunately, none of this neurological rebooting had yet had an effect on his gruesome collection of speech impediments, the last of which would not disappear until his seventeenth year. Now Nathan B. said, "Yeth, Mithuth Nuthbaum, do you know de ageth of duh wefugee chiwuhdwen?"

Upon finishing this labor-intensive inquiry, he peeked over his shoulder to beam at me in triumph. It had been known for some time that Nathan Bitterman was very much in love with me. I didn't smile back. In only a few more months, I would finish sixth grade, graduating from this school. My parents, presented with no other option, would finally be forced to send me away from the Jews, to the promised land of public school, where I planned to throw myself at the biggest, blondest Presbyterian who would have me.

My dream Presbyterian wasn't just any Presbyterian but manufactured to fit my precise specifications, a list of exacting criteria that grew longer each day. As I mentioned, he would be broad and well built (for a seventh-grader, anyway), but he would also wear sweaters ordered from the J. Crew catalogue, smell of Cool Water aftershave, and harbor a secret affinity for the Broadway musical (this last would eventually lead to difficulty). I passed hours dreaming of his first name—something short, masculine, resolutely New Testament. Luke. Tom. Chris. *Chris!* But choosing his surname, along with the ethnicity (or lack thereof) it implied, was more fun. I considered simple occupational/location-related monikers, names bestowed hundreds of years ago in a quaint English hamlet, where his pink-cheeked ancestors drank ale, rode horses, thatched roofs, and burned heretics with uncomplicated gusto. Baker, Taylor, Waters, Woods. When these seemed a bit standard-issue, I experimented with the names of beloved soap opera characters—always an excellent resource for finding the perfect appellation for the WASP/porn star in all of us. I had narrowed the best of these down to two: Walsh, meaning "Welsh" (see "Walsh, Brandon, Brenda, Cindy, and Jim," *Beverly Hills 90210,* FOX), and Abbott, meaning "abbot" (see "Abbott, Ashley, Billy, Jack, Jill, John, Traci," *The Young and the Restless,* CBS), but I was most intrigued by the rich variety of surnames beginning with the inimitably plucky prefix *Mc.* Slap a *Mc* (or a *Mac*) onto your name, and you instantly transform into a Meg Ryan character—cuter, spunkier, and more lovable. And yes, I realize this sounds stupid now, but hindsight is always 20/20. Friends, I beg you, do not pretend innocence. The fate of our great nation begs courage and integrity. There was a time, America, when many among us were held in thrall to the corrupting charms of Meg Ryan. When we fell in love with her endlessly, in movie after movie. Meg Ryan, with her endless procession of adorably "quirky" (wandering forlornly into the kitchen at 3 A.M. to eat peanut butter directly out of the jar—*without even spreading it on a cracker or anything!* Quelle *bizarre!*), hopelessly insecure Katies and Kathleens and Maggies: Kate McKay, Kathleen McGuire, Maggie Mc*Goy.*

And my fantasy boyfriend, Chris McPresbyterian, with his fantasy mother in the Junior League who wore sweaters with Scottie dogs knitted into them and their fantasy family dinners with the McPresbyterian grandparents, who chewed their pork chops and mashed potatoes and peas with their mouth closed and never, ever, inquired about the regularity of the McPresbyterian grandchildren's bowel movements. And Chris and I would go upstairs to his room, which would be decorated all in plaid, and close the door, which would bother no one because the adults would be downstairs, getting lightly tipsy on red wine, *which they imbibed for pleasure and did not refrigerate!*—and kiss with tongues for hours and hours and I would come home reeking of Cool Water and Protestantism and never be forced to participate in what was known as a "*brocha* bee"[†] ever, *ever* again.

But for now, I must languish with the Jews and the Jew Cadets in Jewland, where our Beloved Leader was about to address the mangled query of my Fudd-like suitor.

"I believe the children are both about nine years old," Mrs. Nussbaum announced. "And Nathan, I really think it's inappropriate to refer to them as refugees."

Nathan Finkel, the first to term them *refugees*, smirked at the lesser Nathan. The lesser Nathan's response, as always, was to hit himself violently in the head.

[†] Hello again, Gentiles! Come in and help yourself to the ham salad! *Brocha* is the Hebrew word for "blessing." As you may remember from high school productions of *Fiddler on the Roof,* there is one for almost everything. A "*brocha* bee," then, is a competition much like a spelling bee, in which one might be asked a question such as "First popularized by observant Jews in the Warsaw Ghetto, what is the *brocha* said before eating a potato, raw or rotten?" Obviously this is a trick question, for if a food is eaten in other than its usual manner (i.e., raw or rotten), a different blessing is required than that for the same food prepared and consumed in its customary fashion. And you people wonder why Israeli policy is such an impenetrable pain in the ass.

My maternal grandmother came to this country from a small village in Lithuania in 1922. Her mother had died of tuberculosis several years earlier, during the war, and her aunt, to whose care she and her younger brother had been entrusted, died soon afterward. Left alone with their cousins, the children were sent for by their father, my great-grandfather, in Ohio, whom they barely remembered and who, according to contemporary accounts, was a real bastard. Leaving their orphaned cousins behind, they traveled unaccompanied, the journey from their village to the ship alone lasting several weeks. My grandmother was about twelve at the time; her brother, my great-uncle, was two years younger.

My mother would often tell the story of her great adventure, attempting to leaven its underlying, though not atypical, sadness with amusing shipboard anecdotes. The time my bewildered little *bubbe* tried to eat a banana with the peel still on! The time she followed a woman with false teeth around for days, fascinated by the notion that one could have a full set of teeth and then, just as suddenly, be as toothless as a baby. The time a sailor roughly told her to move from a heap of canvas on the dock, and violently seasick, she threw up all over his chest.

"Isn't that funny?" my mother would bray cheerfully.

"It's still really sad," I would say.

"Well, consider the alternative!"

"What do you mean?"

"If she hadn't come to America?"

I would think for a moment. "We'd be living in Lithuania,[†] in a house with dirt floors?"

[†] According to inter-Jewish ethnographical lore, we Lithuanians, or Litvaks, have certain inherent traits, namely, we are cold, analytical, and unfriendly (particularly in contrast with the warmer and more effusive Jews of Galicia, our sworn enemies). We also prefer our gefilte fish savory, as opposed to sweetened (also in contrast to the Galicians), a difference that could have surely led to centuries of brutal internecine violence à la the Catholic/Protestant or Sunni/Shia conflicts, had it not been for all the other people who were trying to kill us.

My mother would throw her head back with a peal of delight. "No! She'd have been sent to the gas, silly! Just like the rest of her family! We'd never have even been born!"

This is my mother's idea of a funny joke.

For me, the most salient point of these narratives was the simple circumstance of their ages: a twelve-year-old and a ten-year-old coming by themselves to a foreign country to live forever with a strange, mean man. This knowledge was difficult to reconcile with the fact that I was not yet permitted to visit a shopping mall without adult supervision.

"Things were different then," my mother says. "Safer. Except, you know, for the pogroms."

There was a photograph, stained and sepia-tinged, of my grandmother, taken just before they left Europe, and because she died long before I was born, this was the way I always imagined her. Her clothing, undoubtedly her best, is old-fashioned and girlish: a high-waisted dress of indistinct calico, low-heeled boots with a neat row of buttons marching primly up her ankles, a large bow perched stiffly in her bobbed hair. I wonder about her hair in this picture—surely the Jazz Age hadn't reached the shtetl? Was her hair cut off especially for the voyage, to cut down on lice? Had she been ill? I dimly remember a phrase from a storybook in the library about a band of wandering minstrels in the Middle Ages: "Never mind Pearl's hair; it fell out with the fever."

My grandmother was also named Pearl.

Also pictured is her younger brother, who would grow up to become my nonagenarian uncle, who, after a long, happy life of being universally beloved by all who know him, currently occupies his time playing with his dentures and laughing uncontrollably.

"Better than weeping uncontrollably," my mother says.

In the photograph, he sits in front of my grandmother,

clutching for dear life a toy horse he'll have to return at the end of the session, a photographer's prop to lend the illusion of affluence to another unhappy child. They both look so old, so worn. Weary, perhaps, at the prospect of the long journey ahead, of schlepping all that shit, the trunks, the *snacks,* the heirloom menorah, on trains, on boats, across the ocean. Yet they don't look afraid. Something in their dark eyes is strangely opaque, beyond fear, as if after what they have gone through—the fitful deaths of their mother, their aunt, the various and sundry pogroms, the lying in a hole covered in straw so the drunk peasants won't rape you— nothing could ever scare them again.

So, what horrors had Eastern Europe's newest little stateless waifs beheld before embarking on the long road to freedom? Would their faces be as haggard, as dead, as indifferent to further trauma as my beribboned grandmother's? The Soviet Union was the most oppressive and anti-Semitic regime since Nazi Germany—fund-raising letter after fund-raising letter had in-formed us of that. For God's sake, Heather Schneiderman had do-nated a *full third of her Bat Mitzvah profits* (I mean, gifts) to charities that might alleviate the suffering of her "twin," Galina Yevgenova Rifkin, denied a celebration of her own womanhood by a brutal regime that was the Enemy of Joy. *One whole third of her Bat Mitzvah money!* It said so right on the invitation! *And this, even though Heather Schneiderman's parents, Dr. and Mrs. Steven Schneiderman, had made it very clear that Heather was going to be expected to pay for HALF HER CAR HERSELF when she turned sixteen!* That's how serious it was!

Coming out of a situation so dire, I felt certain that these poor children had experienced all manner of intolerable cruelty. I imagined them huddled in the subzero weather, standing on the endless line for hand soap or sardine paste, pulling their shabby furs over their heads to block out the cruel invective hurled by their comrades, the accompanying gobs of spit freezing midair and hitting their faces squarely in icy shards of Jew-hating hail. I imagined them struggling through the snow with their little newspaper-wrapped packages of fish and bread and rolls of toilet paper also suitable for industrial sanding with tears freezing on their cheeks, trudging home to a dank flat in a cinder-block housing complex to find the apartment ransacked, books shredded, the ancient violin smashed to bits, and their elderly grandfather lying unconscious in the middle of it all, blood pouring from his skull. The KGB officer on his way out pauses in the hall to slap them hard across their cheeks with his leather glove and steal their hard-won toilet paper. I imagined them at school, forced to wear unflattering Young Pioneers uniforms with neckerchiefs, reciting *The Communist Manifesto* from memory, performing rigorous calisthenics to a piano recording of the Laureate of the Lenin Komsomol Award, while squat, hard-faced teachers speckled in moles (and facial hair, for the women) crack their braided whips, shouting: *"Faster, Jew-filth! Faster! Faster!"*

"Now remember," Mrs. Nussbaum said, winding down. "They're going to be a little overwhelmed. They'll be in a brand-new place, and they don't speak any English."

Jamie Kirshner—whose mother was a convert†—leaned over

---

† A word about the Jewish attitude toward converts: long known for our steadfast refusal to add to our numbers through proselytizing, the Jews, as a whole, remain somewhat cool on the subject of conversion. A prospective member must thrice approach and be thrice refused by the attending rabbi before being allowed to begin conversion classes, and even long after the process is complete, the shadows of one's provenance continue to hang about the head of the converted, as one might hear such whispers as "I hear the father did some jail time," or "You know, she used to be a man." I'm afraid to say that the simple motivation behind much of this is jealousy. Converts to Judaism are disproportionately Gentile women preparing to marry Jewish men—who as we all know make the best husbands—and the wide-hipped, bushy-haired thirty-four-year-olds still living with their parents would scarcely be human if they didn't glance across the pew Saturday morning at the willowy stranger praying diligently in their midst and think, *What? He couldn't find a real Jewish girl to marry?*

to me and snorted. "They must be pretty stupid if they can't speak English."

Mrs. Nussbaum trained her laser death ray on Jamie immediately, the veins in her neck popping slightly over the collar of her teal knit two-piece. "*Listen to me*," she hissed. "We are going to be on our *very best behavior.* I will *not* hear any negative comments or put-downs. *Is that clear?*"

Exceedingly clear. I flicked Jamie Kirshner hard on the knee. I didn't want to hear any negative comments or put-downs either. I would defend these poor refugee children from the taunts and barbs of mean people like Jamie Kirshner, who if she wanted to see stupid, should really listen to herself sounding out the word *daughter* in reading group sometime. I mean, that was just funny. These children were from the land of Pushkin and Tolstoy, Dostoyevsky and *Doctor Zhivago.* They may not have had the advantages that we'd had, having been discriminated against and denied luxuries like chewing gum and disposable sanitary napkins, but before long they'd be reading circles around retarded half-Lutherans like Jamie Kirshner. And I would teach them.

I, Rachel Shukert, was going to teach the refugees English.

The idea was thrilling. I was thrilled to picture their shining faces turned to me in awe as I unlocked for them the mysteries and grandeur of the English language. I was thrilled as I pictured teachers and parents taking me aside to passionately commend me for what I was doing for these poor children. I was thrilled as I saw them at a podium in front of the whole school, hell, the whole city, delivering a speech in perfect English about the one girl who had really helped them, the girl who had really made a difference; the thundering crescendo of applause as I slowly, shyly rose to my feet, blushing prettily as I made my way to the stage through an ocean of well-wishers. I was thrilled; until I stepped in the puddle of fresh urine in which Danny Edelstein stood, chuckling merrily to himself as he licked his bleeding lips.

My school offered grades K–6; still, the number of students was exceedingly small. This was to be expected of the only Jewish day school in Nebraska, a state not known for its religious diversity, despite achievements throughout its history by prominent local Jews such as Henry Monsky[†] . . . and . . . well, that's all I can think of.[††] Oh wait! Mrs. B.![N]

The arrival of the two Russian students would increase our student body by almost 10 percent. Luckily, we had a third classroom.

Our building was a former country school once attended by the children of small farmers whose property clustered around the

---

[†] The founder of Aleph Zadik Aleph (AZA) #1, the founding chapter of the world-reknowned B'nai B'rith Youth Organization, from whom I received the title of "Sweetheart" in 1996.

[††] A Google search for "famous Jews from Nebraska" returned 0 hits.

[N] Rose Blumkin, affectionately referred to as Mrs. B., a Russian Jewish immigrant of extraordinarily tiny stature, founded the Nebraska Furniture Mart in 1937 with five hundred dollars' worth of furniture and grew the business into the largest and most comprehensive furniture and carpet store in the Midwest. Employees and shoppers alike remember her, still spry in her late eighties, whizzing around her 700,000-square-foot store in a motorized golf cart, seeking out especially stupid or lazy sales associates upon whom to hurl a barrage of Yiddish-inflected criticism. After a well-publicized business dispute with her grandsons, during which she referred to them as "the Hitlers" in the pages of the *Omaha World Herald*, Mrs. Blumkin, at age 95, abandoned the empire she had created and opened up a megastore, Mrs. B's Warehouse, right across the street from the competition, where she worked every day until her death in 1998 at the age of 104. She was also a generous philanthropist, lending her resources and name to a variety of charities, most notably the Rose Blumkin Home for the Jewish Aged, where hundreds of her coreligionists have contentedly lived out their final days transfixed before reruns of *The Cosby Show*, stroking stuffed toys and hurling racial invective at darkcomplected staff members. Rose Blumkin, we salute you. You truly are, as one website I found called you, "the Cornhusker State's Best-Known Jew." This has been "Great Moments in Nebraska History." Good night, and go Huskers!

Omaha city limits in the 1950s. All but abandoned, the building and surrounding land was bought in the 1970s by Congregation Beth Israel (the Orthodox synagogue in town). Its infrastructure was falling into deep disrepair, rife with broken faucets, missing doorstops, and all sorts of other minor dangers. The asbestos level was considered hazardous to our health, and one of the nice things about being the last kid picked up after school was the possibility of seeing Mrs. Nussbaum climbing up into the ceiling in her aluminized hazmat space suit, paid for by us students selling things out of catalogues door-to-door. The fund-raiser was a great success. It's easy for a surly neighbor to slam the door in the faces of a cheerleading squad or a basketball team. Saying no is more difficult when a seven-year-old brandishes a colored pamphlet of merchandise at your door and pleads, "Please buy this caramel corn in an attractive tin the shape of a cat, or we will all die of lung cancer!"

The student body, minuscule as it was, was split into three factions: the young children of harried yuppies desperate for an all-day kindergarten that wouldn't be so strict about the birthday cutoff dates; the outspoken über-Jews, who were too religious for public school—these were mostly males with the charming tendency to throw the weight of the Law behind their playground chau‑vinism—"No girls allowed! It says so in the Talmud!"—and, finally, children so developmentally delayed, socially awkward, and irredeemably dweeby that their parents feared they would come home from the merciless jungle of the public school system missing large sections of skin and having been made to chew and swallow their own soiled underpants.

There was little chance of such things happening here. From the kindergarteners to the sixth-graders, we shared everything as one: recess, assembly, music, gym. We ate lunch together at long tables in a small cafeteria, standing in line to microwave our approved kosher lunches and retrieve our cartons of milk from a communal refrigerator. It felt more like a large, odd family than a school. In retrospect, the experience was an extraordinarily kind one, free from bullies and cruel, rough play, remarkably lacking in cliques and cattiness. Still, I couldn't overcome the suspicion that the whole *Jewish* thing was severely impeding my life's ambition to be a goy.

The evening after Mrs. Nussbaum's announcement, my grandmother stopped by our house to unload several shoe boxes full of stale mandelbrot[†] from the trunk of her car. My mother accepted them with her usual grace: "Great. Now we finally have a reason to build onto the house."

When my grandmother had finished refusing all offers of food and drink and settled onto the sofa, I apprised her of my grand plan to save the Russians.

"Isn't that darling! What a sweet girl you are!" Grandma exclaimed, clasping her knobby hands in delight. "Don't you have a sweet, wonderful daughter?" She gazed at my mother rapturously.

"I think they're required by the state to hire someone for that," said my mother. "Someone who knows what they're doing."

"Don't you worry about that," clucked my grandmother, who in the immortal words of my mother "would watch you grind your own shit into her carpet and tell you you were Picasso." "I think it's just wonderful what you're doing for those poor refugee children. I'm taking you on a shopping spree this weekend, and I don't want to hear any complaining. My little teacher's going to need a whole new wardrobe!"

My mother went upstairs. She didn't come down for a very long time.

Bright and early Monday morning, I sat in the principal's tiny office in a brand-new Esprit flowered-denim jacket with a

[†] A tough, biscotti-like almond cookie, usually coated in sugar or cinnamon, suitable for eating with coffee or for performing minor tooth extractions.

matching flounced miniskirt and a coordinating oversized tote bag. Mrs. Nussbaum toyed pensively with an eraser in the shape of an apple, undoubtedly pondering how best to articulate her praise of my altruism, my generosity of spirit, my clear superiority as a human being and a Future Leader of America.

"Well," she said at last. "We're actually planning to hire someone to help them with their English. I mean, a professional in this sort of thing."

"And now you don't have to! Isn't that great?"

She said nothing.

Why? Why, why was I destined to spend my life in the company of provincial fools, yokels unable to see the greatness that blazed before their empty eyes? "Don't you see? I'M SAVING YOU MONEY!"

"You watch your tone, young lady," she snapped. "No one raises their voice to me in this office."

"I'm just trying to help," I whispered sulkily. "Didn't you tell us we all had to help?"

Her tone softened a little. "Yes," she said. "And I appreciate your good intentions. But we are required by the state of Nebraska to hire a professional ESL teacher. It's the *law.*"

"But I could teach them stuff about our *culture*. It would be good for them learn stuff from, like, a *peer,* you know?" I adjusted my new tote bag, so that the giant E S P R I T emblazoned across the pocket was easier to read. "I mean, after all, I am probably one of the most, if not *the* most . . . *coolest* kids at this school."

What does it mean to be the coolest out of a group of forlorn toddlers, Chasidim-in-training, and borderline autistics? Mrs. Nussbaum didn't attempt an answer, but several days later I was summoned to her office. She informed me that I was to be excused from social studies twice a week to report to the library, where I would help our new students to improve their English vocabulary, and gave me a stack of large cards printed with watercolors of various zoo animals. Below each picture, the corresponding word was spelled in big block letters. LION. ELEPHANT. PENGUIN.

"Is this really what they need to be learning?" I asked. "I mean, if I was a refugee—I mean, an *immigrant*—I would want to know more useful things, like about clothes or—"

"Rachel," said Mrs. Nussbaum wearily. "Don't push it."

Allow me, if you will, to set the scene.

A small school library. A young girl (referred to in the dialogue as ME*), dressed in an oversized sweater of shocking purple covered in pom-poms that look like malignant growths, sits at a low table looking very pleased with herself. Her hair is gathered into a tight ponytail that sticks directly out the side of her head like the handle of a watering can and is adorned with a bright turquoise ribbon rosette the size of a large man's fist. On the table before her are some notebooks, pencils, and two stacks of flash cards, one of which appears to have been manufactured by a genuine educational entity; the other a mess of index cards and magazine clippings, sticking together a bit from the excess rubber cement dribbling from the side. She straightens the piles, fusses with her pencils, and smugly sits back in her chair, admiring the arrangement. Two children, a boy and a girl perhaps eight or nine years old, enter. They approach the insanely dressed girl, and at once her satisfied smirk is replaced by a look of dismay. These are the Russians? Some refugees. They're not even dressed right. Sure, they have ugly shoes and sweatshirts featuring unfamiliar cartoon characters, but no shawls? No patches? No babushkas? Where are their babushkas? And what happened to their big dark eyes, full of sorrow, and their thin, pinched faces that tell of years of hunger and humiliation? They look awfully well fed—especially the boy, she notes, taking in his round belly and large, flaccid cheeks with disapproval. Instinctively she tightens her grip* *around the bag of plain M&M's concealed in her lap. They sit and stare at her impassively, not even a flicker of gratefulness or admiration on their faces; not even for her sweater that cost seventy-eight dollars, even though her mother said that was an obscene amount to spend on a sweater for an eleven-year-old, that* she *didn't even have a sweater that cost seventy-eight dollars even though she had a Ph.D. and was finished growing. "Except for out!" the girl had responded and had been sent to her room and made to stay there all night even though it was a Must See TV Thursday, which meant missing* 227, Amen, The Golden Girls, Empty Nest, *and* L.A. Law. *Oh well. They're Communists. They don't understand the importance of labels. The girl decides to give them a second chance.*

ME *(pointing to her chest)*: My name is Rachel. Rachel. What's your name?

(The refugees do not respond.)

ME *(louder and slower, still pointing)*: Rachel. Ray-chul.

BOY *(pointing to himself)*: Ray-chul.

ME *(even louder)*: No! Rachel. Me. *I'm* Rachel.

(No response)

ME *(shouting)*: RACHEL! RACHEL!

BOY *(also shouting)*: RAY-CHUL! RAY-CHUL!

A WOMAN'S VOICE: RACHEL!

(MRS. OLSEN, the second- and third- grade teacher, has stuck her head inside the library.)

MRS. OLSEN: Could you keep it down? Please? I am *trying* to teach a lesson to my class.

ME: Sorry.

MRS. OLSEN: Sorry what?

ME: Sorry, Mrs. Olsen. I'll be quieter.

MRS. OLSEN: Thank you.

(She disappears back into her classroom. ME turns back to the suspiciously chubby "refugees.")

ME *(whispering)*: My name is Rachel.

(The girl, perhaps a bit sharper than the boy, seems to have figured out at last what is being communicated.)

GIRL *(whispering, points at self)*: Yelena.

BOY *(also whispering, points at self)*: Ray-chul.

(Disgusted, the girl, YELENA, shakes her head and confers with him in Russian.)

GIRL: *Brezhnev stolichnaya. Blini dosteyevsky glasnost nyet.*

BOY: *Brezhnev vodka smirnoff?*

GIRL: *Dah.*

BOY: Ah! *(points at self)* EUGENE! EUGENE!

ME: Great! Your name is Eugene, and your name is Yelena, and my name is Rachel!

BOY: *Dah, dah!* EUGENE!

(They sit in silence.)
(Finally, ME, still unaware that her sweater has metastasized, picks up the animal flash cards.)

ME: Lion.

GIRL and BOY: Lion.

ME: Tiger.

GIRL and BOY: Tiger.

ME: Ostrich.

> *(There is some laughter. Perhaps* ostrich *means something different in Russian, like "vomit" or "penis"? After they have worked their way through the entire stack of flash cards, they again sit in silence for five minutes. ME, who is in way over her head, picks up the mass of rubber-cement-covered flash cards and holds one up.)*

ME: I made some of my own flash cards, just in case we got through those . . . just some stuff I thought you guys should know . . .

> *(They stare at her in silence. Pensively, the boy begins to pick his nose.)*

ME *(pointing to flash card)*: Jason Priestley.

GIRL and BOY: Jason Priestley.

ME: Fred Savage.

GIRL and BOY: Fred Sawage.

ME: Jordan Knight.

GIRL and BOY: Jordan Knight.

ME: I actually kind of hate the New Kids on the Block. I'm, like, more into musicals, you know, like *Camelot*? Or like *The Phantom of the Opera*? That's mostly what I listen to, on my Sony boom box that my parents bought me that cost like fifty dollars? You guys probably don't have those in Russia. Anyway, I just think musical theater is so much more articulate and, like, intelligent than pop music or whatever. Possibly with the exception of Whitney Houston, because her songs are like, really emotional. But whatever you think about them, I put Jordan in here because New Kids on the Block is probably like, one of the *most* influential music groups of all time. I mean, everybody says so, like even *Time* magazine, and a lot of people are really into them, so you should know who they are and which one you think is the cutest in case anybody asks you. I think Jordan is the cutest. But there's this one girl I know who thinks Danny's the cutest. Isn't that gross? Like, gag me. He looks like a *monkey*! But actually, that's not even the grossest thing, because the grossest thing ever is that her parents gave her New Kids on the Block sheets, like to sleep on, for Hanukah, and she says how it's awesome because there's a big picture of Danny on her *pillowcase* and she likes that *she drools on him while she's asleep*. Ew! She's disgusting. But I'm not going to tell you her name or anything, because she's seriously my best friend.

(They sit in silence for several minutes.)

Mrs. Olsen stuck her head back into the library. I marveled at how her perm wobbled gently in one piece with even the slightest motion of her head. Might one find a metaphor for this occurrence in nature—the crest of a French poodle, the puff of dandelion in a weak breeze? No. There was no precedent for Mrs. Olsen's hair, in either the animal or botanical kingdoms. It was magical.

"Time for lunch," she said.

Gleefully, I jumped to my feet, the forgotten package of M&M's in my lap dropping to the floor.

"M&M's!" cried Eugene.

"Yes, thank you," I said, scooping them up. "Come on. It's time to eat our lunches now." I mimed bringing a fork to my lips. They mirrored my gesture.

"No, not here. IN THE LUNCHROOM."

Why do we assume those unable to speak our language are

hearing-impaired? Has anyone actually met a person from another country who is hearing-impaired, and would our manner of
addressing them change? Would we change our tactics entirely
and whisper at them, rapidly and unintelligibly?

"M&M's!" Eugene cried, more insistently. "M&M's!" He
pointed a chubby finger toward the bag clutched in my hand.

Were we impelled to be especially nice to these people, for no
tangible reason other than an accident of birth? An accident of
history? If it was the United States that collapsed under the weight
of its own disastrous policies (as it threatens to any day) and its
citizens were obliged to take up residence in formerly hostile or
indifferent countries, if an influx of American refugees—excuse
me, *expatriates*—suddenly flooded Bucharest, or Lyons, or Islam-
abad, would they be extra nice to us? Would they bother to pro-
vide us with valuable cultural insight into their television
programs, teen idols, and fashionable footwear—to spend *forty-
five minutes of their life that they would never get back ON A
WEEKEND* making them flash cards to educate them to this effect? Would they feel like they had to give us their M&M's?

"M&M's!" He was shouting now. *"M&M's!"*

"For heaven's sake, Rachel," cried Mrs. Olsen, shepherding her
class through the library. "Give that poor Russian boy your M&M's!"

The next week, the ESL teacher arrived.

Some time later, I arrived at school one morning and found a
small group clustered around my locker, giggling, and for a terrible moment I thought that someone had found the picture of
Fred Savage that hung inside the door, his wrinkled newspaper
face sticky with Bonne Belle watermelon lip balm. Such a discov-
ery would mean dishonor. If my Jewish day school in Omaha
transformed into ancient Rome, and instead of a sixth-grader
with a disfiguring scrunchie I was a senator in a chalk-whitened

toga, I would have no choice but to fall upon my sword in the Forum to redeem my name and my family from the cruel master of ignominy.

Naturally, the reality was much, much more shameful.

On the door of my locker was a sheet of notebook paper, held there by the application of stickers—a badgers-and-other-small-woodland-creatures-on-skateboards motif—that I recognized as belonging to Mrs. Olsen. Pilfered from her desk? If this was the scene of a crime, I wanted no part of it. On the paper, somebody had carefully lettered his newly acquired English vocabulary in the following message:

RACHEL.
I LOVE HER. BY EUGENE.

Underneath were three small drawings done in colored pencil: a pink heart, a purple flower, and several small colored dots that, horrified, I realized were M&M's.

Oh dear.

"Ooooh! Rachel and Eugene are in LOVE!"

The taunt burned my ears. So much for the kindness of the socially impaired. They smelled blood, and now they swarmed around the carrion like vultures. Scrawny, adenoidal vultures with speech impediments and bladder-control issues, but vultures nonetheless.

"Hey Wachuwh! Aw you going to wet Eugene touch youhw butt?"

"Rachel and Eugene sitting in a tree, K-I-S-S-I-N- . . . wait. How do you say *kissing* in Russian?"

"*Celovanya*" was the smooth reply.

Et tu, Yelena? Will you too betray me?

From the middle of the crowd emerged Eugene himself, rosy and smiling. He beamed at me. He wasn't ashamed at expressing his feelings in a public forum; on the contrary, he looked proud, glowing like a man who has just proposed marriage on a talk show. Perhaps life in a rapidly destabilizing country, a life filled with prejudice and deprivation, had taught him to seize the day. Life, even at nine, was too short, too precious to hide your feelings, to spend weeks swiping the schoolbooks of your beloved and defacing her art projects with glue, prank-calling her house at sleepover parties and telling your friend to tell her she's ugly. Love was a cause for joyful celebration, something exquisite and rare, meant to be shouted from the rooftops: I'M IN LOVE AND IT'S BEAUTIFUL AND I DON'T CARE WHO KNOWS IT!

If that was the case, America was going to turn his ass so far inside out it would swallow his head. When even the autistics are laughing at you, it's time to learn a hard lesson.

I'd certainly learned mine. Several years later, in the tenth grade, boys fleeing the civil war in Sudan started trickling into our high school. These new students, warned my homeroom teacher, had suffered unimaginable trauma. They were certain to experience severe culture shock, and any help we might offer them—tutoring, language assistance, or even just refraining from acting like a total asshole in their presence (it was a public school, we didn't aim that high) would be greatly appreciated.

Had I been the person I was five years earlier, I'd have been the first to the office to sign up to help. I'd offer rides, food, clothing. I might even collaborate with one of them on a heart-wrenching novelized version of his experience with an obtuse title and highly conceptual jacket design that would salvage my literary reputation and cement my position as an Important Humanist of Our Time. I mean, before somebody else did it first.

But alas, that person was no more. In her place was a new person, who twisted a lock of hair around her finger, frowned, and popped the tab of acid she'd been keeping in her wallet for a special occasion.

Fuck it, the person thought. *We've all got problems.*

Four

A Very Goyische Christmas

1

A long, long time ago, in a land far away, there lived a little girl named Mary.

Mary was a very good girl. She always helped her mother with chores. She was also very beautiful, with long hair and a fair skin, and all the villagers admired her.

"What a beauty!" they would exclaim as she walked by to get water from the well. "She'll make a lucky man a fine wife someday."

One day, her father summoned her to him. "Daughter," he said, "I have some news for you. Smile, for you are to be a bride!"

Mary was to marry Joseph, a fine man, with kind eyes and a soft black beard. He was a carpenter and spent all day making things with his hands, like stools and tables and bookshelves. Mary thought she was very lucky indeed.

But little did she know that her life was about to change forever. For one day, as Mary sat chopping onions for the evening meal, the angel Gabriel appeared before her. She knew he was an angel, because wings sprouted from his back and his hair was spun from gold as pure as fire, and also he had with him many naked babies, who also had wings. Mary fell to her knees in worship.

"Rise, child," said Gabriel, after he had blown one long note on his golden trumpet, a note more pure and beautiful than the laughter of children, the tears of brides, and the song of the thorn bird combined. "Blessed you are, for you have been chosen from all women. The Holy Spirit has implanted in your womb His sacred seed, for the child you shall bear shall be the child of our Lord!"

Mary knew at once that the angel spoke the truth. She bowed her head and said, "Here am I, servant of the Lord; let it be with me according to His will."

But the angel Gabriel and all of his nude flying children were gone.

And lo, so went the Annunciation.

The next day Mary confessed to Joseph, her betrothed, of the angel's holy visit.

"Mary, truly you are blessed!" he exclaimed. "For in the night I have dreamed this very thing!"

And Mary and Joseph rejoiced together, in a pure, pious, and fully clothed way, and soon thereafter they became man and wife in the holy eyes of God.

Many months passed, and Mary grew heavy with child.

For some reason no one is sure about except it has something to do with paying taxes, they set out on a long and treacherous journey. When at last they reached the village of Bethlehem, Mary's birthing pains began. Desperately, they searched for a place that she might be brought to bed, but there was no room at the inn, or the next inn, until finally, at the poorest of them all, the innkeeper took pity on them.

"Alas, I have not a room for you," said the innkeeper. "But go ye unto my manger, that you may lie and bring forth your child there."

And lo, Mary and Joseph entered the manger, and there upon the straw, our Lord and Savior, Jesus Christ, was born.

In the east, three kings of the faraway Orient had prophesied that soon the King of all Kings would arrive in the world, and no sooner had the babe Jesus been swaddled than they appeared before him, offering the rich treasures of their lands—gold, frankincense, and fragrant myrrh. And knelt they before Mary and her babe, and a heavenly host of angels sang from on high, rejoicing: "Glory be to God in the highest, and upon the earth let there be peace!"

But someone else had heard of the birth of the baby Jesus, our most Holy Lord. The wicked Herod, king of the Jews, and he did not rejoice, for he desired to be more powerful than even the Lord himself. And so the wicked Herod, king of the Jews, desired to harm the baby Jesus, and commanded he that all the male children in Bethlehem be slaughtered, that he might keep the power he craved. And so the men of wicked Herod, king of the Jews, began to search for—

"That's enough," my mother said, white-faced. How long had she been standing there anyway? "We're going home now."

And thus, with this recitation in the winter of 1984 to the students of her preschool in the Share-a-Story corner, did little Rachel Shukert crush whatever slim chance she may have had of visiting Santa in his magical village near the Sbarro's in the mall.

"Santa?" my mother scoffed. "You're lucky we didn't send you to some Chasidic boarding school in Borough Park."

2

It's December. We did it, all of us, except the dead ones. We made it through another year alive.

January is around the corner, yet a distant memory. We spent

February trying to hang on to the last, withering remnants of our New Year's resolutions, wondering if our boyfriend was going to forget about Valentine's Day and why it was almost March already, and "oh yeah, Black History Month." In March and April we started writing the correct year on our checks and began to get some work done, only to set it aside in May, because "fuck it, it's almost summer." June flew by, as we planned our vacation and drank summer cocktails, and in July we visited our parents (some vacation), and in August we walked around sweating and moaning and being boring and, to combat the boredom, slept with six out of the seven people still in town, which left us even more bored. With September came a new year, for the students and the Jews, bringing with it a whiff of hope. In October we finally got to start wearing our cute new fall clothes, and we spent November eating pie and avoiding the six people we slept with in August who started calling out of the blue, and suddenly, it's time to celebrate! Let us smile crazily at cashiers and adorn our bodies with sequins. One more year gone, and next year, next year will be better. Next year we could be rich! Next year we could be famous!

But another year ending brings us all another year closer to . . . you know. So we drink, and eat, and accumulate debt, and bestow a hand job in the ladies' room upon the guy from marketing who just got engaged because these things will temporarily stave off the inevitable, and because we have been driven mad, *mad,* by the music.

The Christmas Music.

Hark how the bells sweet silver bells all seem to say throw cares away . . . have a holly jolly . . . just like the ones I used to know, where the . . . sleigh bells jing-a-ling ting-ting-ting-a-ling . . . silver bells, silver bells, it's Christmastime in the . . . jingle bells jingle bells jingle all the BELLS BELLS JESUS BELLS BOY CHILD GAY SNOW AND SLEIGH BELLS BELLS BELLS BELLS

BELLS BELLS BELLS REDRUM REDRUM GOD DEAD
SANTA SATAN BELLS!

In the Midwestern public school system, where the line between church and state is blurry and drawn in chalk, Jewish children navigate a slippery course at Christmas.

Choir poses a particular challenge at this time of year for
those squeamish about words like *Savior* or *Christ* passing their
lips. Some Jewish children—for example, my father as a boy—
employ a selective editing technique, giving us beloved holiday
classics like "Silent Night, ___ Night" and "Onward ___ ian Soldiers!" Others, particularly those of us with a shot at a solo, choose
a different approach; we sing the phrases in full, in a voice pure
and clear as a cantor's on Kol Nidre,[†] all the while thinking: *They
think a virgin had a baby? No wonder these people can't do their own
damn taxes.*

Personally, I enjoy Christmas music. Some of it, anyway. The
gorgeous "Christmas Time Is Here," the song the Peanuts gang
sings in *A Charlie Brown Christmas* that sounds like the feeling of
watching two drops of sleet race each other to the bottom of the
glass pane. Or Judy Garland singing "Have Yourself a Merry Little Christmas" in *Meet Me in St. Louis,* which rarely fails to make
me cry. Judy knew that each Christmas could easily be your last.
That's what amphetamine addiction does: it makes people wise.

There was a time when I, too, was a singer, a fiction perpetuated by my membership in the Omaha High School Minstrels,

---

[†] Kol Nidre is chanted by the cantor before sunset on the eve of Yom Kippur, the
day of Atonement. It is an ancient prayer in which the congregation publicly re-
nounces all vows or promises made in the past year, so as to begin the new year
with a clean slate and a clear conscience. Naturally, it has often been used by our
enemies as evidence of our inherent untrustworthiness; it seems that metaphor is
lost on the Jew-haters. But despite the controversy, it remains the holiest service
on the holiest night of the year, so powerful that it is said even the dead in their
graves can hear it. The living, on the other hand, must jostle for seats, commit
their names to long waiting lists, or make sizable financial contributions to the
synagogue to get a pew.

the highest caste of my high school's expansive choral system. While this carried with it some inarguably negative points—the ridicule of one's peers; the uniform "gown," a partial-birth abortion of a dress in purple sateen with a large, synthetic pearl at the bosom—the investment paid major dividends around the holiday season. No trig homework? No problem! Pesky chemistry final? Forget about it! When test day rolls around, you're very likely to be standing surrounded by artificial plants in a cheery sunroom singing "O Come, O Come, Emmanuel" to the lunatics at the Douglas County Hospital.[N]

I loved, loved, *loved* singing for the lunatics. I loved singing for them so much that I would fill an entire page just typing the word *love* over and over again, except I'm not a schizophrenic, or a top postmodernist.

The lunatics were charming, picturesque, supine on stretchers, heads wrapped in bandages from fresh lobotomies, their mad eyes as wide as a child's on Christmas morn. Some of them even sang along. I imagined the caressing melody of "What Child Is This?" would soothe their anguished spirits; the soaring, commanding blockade of "O Holy Night" (*Fall on your knees!/O hear the angel voices!*) might obscure the demons urging them to set fire to their earlobe or cut the baby up with scissors. We sang and sang, and the lunatics would sway and weep, and a few of the unrestrained ones would crouch on the floor to engage in some

---

[N] Now masquerading under the kinder, gentler name of the Douglas County Health Center. Built in 1886 as a "pest house," where penniless unfortunates were sent to die of communicable diseases such as smallpox, tuberculosis, and the plague, isolated from the healthy population, it had a stone façade that loomed threateningly over the stretch of lawn separating it from my favorite Goodwill store. One afternoon, returning in my car with plastic bags stuffed with my purchases—clothing, records, and other relics of the dead—I heard the sound of the thunderclaps mingled with the cries of the mad issuing from its turrets and had quite a fright, until I realized the sound was coming from inside my car, where I had left the key in the ignition with the stereo still on, as I had been distracted while parking by the appearance of a new and unexplained bruise on my forearm that seemed clearly indicative of advanced leukemia.

autoerotic rocking and moaning. After we finished, the staff would offer us punch and few a plates of damp cookies as we enjoyed the frenzied cheers of our grateful audience.

"Thank you so much, and merry Christmas," our choir director said, giving a little salute. "It was great to sing for you all."

"I HOPE YOUR PUSSY FALLS OUT, YOU FUCKING WHORE!" the lunatics replied.

All in all, a perfectly lovely way to spend an afternoon.

The elderly, on the other hand, were another matter. There were several fairly upscale nursing homes in Omaha (among them the Rose Blumkin Jewish Home,[N] though the gnarled old Jews who made their home there were not the target audience for our little band of carolers), but we rarely performed in these; rather, we seemed to entertain the old people who had nowhere to go for Christmas, no children or families to torment—people who had reached the winter of their lives to find themselves no more loved or wanted than they had been in the spring.

The elderly never seemed particularly glad to see us. Bundles of brittle old bones trundled together in the common room, they regarded us through rheumy eyes with a mixture of suspicion and indifference. I imagined how I'd feel if I were an ailing octogenarian, broke, alone, ripped from one of my few remaining pleasures— a particularly good *Trapper John* rerun, a refreshing nap, a happy bout of self-gratification with a plastic fork smuggled from the cafeteria—and forced to listen to a fucking *glee* club sing "Here We Come A-Wassailing" for over an hour of one of my waning days on earth. And also burdened, of course, with the knowledge that if I even made it to Christmas this year, I'd just be sitting with the other hags here in God's Waiting Room consuming green Jell-O and slices of drinkable ham, bombarded with gusts of false cheer from fat nurses who resented me.

[N] See footnote p. 61.

I imagine I might be a tough customer.

It was during Melinda Lembeck's solo verse in "Here We Come A-Wassailing" that the old man vomited. He was sitting just a few feet from me in the front row. I watched as the sick, runny and vibrantly pink, trickled onto his flannel shirt and he retched again, this time splattering liberally the gears of his wheelchair and the rubber toe of my green Converse sneaker. Trying to hold in my laughter, I searched the crowd for an orderly, and our choir director shot me a look. It was time for my solo.

Love and joy come to you
And to you your wassail too
And God bless you and send you a happy new year
And God send you a happy new year.

The old man stared away from us at something unseen, the pink vomit still gumming his beard. It seemed this sort of thing happened all the time. From a middle row, a woman shouted at the top of her voice, over and over: *"When will it be over? Somebody tell me, when will it be over?"* No one answered her. She began to weep.

O little town of Bethlehem
How still we see thee lie!
Above thy deep and dreamless sleep
The silent stars go by.

It was still early, but outside, the sky was already getting dark. The days are so short that time of year.

3

The feast of Hanukah, a pleasant, undemanding winter festival celebrating one of the precious few times in our history that we were not horribly, brutally massacred or victimized, is actually a relatively minor holiday. This is not terribly surprising. The Jews, after all, are a group who have chosen to observe our most important holiday by denying ourselves food and drink while standing in synagogue for hours listening to the rabbi recite the grisly martyrology of our people—those who were burned in the ovens or sent to the gas, those who were flayed by the Romans and crushed by the Greeks, murdered by peasants and tortured by priests. It's all very festive, particularly when punctuated by the frequent punches to the breast that we are expected to administer in penance, leaving a knuckle-shaped black-and-blue mark just above one's bra.

"Don't hit yourself so hard there, honey," my grandmother would say. "What could you have done so wrong?"

"Let her hit herself," my mother would chime in. "She'll save up for next year."

It was one of the great disappointments of my grandmother's life to be born halakhically† ineligible for participation in the cheerier festivals celebrated by the rest of the world. The Christmas season left her especially torn. While never one to adhere too closely to the letter of the law—cheeseburgers were served unashamedly in her home, right under the I KEEP A KOSHER KITCHEN needlepoint—an acknowledged celebration of Christmas would be too much, even for her. As the saying goes: "Shrimp may be *treyf,* but pork is anti-Semitic."

---

† Gentiles! Welcome! I bid you, wash the dust from your feet in my tents and my women shall fetch three *seahs* of fine flours, and knead it and bake it that you might eat of the bread and be refreshed! This anglicized adverb refers to halakha, the body of Jewish law, which determines everything from which foods are acceptable to eat to which activities are expressly forbidden on the Sabbath to the precise degrees of Judaic matrilineal descent. There is even a special court that follows the principles of halakha, called a *Bet Din,* that passes judgment on individual cases pertaining to Jewish law—somewhat like the shari'a, or Islamic law, that we hear so much about—only these cases tend to have less to do with family honor/corporal punishment and more about which delicatessen may have let a slice of cheese get near the cold cuts.

But she did her best. A curious grandchild might explore a downstairs closet—an expedition fraught with danger, as a small child could easily be crushed by the avalanche of unused yarn—to find racks heaped with rolls of smooth, shining wrapping paper; crisp plaids in red and green, frolicking teams of sparkling reindeer, silver wreaths studded with pearlized poinsettias, waiting to adorn the gifts she distributed. Every Gentile of her acquaintance—area merchants, the nurses at the Home, my aunt—would receive the gifts she made: marble cakes and fruitcakes; Christmas needle-points; miniature ceramic trees, glazed by hand and outfitted with working fairy lights no bigger than a baby's fingertip. Not to be outdone in holiday spirit by the festive Santa sweaters and the baby Jesus shoelaces one spotted on ladies about town, my grand-mother was a vision in blue and gold and silver, festooned with glittering menorahs and Stars of David. Sparkling dreidels danced at her ears, strings of smiling latkes marched about her hips. Her chest streaked with puff paint and shoulders with lamé, she was a beacon unto her people, a beam of strength and light, like Debo-rah, like Judith. Oh, Grandma. Many women have done valiantly, but you surpass them all.

Hanukah at Grandma's typically occurred near the end of the holiday, and we waited for it with mounting excitement. After a few nights of Hanukah at home, the interminable wait for my fa-ther to arrive, then waiting *again* for him to shower and change (to my knowledge, he is the only person in the Omaha area to ride his bike home from work in the middle of December), after the initial excitement of presents had given way to socks and underwear and a fifth copy of *Hershel and the Hanukkah Goblins,*[†] after my mother

[†] The Hershel in question is the folkloric Hershel of Ostropol. A cunning trick-ster, he is sort of a Pale of Settlement Anansi or Coyote, based on a historic fig-ure who served as a kind of court jester in Ukraine. Although Hershel eventually met a violent death at the hands of an enraged rabbi, he lives on in the libraries of disappointed Jewish children, who often receive illustrated accounts of

and father looked at the sweaters they had bought for each other and immediately requested a gift receipt, it was at last time for . . .

"The Festival of Greed!" my father cries, as we pull into my grandparents' driveway. Above us, the twin flags of the United States and Israel flutter majestically in the winter wind, framing a collection of stained-glass clowns in various states of leering. Streamers of blue and white snake around the drainpipe, and the garage door boasts brightly colored paper cutouts—dreidels, menorahs, bags of money;† —all the symbols of our people.

"The Festival of Greed," my father repeats, more quietly.

"Did she really put a *yellow* Star of David on the garage door?" asks my mother.

There's some tension between them; things got a little ugly when my father was informed that he would not be traveling to and from his parents' house by bicycle, as we would need to take the minivan in order to "U-Haul" home all the "shit" we would be receiving from "her." As my mother was "scared shitless" of driving "that huge fucking car," his assistance in "transporting *your* children to *your* parents" was required. As this meant my father would have managed a mere 120 minutes of cardiovascular activity on a day when tradition mandated he eat starchy foods fried in oil, acquiescence had not come easy.

The smell of cooking oil reaches us before Grandma does. "Happy Hanukah!" she cries, and engulfs us, pressing each of us in turn to her bosom, imprinting our cheeks with the heavy gold of her necklaces as we turn our faces so that her kisses land in our

---

his vaguely amusing exploits on Hanukah and other holidays in place of the real gifts they were hoping for, with a hearty "You like Adam Sandler? Well, here's a real Jewish comedian for you!" If you asked me, I would rank "Hershel of Ostropol" number three on the list of why young Jews reject their heritage, "Hebrew school" and "parents" being numbers one and two, respectively.

† Obviously, this is a reference to the Hanukah gelt, a few coins traditionally given in lieu of gifts to children in the Hanukah celebrations of the old country, and not at all about the character or financial situations of the Jews in general. And if you thought otherwise, then you, sir, are an anti-Semite.

hair, where the saliva can't hurt us, although this maneuver is far more crucial when greeting my grandfather, whose salivary glands could prove the answer to African drought.

"Happy Hanukah!" says my father, smiling.

"Hello," says my mother.

As she mentioned in the car, we would not be spending a night of Hanukah with her parents. Her parents were dead.

My grandfather is splayed majestically in his Chair in the TV room, watching intently as the College Bowling Championships hurtle along to their thrilling conclusion. The detritus of the day's snacks obscures the slogan on his T-shirt so it reads I ONLY PLAY OLF ON DAYS THAT ND WITH Y. Much saliva is spilled and deflected. We are pronounced pretty, then ugly, then prettier all the time, and permitted to go about our business until summoned back for dinner.

My grandmother's latkes are small and very dense. She likes to fry them a few days ahead of time, pop them in the refrigerator—makes things easier, she says—then reheat them in the oven with several cloves of garlic thrown in just before serving. A large serving dish partially wrapped in foil contains grayish slivers of brisket bathed in gravy for the meat eaters. My grandfather settles at the head of the table and surrenders himself.

"I'll tell you one thing," he clucks, his speech punctuated with appreciative suckling. "That Grandma knows how to make a nice brisket."

Unfortunately, my grandmother, bringing dish after dish from the kitchen, is unable to hear his compliment. There are heaping bowls of kasha with bow-tie noodles. A noodle kugel the size of an unfolded newspaper. Two chickens, roasted, and marinated in Italian dressing. Cubes of watermelon, served in a bowl she glazed herself in her ceramics class to look like a watermelon. And there is a mysterious concoction for the vegetarians among us. We look at each other in trepidation as my father breaks through its thick crust to discover several more cloves of garlic bobbing expectantly in a watery corn-studded filling.

"How much water did the recipe call for?" he asks.

"Oh, the recipes in *Redbook* always make everything too dry," my grandmother replies breezily.

"And the garlic?"

Her blue eyes narrow quicky, then open wide, disingenuously, like a clever child avoiding a blow. "What do you mean?" she exclaims. "Garlic is very healthy for you!"

"Healthful," my mother mutters. *"Healthful."* Only my sister and I can hear her. Everyone else is deaf.

With enough of the meal eaten to satisfy her, my grandmother begins the endless task of wrapping up the leftovers in several layers of used aluminum foil and packing them into one of her three refrigerators, where they will remain until the event of her death. The rest of us amble into the living room to light the Hanukah candles, my father leading the benediction, my grandfather fumbling a velveteen yarmulke over his bald spot and echoing him in a gruff drawl, my uncle blinking rapidly, blank and bewildered as a recent arrival from outer space. Who are these men in the funny hats? What is this strange language they speak? What has all this to do with me?

And finally, presents. Presents!

"Are you ready?" my father whispers to my mother.

"Oh, I'm about as ready as I'll ever be," she mutters back.

My grandparents' basement is carpeted wall to wall in synthetic orange shag that looks like the skin of a discontinued Muppet. Framed prints of lugubrious rabbis adorn the walls, and a pair of slatted doors hide a wet bar and several bottles of barnacled mai tai mix. And featured dramatically under a hanging lamp with a casino motif is the pool table.

Who needs a Christmas tree when you have the Hanukah pool table? Never actually used for playing the game of pool, it serves during the rest of the year as a gift-wrapping station, an iron-ing board, an impromptu fashion runway. Now it is scarcely visible under stacks and stacks of packages, glittering blue and gold under sinuous coils of metallic ribbon. Heaps of chocolate coins in golden foil flicker their reflected light across the ecstatic faces of the grandchildren, each of whom has a tower of splendidly wrapped gifts awaiting opening, a tower reaching far above their heads to the flakes of mica glinting in the starry, stucco ceiling.

"Wow!" I exclaim, and look for my pile. It's where it always is, next to the shelf with the Little Maids of the Thirteen Colonies porcelain doll series from the Franklin Mint.

"Wow, wow, wow!" exclaims my sister, clapping her little hands in glee.

My grandmother beams. She has imagined this moment of our delight through months of preparation, list making, and shopping, weeks of wrapping and cutting and tying and taping.

"Happy, happy Hanukah, darlings," she says.

"That grandma of yours is some grandma, huh?" my grandfa-ther pipes up. "Where are mine?"

The grown-ups try to keep things orderly, of course, but no sooner has my littlest cousin unwrapped a baby doll the size of an Irish setter than we crack, tearing into the gifts with desperation. The room begins to fill with paper and trimmings, which we throw at one another gleefully and roll around in like a gangster's moll in a mountain of ill-gotten cash. A chorus of "Thank yous" fills the air.

"*Thank you, Grandma!*" shrieks my sister, tearing the paper off a truly awesome Playmobil circus set.

"Thank you, Grandma," I say with a sigh, unpacking a pur-ple china unicorn with silver stars on its forehead and rump.

"Thank you, Grandma," says my cousin, nodding his hairless chin in her direction as he inspects his Junior Deluxe Shaving Kit, complete with monogrammed case and badger-hair shaving brush.

Coordinating sweater-and-slacks sets. A pretty wicker sewing basket, outfitted with a squat pincushion of Chinese silk, cloisonné thimbles, spools of gorgeously colored thread. Child-sized dressing gowns and furniture. Books. Dolls. Movies. Games. My mother studies a loudly patterned umbrella and sighs audibly when she is presented with a ceramic cookie jar shaped like a bearded rabbi holding a Torah scroll.

"I made that. Isn't is adorable?" Grandma crows. "They have a whole set of dessert plates at the center that match. Do you want me to make you those, to go?"

"No," says my mother. "Thank you."

My father carefully frees the Major League Baseball All-Star chess set from its bubble wrap.

"I don't know how to play chess," he says, placing a miniature Roger Maris in the rook's square beside a wee Yogi Berra.

"You don't?" Grandma looks worried for a moment.

"No."

"Oh, well. You can learn. And besides, it's a collector's item! Keep the box!"

Keep the box. Folk wisdom passed down through the ages. Keep the box. And the ribbons. And the wrapping paper. And the shopping bags. They'll come in handy someday, you'll see. What if someday you need a piece of string, and it's a matter of life and death, G-d† forbid, and you threw away the string? You can't just go to the store and buy another piece of string—who knows if the store's even there anymore, G-d forbid? No stores, no neighbors

---

† For the Gentiles: In the Jewish tradition, the name of God is so holy it cannot be spoken. If it is written in its entirety, as in a Torah or prayer book, when the book can no longer be used it must be buried in a cemetery, like a dead person, complete with blessings and a eulogy (but you don't have to wear black). While this condition really applies only to the name of God as it is written in Hebrew, the authors of English-language Judaica, such as textbooks, song sheets, and the paper Haggadahs—the book used during the Passover, printed by Maxwell House as a promotional in the late seventies and still used by seder attendees to this day—aren't taking any chances, hence the hyphen.

anywhere, it's life or death, and then what are you going to do? G-d forbid it should happen, so wouldn't you rather just hold on to the string in the first place and not have this kind of tsuris?[†]

Because shouldn't having as many possessions as possible protect you from any harm (G-d forbid) that may befall you? Shouldn't it guarantee that everything, for the babies, for the person who loves you *so, so much,* shouldn't it guarantee that everything will always be okay?

"The Festival of Greed," my father says with a sigh as he pulls down the backseat of the van to make room for the boxes and bags we have acquired over the last few hours.

"Over until next year," says my mother, slipping an arm around his slim waist.

My sister is asleep in her car seat. I cradle my purple porcelain unicorn in my palm and caress its silver stars with my thumb. I won't let anyone give it away. It could be a matter of life and death.

The white lights shimmer against the dark of the tree, illuminating the silver globes dangling from the branches. The pine smell is overwhelming. I sneeze.

Around me, the goyim related to my new friend at my new public school are opening their gifts. My friend opens a box from her grandmother to find a sweater a couple of sizes too small knitted with the grinning visage of Minnie Mouse. Pinned to the sleeve is a five-dollar bill.

"What else did she give you?" I murmur.

She frowns at me, confused. "Nothing. Thank you, Grandma!"

[†] This is the Yiddish word for "trouble." Peculiarly Jewish troubles. For example, being evicted from your home by order of the tsar is tsuris. The Arabs kidnapping an Israeli soldier from the Lebanese border is tsuris (for the American Jews, at least; I can't speak for the Israelis, who generally have a different, less panicked way of looking at things). And yes, no matter what your in-laws have assured you, having your child marry an Episcopalian is tsuris.

"You're welcome, honey," says her grandma, adjusting her bad hip more firmly in the rocking chair. "Merry Christmas."

Alone under the tree is a tiny package wrapped in nondenominational paper. Snowmen. Everyone likes snowmen. Even *Muslims* are okay with snowmen. It is addressed to me.

"Open it," urges my friend's mother. She smiles. Her teeth are slicked with lipstick and eggnog.

"Open it!" says my friend.

I open it slowly, smoothing out the paper carefully. Inside is a glass tree ornament, shaped like a snowflake.

"We wanted to get you something that wasn't too Christmasy," says my friend's father.

"But still, you can put it on your tree," my friend's mother chimes in. She beams at her husband, the red fairy lights embedded in her Rudolph sweater blinking on and off. In a movie theater nearby, my own mother and father are gorging themselves on popcorn and Diet Coke, watching the latest Woody Allen movie without me.

I hold the ornament up to the light.

"Thank you," I say. "It's just what I needed."

Baby Jesus in the crèche shoots me a look. He knows bullshit when he hears it. I glance at the clock. If my father comes to pick me up right now, I just might make the second show.

Five

Typical Bat Mitzvah Speech, United States, c. 1992–1995

Extremely important in Jewish communities of the late twentieth-century Clintonian Dynasty was the widespread practice of Bar and Bat Mitzvah, in which participants were made to engage in feats of strength and stamina, and other physical trials in order to prove their fertility (in the males' case, virility), followed by an elaborate celebration designed to display the wealth and power of the clan, known as the "witz" or "vitz."[1] While archeologists have unearthed ample evidence of written and oral examinations administered throughout adolescence in nearly all ethnic and religious divisions of the period, among Jews, a people known to place an unusually high premium on intellect and academic achievement, such displays of intellectual prowess were of particular import. The follow-

---

1. Anthropologists are divided on this appellation; while *witz* is the most frequently used term for the familial groups or clans that made up the Jewish society of the period, such a group may also be known as a *stein* or a *feld*. Most mainstream historians agree that the three terms are equally correct.

ing text is a simulation of one such address a typical female adolescent may have delivered to her family's guests at the conclusion of Bat Mitzvah, reconstructed by a team of ethnohistorians and paleontologists at the University of Shanghai, using the surviving literature, television, and electronic communication of the period, as well as the landmark archaeological find known as the Shukert Cache, excavated from ruins in the region of Oma-Ha in the former United States of America, a collection of fragmented letters, diaries, and other documents seemingly preserved by the large amounts of radioactive fallout in the area. This text first appeared as part of the Shanghai Historical Society's traveling exhibition "When God Mattered: Understanding Religion and Magic in the American Empire." The exhibit's text has been translated from the original Mandarin by the author.

Dear Friends, Family, Jewish Kids from Hebrew School That, No Offense, I Don't Really Consider Friends, Distant Cousins I Have Never Met Before, and All the Old People Who Are Friends of My Grandparents That My Parents Didn't Want to Invite:

Thank you all for celebrating with me as I become a Bat Mitzvah!

G-d! Old People, do you mind? Already with the sucking candy[2] and the dentures? Do you know how repulsive that is to people who can still hear? Slurp, slurp, slurp—it's like we can *feel* your teeth sliding around against your gums. Come on! It's one thing when the rabbi is speaking. He gets to do this every week. But this is me! This is my only chance to make a speech like, ever, and my mom bought me this suit that cost like almost two hundred dollars[3] and God! I mean, G-d!

2. *Sucking candy*: small marble-like objects often found still clenched in the jaws of skeletons of persons who reached seventy-five or more years of age. Their purpose is not known, but evidence points to the idea that they may have had alleviated the rudimentarily treated aches and pains of the geriatric.
3. Equivalent to roughly twenty million *jiao*.

Okay, fine. Don't mind me. Go ahead and suck. Slurp those root beer barrels[4] that have been in your purse since the Carter administration during my speech. My speech of the only Bat Mitzvah I will ever have. Just go ahead. I don't care if you hate me. You think I care? Everybody already hates me anyway, especially my mother. But not as much as I hate her.

Maybe that was a mistake. Saying how much I hate my mother, right here on the bimah,[5] in front of the big thing of the Ten Commandments, one of which is "Honor thy Father and Mother." G-d is probably pissed. He's probably staring down through that window at the very top of the ceiling where I thought He lived when I was little, planning His revenge, because what kind of a person thinks such things about her mother? Instant death would be too good for such a person. He'll probably give me leukemia, or juvenile diabetes, or make me get, like, really fucking fat, like, out of nowhere. Oh shit! I just cussed. I'm sorry! And now I said *shit* too, although everyone, even G-d, knows that *shit* isn't as bad a word as *fuck,* because *fuck* is the worst cussword except I hear they can say it on TV now in England. America is so lame sometimes. Anyway, I'm sorry. I didn't mean to cuss, not standing here in front of the ark with all the Torahs that they saved from synagogues in Poland where all the Jews got killed by the Nazis.[6]

I should have made this speech have something to do with Nazis—that's always a crowd-pleaser, and at least something I know a lot about. But people might think I'm weird, like one of

4. Further evidence that this "sucking candy" may have had an alcoholic or narcotic effect, particularly upon the weakened constitutions of the elderly. See Dr. Eric Johnston, *Pervasive Social Ills in the Early Clintonian Period* (Baghdad: University of Baghdad Press, 2998), pp. 223–28.
5. The stage or podium in a house of worship; probably soaked in animal blood and entrails from frequent sacrifice.
6. Typically inaccurate reference to the "Jewish Holocaust," which archaeologists today know to be an elaborate hoax perpetuated by the ruling classes to further subjugate the proletariat.

those weird militaristic semi-goths who wear, like, old Wehrmacht jackets and eyeliner to school, and besides, the Nazis aren't in the Torah, at least, not yet. Probably someday. In Hebrew school they're all basically just Nazis under another name, the Canaanites and the Amalekites and the Philistines and the Jebusites, all the people in the Bible who tried to destroy us. There sure have been a lot of them. I mean, standing here in front of you all, it's kind of amazing that we're still here, doing our traditions and everything. Oh well. I guess it's just a matter of time.

So anyway, the Torah portion today is Naso, which means— um, I thought I had this written down, and now the rabbi is giving me the dirtiest look . . . well, whatever. I'm sorry! Okay. The Torah portion today is Naso, which is in the book of Bamidbar, which actually means "In the Desert" but in English is called Numbers, so even if I could tell you what it means, it probably wouldn't mean what it really means anyway.

You know what I wonder sometimes? What if the whole thing is a mistranslation? I mean, like, the entire Torah? Because you know how people who are anti-Semitic are always all, like, "Jews have horns"? I mean, I guess they don't say that so much now. Today people who are anti-Semites say things like "You're Jewish? My church says that you're going to Hell"[7] or "Zionism is racism" or "No, you can't make up the biology midterm I specifically scheduled on Yom Kippur; you people are always asking for special treatment and I'm sick of it." That really happened, that last one, and Lisa Schneiderman's dad (who is a partner in the law

7. This theory, highly prevalent throughout first and second millennium Christendom, was abandoned with Dr. Gary Oppenheim's Nobel Prize–winning work, *Fire and Brimstone: A Ph.D.'s Journey Through the Gates of Hell* (New York: Random House, 3012), proving conclusively the material existence of Hell, not in a fiery pit situated somewhere within the earth's crust but rather in a nondescript warehouse some 50 miles west of Lubbock, Texas, with a population, while boasting a handful of Jews, comprising a disproportionate number of former oil executives, right-wing radio commentators, and a pesky overabundance of deer.

firm of Schneiderman, Abrams and Katz, all of whom I see sitting before me in the pews today) called the principal and tried to get that teacher fired, but the principal said he was very sorry, but the teacher had tenure so the only way he could fire him was if he had some kind of inappropriate contact with the aggrieved party. Hugging, for example. This biology teacher was not a hugger. He would, however, be forced to allow us to make up the exam, and Lisa Schneiderman and I had to go down to his creepy office in the basement to take the test after school, and he had already changed into his basketball-coach outfit or whatever, with these really, really tight red shorts made out of polyester or whatever, you know, with the snaps on the front, and the whole time, even though it almost seriously made us puke, Lisa Schneiderman and I, like, stared at his crotch, because Lisa said her dad said if his dick[8] or anything, like, fell out of his shorts and we saw it, or if it (and this is Mr. Schneiderman's word, not mine) *stirred,* to tell him and he'd get the "fucking bastard" (again, Mr. Schneiderman cussing, G-d, not me!) "thrown out on his Nazi ass."

But nothing happened, except that Lisa Schneiderman and I both got C's on the exam, because the fucking bastard hates Jews, and he probably doesn't even have anything there to fall out anyway. He's probably flat in the front like Ken.[9]

You know who's definitely not flat in the front like Ken? Eric Moffat. You want to know how I know? Because when he hugged me right after our last class got out before winter break, I totally felt it on my leg. But whatever, we're just friends.

Oh! But from before, about how anti-Semitic people are all,

8. Meaning unclear, perhaps a slang reference to the pet name of Richard Milhous Nixon, a well-loved nation-state consul of the period.
9. Unknown reference, although clearly derisive—there are a variety of "Kens" in this period—perhaps a bawdy allusion to the perceived masculinity (or lack thereof) of independent White House counsel Ken Starr, disgraced Enron chief Ken Lay, or the still-running U.K. soap opera *Coronation Street*'s bequiffed Ken Barlow.

like, Jews have horns? And the reason they say that is because Michaelangelo or one of the guys they named after the Ninja Turtles[10] but I think it was Michelangelo made that sculpture of Moses coming off Mount Sinai with horns on his head? And the whole reason that he did that was because in that actual part of the Torah it's supposed to say "Moses came down from Mount Sinai with rays coming out of his head" like he was glowing because he'd seen G-d? But instead it was mistranslated to say that he "came down from Mount Sinai with *horns* coming out of his head" like the devil, so then people were all, like, Jews are devils and have horns and we all know that's not true.[11]

So what if everything in the Torah was mistranslated? Instead of it saying "Don't eat pork" what if it really says "Bacon is good!" Or instead of "Honor the Sabbath day and keep it holy" it says "The Sabbath is the least holy day of the week, so you should go to Alison Waterman's birthday party at Skateland on Friday night no matter what your mother says"? And what if instead of "Honor thy father and mother" it says "Your father and mother are old and lame and don't understand anything that's important, so just forget about whatever they say, because they (especially your mother) are probably just jealous of you anyway"?

Doesn't that kind of blow your mind? And also, what if I got my period up here? That would be *so* embarrassing.

So, yeah, my Torah portion today is called Naso. The first part of it is all about how many people there are in the tribe of Gershon, and how if your wife cheats on you in a sexual manner you have to bring the high priest some food, like, to cleanse yourself from being cheated on. But the part I read is about the Nazirites.

For the lay Israelite (that is, not a *Cohen,* or high priest by

10. A group of minor deities.
11. This was, in fact, proven to be true by a group of award-winning scientists at MIT.

birth—and believe me, if you think it's insane that Josh Cohen, who used to eat dirt and wet the bed every night at sleepaway camp, is supposed to be holy, you're not the only one), a Nazirite (and not an oncologist!) is the most holy, most precious thing to be.

To become a Nazirite, one must maintain certain guidelines, in order to achieve this pure and holy state.

One: He may never consume any grape product, be it wine, grape juice, vinegar, fresh grapes, raisins, and if they had been invented then, probably not even grape Kool-Aid, grape Bubble Yum, or even, no matter how sick he gets, Dimetapp.[12] When I told her this, my mother said, "No raisins? What if they get constipated?" What a wit. She thinks she's so funny, except she's not. And when I don't laugh, she laughs at me because she thinks I'm embarrassed or something. I'm not embarrassed. The only person she embarrasses is herself.

Two: A Nazirite must never allow a razor to come upon his head or allow his hair to be cut in any way. Ugh. That's another thing my mom kept saying for the past two weeks when she was trying to get my dad to get a haircut for the party: "What are you, a Nazirite?" Ha ha ha, Mom, you're so hysterical. No, seriously, have you ever thought of taking your show on the road? There she is, sitting right in the front row, smiling. What is that? Is she crying? *G-d! Why is she so embarrassing?*

Okay.

Also, not only is a Nazirite not supposed to cut his hair, he's not supposed to comb it with a brush or wash it, because this will certainly result in some hair being extracted from his head.

---

12. Historians are split on the interpretation of this term: the Viswanathan school states that it refers to a flavored syrup or serum given to children to relieve coughs, sore throats, and other such afflictions, while the school of thought led by Dr. Franz Liebenhoff maintains that it alludes to the recreational practice of preparing or "tapping" one's vein to receive an injection distilled from a "dime bag" of heroin or other such narcotic.

Um, I didn't wash my hair this morning. I was kind of too busy.

Actually, I don't always wash my hair every day. I mean to, but it gets so crazy in the morning before school. Sometimes I don't even wash it every other day. Is that gross? It's probably gross.

Look at my friends sitting out there. They all washed their hair this morning. They probably wash their hair every day. I really hope none of them can tell I didn't wash my hair. I don't think they'd still be my friends. Seriously. They'd call me dirty, like that girl Lacey who lives behind the supermarket.

Okay. Also, a Nazirite is not to have any contact with a dead body, and is meant to avoid all situations where such contact is inevitable—for example, visits to the cemetery or the Rose Blumkin Home for the Jewish Aged[13] are strictly forbidden. However, if said contact happens outside of his control—for example, someone just drops dead in front of him in line or something— then he must cleanse himself by fasting for seven days, and on the seventh day he has to shave his head, and then he has to bring a young lamb and a large basket of assorted breads to the temple for the high priest to sacrifice, and then he can go back to being a Nazirite, which . . . well, what the Nazirite gets out of this is kind

---

13. This is extremely significant, as it is the earliest known reference to the site first excavated by Dr. Akeno Mpugwale and his team from the University of Lagos, and corresponds to Dr. Mpugwale's published hypothesis that the site termed here "Rose Blumkin Home for the Jewish Aged" was in fact a kind of sacred holding place for the bodies of high-caste members of society as they were prepared for burial. The bodies would be placed in beds or chairs with wheels affixed, symbolizing mobility and the transitory nature of the life cycle, surrounded by stuffed toys, mainly animals, representative of the various deities that had protected the deceased in life. Additionally, according to Dr. Mpugwale, the teeth would be removed and soft food smeared ceremonially on the gums, and the pelvis would be dressed in a padded garment (found to be remarkably well preserved) in a ritual similar to the swaddling of a baby, all of this symbolizing a return to infancy for the deceased in a culture that worshipped the concept of Youth. These findings are somewhat controversial, as several eminent archaeologists have disagreed with Dr. Mpugwale's findings, most famously Dr. Leonid Braslavsky of Krakow University, who has argued that the site of the alleged "Rose Blumkin Home for the Jewish Aged" is clearly the remains of an ancient bazaar, notorious for its slave trade.

of unclear. Maybe it was like being a celebrity back then. Maybe people sent you free clothes and stuff.

So, that's done. Now comes the money shot.

No, but not like that! That's not what I meant! Ew! Eric Moffat told me what that was when we broke into discussion groups in language arts last week. He was all, "Hey, Rachel," and I was like, "Yeah?" and he was like, "Do you know what a money shot is?" and I was like, "Yeah," and he was like, "What is it, then?" and I was like, "It's like the main part of something" and he was all, "Yeah, I guess you could look at it that way" and kind of snickered, and I was like, "Well, what do you think it is?" and he said— well, I'm not even going to think about what he said because it's too gross and deeply inappropriate for synagogue but it had something to do with porno. And then I told Kelly what Eric Moffat said, and she said she can't help it, she still likes him even though he's a total perv because that's how it is when you're in love. And we both agreed that we would never, in our whole lives, do a money shot, and probably not ever a blow job either, because that's also really gross, but we might sometime give someone a hand job and we practiced giving hand jobs on a curling iron and the handle of a hairbrush, and she said she would probably give Eric Moffat a hand job if he wanted her to and I said I would give Justin Connolly one, because I am seriously, deeply in love with Justin Connolly but I would probably maybe give Eric Moffat a hand job too, as long as Kelly didn't find out.[14]

Today, I become a Jewish woman.

I was already a woman, because I've had my period twice now—I thought it was three times, because a couple of weeks ago

---

14. The unusual linguistic and grammatical structure of the passage has been painstakingly studied and reconstructed here by scholars of the period, who have concluded that it may be an early or crude form of the epic poetry or heroic verse we find in the surviving works of the blind rhapsode of the period popularly known today as "Fiddy," although their true authorship may never be known.

some weird brown stuff came out but my mom said that was some other discharge—*like she knows.*

Mr. Paulsen, my Human Growth and Development teacher, said that sometimes girls can feel embarrassed after first getting their periods, like everyone can tell they have it just from looking at them, but I don't think Mr. Paulsen, who has a picture of Jesus on his desk next to this big chunk of glass proclaiming his membership in the National Association of Christian Athletes, knows very much about women. He was pretty weird when he was talking about sex and stuff, he was all, "Sexual intercourse feels good, I'm not going to lie to you and say it doesn't. It's supposed to feel good. That's part of G-d's plan. But it is best enjoyed between a man and a woman who love each other very much."

And in the back, David Carlson was like, "What about gay people?"

And Mr. Paulsen was like, "We're not going to discuss that."

Poor David Carlson. I think he's gay. I was in the chorus of *Hello, Dolly!* at the Omaha Community Playhouse last summer, so I know who's gay and who's not and David Carlson is definitely gay because not only does he take, like, really good care of his clothes but we were lab partners all of last semester and he never, ever, once had a crush on me, so he must be gay. Does that sound conceited? I'm not conceited, totally I'm not! I just mean that mostly guys get crushes on girls that they have to talk to a lot, especially girls that are more popular than them. I mean, I'm not super popular, but I'm more popular than David Carlson. I wish David Carlson was more popular though, because I really like talking to him. But if he was more popular, we could actually be friends. I mean, I don't want to sound like a bitch, but I just can't afford to be friends with people who are less popular than me right now, not if I want Justin Connolly to ask me out by the end of the year.

So anyway, then Mr. Paulsen started talking (pretty reluctantly, may I add) about birth control and said, "Of course, abstinence is the only method that makes absolutely one hundred percent sure you won't have a baby," and I said, "What about abortion?" and Mr. Paulsen said, "We are absolutely, one hundred percent not going to discuss that either."

"I would never, ever, *ever* kill my baby," said that girl Lacey who lives behind the supermarket. "Because I'm a Christian." She was looking right at me when she said it.

"I feel sorry for the baby," I said.

"We are not going to discuss this!" said Mr. Paulsen.

Did I mention that Mr. Paulsen always wears one of those lapel pins shaped like the little baby feet? That means he's pro-life. Pardon my French, G-d, but I think that's fucked up. I don't think a man has any right to tell a woman that she has to have a baby that she doesn't want. And that girl Lacey is just pro-life because she doesn't have a future.

It bothered me, though, how she looked at me when she was like, *"I'm a Christian."* I don't mind so much if people can tell that I've had my period just from looking at me, but I do kind of worry that they can tell I'm Jewish. Probably because I have horns. No, it's a joke! G-d!

Today, as the Nazirites took their vows of holiness, I undertake my obligations as a Jewish woman. These include being nice to my family and committed to social justice and to getting all A's so, unlike that girl Lacey who lives behind the supermarket, I will get into a good college. According to my mother, it also means only liking or dating Jewish boys for my whole life until I finally get married to one. To her I say, "Mom, turn your head to the back pew and behold the radiant, golden god that is Justin Connolly and say that again. Look into my eyes and say it."

Besides, Jewish boys aren't all so nice. Heather Posner's brother Andy sells pot after swim team, and I heard he had sex with some black girl.

Well, the cantor is looking at his watch and the old people are crackling their wrappers, so I guess it's time for the thank-yous.

First of all, I'd like to thank my parents.

Mom, seriously, you need to stop crying. You are humiliating yourself and everyone around you, and this isn't, like, the mall,[15] where I can pretend I've never seen you before. For real—check yourself before you wreck yourself.

Okay. Thank you, Mom and Dad, for driving me back and forth from Hebrew school and tutoring in the cantor's office, although you were the ones who wanted me to go, not me, so it's not like you did me a big favor or anything.

Also, thank you for paying for this whole thing. The party tonight is going to be sweet. I mean, it's not going to be crazy or anything, but I wouldn't want it to be. I think that's tacky. Especially here—I mean, come on. It's Omaha, not Beverly Hills, and your dad is not Steven Spielberg,[16] he's an orthodontist from Kansas City. You don't need to enter on a stallion and have a glass-blower.

That kind of sounds like medieval times, right? I actually read about a medieval-themed Bar Mitzvah in one of those articles my mom is always cutting out from the *Forward*. We don't agree on much these days, but both of us thought that medieval Europe was a deeply inappropriate theme for a Bar Mitzvah.

"What do they do?" I asked. "Bind everyone to stakes and make them watch the slide show?"

"Only if they won't accept baptism," she said. "Then a bunch of monks come in and set everyone on fire."

It's a slippery slope. I mean, what will the next big theme

15. Reference to the Mall of Washington, D.C., a meeting place and forum for those involved in government; this has led scholars to infer that the family in question may have been politically important.
16. A despotic ruler or warlord, of the Late Middle American Empire, famed for his great wealth.

be—the Yom Kippur War? How about the Warsaw Ghetto? Just imagine. Rented rottweilers prowling around the lobby. There's food, but you have to crawl under a fence of barbed wire to get it. The deejay just keeps playing that "C'mon 'n' Ride It (the Train)" song over and over again, and then at the end, everyone gets a T-shirt that says I HAD A GAS AT ANDREA'S BAT MITZVAH!

Wait, where was I? Yes. Thank you to my parents for instilling in me a positive Jewish identity.

Thank you to my grandparents, and also to my mother's parents, who are dead, so I'm not sure why I'm thanking them, but Mrs. Rothman told me to. But especially thank you to the living ones that I have actually met, and who hosted the Shabbat dinner last night. And a special shout-out to Grandma for making those insane ceramic centerpieces with the disembodied hands that some of you may have taken home.

Thanks to Mrs. Rothman for helping me write my speech. Thank you to the rabbi and the cantor. Thanks to all the family and friends who came from out of town to celebrate with me on my special day. I look forward to learning your names and picturing your happy faces as I open the colorful envelopes with checks enclosed that you will give me.

And speaking of presents, I would now like to take a moment to address my Gentile classmates in the back pews.

Some of you are good friends. Others of you are not. If you have discussed among yourselves the undeniable fact that I invited several individuals more popular than I am in the hopes that we might become friends as a result, you have not allowed me to be aware of your ridicule, and for this I am truly grateful. But there is something else I ask you to give me now, something far more precious than the journals and earrings and picture frames your mothers have prepared for you to give me. It is an altogether different gift, and there is only one among you who may deliver it.

I want Justin Connolly to slow dance with me at my party to-night.

Alone, and of his own free will. Without prodding, be it catty or well-intentioned. Without the deejay announcing Ladies' Choice. Without me having to ask him, knowing full well he can't refuse because it's my party and my day. Because I will, but I really don't want to. But like I said, I will.

Justin Connolly! I beg you! Look up from playing Eric Mof-fat's Game Boy on silent in the back row and heed me. Today I am a woman, Justin Connolly. My future as such is in your hands. Do not let me become the kind who has to ask men to dance with her. The kind who impresses them initially with her rowdy candor and forthright sexuality, her bawdy humor and disarming intelligence, the kind they sleep with for a couple of months before dumping her for a wan, aloof sort who can go braless in a tank top without looking like a prostitute, saying "You and I, you know, we're like, *buddies,* but Catherine (or Caitlin, or Crucifix) is just . . . really *different*—but don't worry, I'll still call you for casual sex now and then over the next few years." I'm putting the fate of my Jewish womanhood in your Game Boy–playing, masturbation-seasoned hands, Justin Connolly. Do not fail me.

I would like to conclude with the beautiful final section of my *parsha,* which is also the blessing bestowed by Jewish fathers upon their daughters every Friday night:

May the Lord bless you and keep you.

May the Lord make his face to shine upon you and be gra-cious unto you.

May the Lord lift up his countenance upon you and grant you peace.

Amen, and *Shabbat Shalom.*

WARNING

The Following Chapters Contain Explicit Content

If you are my parent, or a close friend or relative of one of my parents, please consider and proceed accordingly.

Should you fall into the latter category, and fear that after reading said explicit material, you will be unable to resist approaching one or both of my parents by telephone/at synagogue/in the locker room at the Jewish Community Center to discuss the appropriate level of shame they should feel, as well as your own undoubtedly sterling and impartial judgment of their daughter's authorship and publication of such material, please skip the following two chapters altogether and proceed immediately to page 142 and begin Chapter 8, "On the Question of My Obscurity."

THANK YOU.

Six

For the Good and Welfare

"Impossible," I told my mother smugly, after she mentioned one evening that I might consider hanging around more with other Members of the Tribe. How could she be so blind? Couldn't she see that this kind of narrow-minded insularity, this rancorous focus on the superficial divisions between peoples was ripping the rich tapestry of the world asunder, all but assuring the total destruction of the divine human experiment? I went to high school now, *public* high school, where adolescents of all colors and creeds gathered together in mutual admiration and wonder for the glorious melting pot we call America. "There are only five Jewish kids at my school, and none of them even listen to the same music as me!"

My mother, several steps ahead as usual, was prepared for this response. In an hour's time, I would be collected by a girl who had snubbed me cruelly at the Jewish Community Center day camp in 1987, and driven by her in her motorcar to an undisclosed

location where we would rendezvous with several other teenage
Jewesses to participate in undisclosed activities for an indetermi-
nate period. For a certain mysterious group that for legal reasons
I shall refer to only as Youth Organization (or YO), this was a phe-
nomenon called "rush."

"Rush?" I said. "Like a sorority?"

"Yes," my mother said.

"I'm not going."

"Oh, you're going," she said.

"It's a school night!" I protested. "I have *homework!*"

She snorted. "Good thing you brought your books home
with you then. Do you even carry a backpack anymore, or have
we dropped all pretense of academic life?"

"*I don't want to go to some stupid sorority meeting with a bunch
of lame JAPs!*" I shouted.

"*Fine! Then I'll go!*" She shouted back. "*And you can cook dinner,
do the dishes, take out the trash, and watch your father fall asleep
watching fucking* Star Trek*!*"

"What?" my father briefly paused the verbal assault he was
delivering to his computer to call down the steps. "What was
that?"

"Nothing!" my mother and I snapped in unison.

Satisfied, he returned to his Microsoft-induced fury. A series
of faint, profanity-laced yelps drifted down the staircase, as
though one of our closets contained a torture chamber for miniature schnauzers.

I glared at my mother. "Go to hell," I snarled. "You can't
make me do anything I don't want to do."

Three quarters of an hour later, a cream-colored BMW pulled
into the driveway. A single manicured hand stretched out the
open window to lazily ash a Marlboro Light as the other laid on
the horn. Squinting, I could make out two dark shapes huddled
together in the backseat.

"Have fun!" yelled my mother.

"Don't you want them to come to the door or—"

Like the shofar blast at the End of Days, the beckoning horn of the BMW ripped through the house. Even the crystal panda bears frolicking on the wall unit trembled in awe.

"Jesus Christ!" my father shrieked from the top of the stairs. "COULD YOU FUCKING LEAVE ALREADY?"

"No, really, Jeeves, don't bother!" I shouted back. "I'll show myself out."

Gingerly, I joined the two dark shapes huddled in the leather interior. One of the shapes was an old friend, Missy Paskowitz, a pathologically friendly girl whom I had known since we were slightly portly ballerinas together in the JCC *Dance!* Level Two. The other shape I did not recognize.

"Hi!" Missy squealed, pressing me fiercely to her wide bosom with crushing force. "Are you so excited? I'm so excited! Do you believe we're finally in high school? I don't believe it sometimes! Do you? DO YOU BELIEVE WE'RE IN HIGH SCHOOL?"

Every day in homeroom, I thought, *when another bit of my soul is skimmed away, like foamy scum from a pot of chicken soup, I am not only forced to believe; I am painfully, mercilessly unable to forget.*

But instead I said: "EEEEEEEE!"

Missy indicated the dark shape to her left. It turned slightly, revealing a round pale face with a long nose.

"This is Amanda Gellman," said Missy. "She just moved here from Montana."

"Virginia," whispered Amanda Gellman.

"Virginia, that's what I said," said Missy.

"Oh, you know each other," drawled the head of highlights in the driver's seat. "That's nice. Do you mind if I smoke?"

"Do you mind if I bum one?" I asked.

The highlights spun around to glare at me with narrowed, expertly made-up eyes. She was the younger daughter of a prominent family whose appearance at High Holiday services would occasion my grandmother to pause in her struggle to separate the wrapper of a three-year-old Jolly Rancher from its sticky host and murmur: "You know, they're *very* wealthy." The family had fallen into some ignominy of late (a divorce that may have caused the contract termination of one of the Jewish country club's most beloved tennis pros and the marriage of the eldest son to a born-again dental hygienist from Alabama), but scandal had only served to lend a hint of welcome pathos to a clan who presented their children with off-the-lot Beemers for their sixteenth birthdays, and they remained one of the most talked-about and grudgingly admired families in our little shtetl on the prairie.

"Marlboro Lights okay?" she asked finally.

Missy Paskowitz looked at me, her eyes wide. The mysterious Gellman turned back to stare emptily out the window.

"I prefer Reds," I replied. "But I guess so. If that's all you have."

She tossed the pack at me. "Help yourself. I buy them by the *carton.*"

And we disappeared into the night.

The Jewish youth group of which I would soon be a member was organized roughly after the Greek system. Boys and girls are segregated into two separate entities, which are then divided into chapters that one must "rush," each with its own illustrious history and character. For example: Girls' Chapter *Perahim Ha-Shalom*[†] #262 was founded in 1943 by the late Mrs. Doris Showalter Stein. Begun at the height of World War II, *Perahim Ha-Shalom* cited a renewed commitment to international peace and freedom in its mission statement and asserted both its religious and cultural identity at a time of

---

[†] Hebrew for "Flowers of Peace."

unparalleled Jewish suffering, and as the preferred chapter of excitable fat girls with skin problems in the greater Cincinnati area. Or Girls' Chapter Golda Meir #1099, founded in 1973 by Mrs. Susan Cohen Peretz and Barbara Levine (rest her soul, she died in that horrible car accident in Tel Aviv with that hippie who said he was Sephardic but everyone, including her aunt Mrs. Levine—remember her? She used to work in the synagogue gift shop—thought he was probably an Arab) in solidarity with the people of Israel at the onset of the Yom Kippur War and whose members are known today as the undisputed Hand Job Queens of suburban Baltimore.

The chapter I joined, along with Missy Paskowitz and Silent Gellman, was not the one to which we were whisked away in the BMW that night to share low-fat snacks in the company of girls with perfect manicures and deep tans, but the other Omaha girls' chapter, where the members were more pizza-friendly and indifferently groomed. I was at a period in my adolescent development when I had experimentally cut my own hair with a sharp kitchen knife before dying sections of it a color that was most aptly described as Menstrual Red, and this lack of rigor toward personal appearance proved a much better fit. When I learned that the smoking of cigarettes was tolerated at all official chapter functions, my decision was made. I would rush.

When I informed my mother of this development, she squealed in delight, using a register of her voice that had not seen action since 1956, when her father died and she became a preternaturally middle-aged first-grader. "That's wonderful!" she trilled. "I'm so excited for you! You're going to have so much fun and make lifelong friends!"

Lifelong. What a horrible word. Meant to signify eternity, something everlasting and solid, yet an inescapable reminder that life has a length. One day it will be over, and you will die. And what will you die from? A person spends his whole life waiting to find out; will it be cancer, God forbid, or a heart attack, or maybe one day you just keel over and they won't even know what happened to you, because Jews aren't supposed to do autopsies.[†]

"Don't count on it," I said. "I'm not a big fan of Jewish people."

Her face darkened slightly, but the love in her eyes stayed bright. "Honey, you don't know it yet, but you are one of the most Jewish people I have ever known."

We met every Thursday after school in a cordoned-off area of the JCC. After a brief period of socializing and engagement in the kind of fervent opposite-sex hugging with which adolescents briefly slake their raging hormones, we adjourned to separate meeting rooms—the very same rooms in which we had previously suffered through hour after tedious hour of afternoon Hebrew school—for our chapter meetings. The girls' meetings, while gossipy and generally tinged with a constant sense of crisis, were conducted with crisp attention to parliamentary procedure. We had elected offices—president, treasurer, Defender of the Faith—each with a particular list of duties: the secretary would pretend to take minutes that would go into a sticker-festooned Trapper Keeper that no one would ever open. The treasurer counted out bills from a worn envelope and reported the tally. The president ran the meeting. The vice president sat in a plastic chair and did not speak. There was a small gavel, which the president would bang on the table with great relish, and at the end of her term, she would tie a colorful grosgrain ribbon, her name and dates of service clearly marked on it in paint pen, to the handle, that future generations might remember what had been.

[†] Philo-Semites and other fans of the Ashkenazi misanthropy of Larry David may recall the hilarious episode of *Curb Your Enthusiasm* in which a small tattoo discovered on the corpse of Larry's recently deceased mother necessitated her burial in the "special" section of the cemetery, alongside suicides and criminals. The autopsy prohibition is along the same line; any mortification of the body and one is declared unfit for eternal slumber among one's *respectable,* untattooed co-religionists. Of course, if the tattoo in question was acquired in, say, Poland between the years of 1941 and 1945, you get a pass. I think.

Our advisor, an adult paid by the organization to lend expertise and make sure no one snuck in any beer, assured us that all
this pageantry would look great on our college résumés. It would
also help us with our leadership skills, particularly for the Jewish
Federation scholarship boards and National Council of Jewish
Women public-service symposiums and the Beth Shalom Sister-
hood's "A Night in Marrakech" Charity Auction Benefit Commit-
tee meetings we would be expected to attend once we had put
away childish things, the hemp jewelry and the six-foot blown-
glass bongs, and married the nice podiatrist we dated at the University of Wisconsin and settled down in Overland Park with five
bedrooms and a lap pool and an eerily empty living room decorated to match our shih tzus, Klezmer and Hanukah.

What the boys did in their meetings I cannot say, but I assumed
it had something to do with masturbation, literal or figurative.

Our other activities varied. We would venture out into the
world of the less fortunate, spearheading a shampoo drive or delivering three hundred badly constructed peanut butter sandwiches
to the homeless. There were "social" events, usually with another
chapter, involving bowling or pizza or something else reminiscent
of an elementary school birthday party, apart, of course, from the
fiendish smoking of cigarettes. But most eagerly anticipated by far
were the elaborate dinner dances that each chapter hosted in turn.
The older girls described them to us breathlessly, their faces shining as brightly as their lovingly conditioned hair.

"The best night of the whole year," one said.

"*So* much fun," said another. "And very, very important to the
organization."

Between the tickets and the sale of ad space in the thick souvenir booklets, a chapter could make most of its money for the
year off these little Semitic proms. They were also formal and
expensive, requiring not only months of careful committee-led
planning but corsages, limos, and costly party frocks, all of which

the kvelling parents of our tight-knit Jewish community were ecstatic to shell out for several times a year.

"Karen! Your Rebecca! So adorable with my Jonathan!" a tear-
ful mother would exclaim, shoving a camera into the face of her
grimacing son, his braces gleaming as he attempts to affix a rubber band laden with baby's breath to the plump wrist of his un-
smiling date. A parade of family members, neighbors, even the
goyim across the street, drawn by the presence of the stretch limo,
had traipsed over to admire the happy couple, who took care not
to touch each other under the imaginary wedding canopy as camera bulbs flashed around them.

"Ruthie, I'm telling you, he is such a handsome boy. And
from a good family," the other would say. "I think we'd better call
the caterers! It's a match!"

They were joking, of course, lampooning the old-world match-
making of their great-grandparents, the Yiddish-speaking *bubbes*
and *zaydes* strapped to their wheelchairs in the Home, surrounded
by dusty gift platters of dried fruit as they tearfully begged visitors
for five dollars with which to buy off the Cossacks. They were kidding, these baby-boomer, tennis-playing mothers, with bachelor's,
even master's degrees, far enough removed from the Old Country
to have one set of dishes[†] and four different diaphragms. They were
joking, but that didn't mean they were funny.

In September of the ninth grade, after the first of these
dances, I was asked to an all-night after-party by some of the

---

[†] For the Gentiles, if you don't already know this: in yet another masochistic
twist on the day-to-day business of running a house, a kosher home is required
to have two sets of dishes, pots, utensils, and other cooking implements—one
for milk products, and one for meat. Some very religious homes (and synagogue
kitchens) even go so far as to have separate appliances. While such a separation
is prescribed in the dietary laws set down in the Torah, it does make one understand, at least in part, why conversion to Christianity proved so tempting to
Saint Paul and the like—there is something very appealing about a dogma that
requires only an unshakable faith to achieve salvation, and not several different
refrigerators.

juniors and seniors. The drinking of alcohol was expected to occur, and only the very coolest of the underclassmen were invited. I could think of no reason why I had been chosen to attend, except that I went to school downtown and therefore was viewed to have easy access to marijuana; still, I was delighted to be asked. Unfortunately, there was no way my parents would let me go.

"Not in a million years," I said ruefully.

"Just call and ask them," said my popular friend Liz, who was two years older and had kindly, if inexplicably, taken me on as her protégée. "Don't you want to go?"

"Yes!" I cried.

"Then call them," she said.

"Well, I'll have to lie. I'll have to tell them something, that I'm spending the night at your house or . . . but then they'll call your mother and find out I lied, and I'll be grounded forever."

"Don't lie," Liz said firmly, handing me the cell phone from her car. I held it gingerly, as though it might pee on my hand if startled. "Just tell them everyone's going to a party somewhere and you'll be back in the morning."

Since I had left the ethnically guarded confines of my Jewish elementary school, my mother had distinguished herself among my friends and acquaintances as a severely crazy person. I might casually mention a plan to grab a snack or a coffee with someone after school, and her internal Goy Alarm would go off.

"Who's that?"

"A friend."

"Well, I've never heard of this person."

"She's my friend. She's in my homeroom."

"Well, you've never mentioned her before. I swear, every day you bring up some new person, from God *knows* where—"

"From school! I'm at a new school! I'm making *new friends*!"

"Well, I'm very uncomfortable with this. Does this friend smoke cigarettes?"

"I don't know!"

"You better know. I'm going to need her phone number, her parents' phone number, her parents' work number, a Social Security number, a blood type, a complete medical history, a—God forbid, that I should even have to say this—*criminal* history—"

"Mom!"

"What? Is this person hiding something? If she's not hiding anything, then why should she and her parents mind answering a few reasonable questions? I mean, you're going God knows where to do God knows what, and I'm not supposed to be worried? Tell me, who is this girl's mother that she doesn't worry? Someone who isn't fit to be a parent, that's who. Probably running around with different men all over the place, leaving her kids with no supervision—you know what? You're not going. Did you hear me? *You're not going!*"

The phone was ringing. "Just tell her the truth," Liz urged.

"Mom?"

"Hi, sweetie! Are you having a nice time?"

"Yes. Listen, I've been invited to a party."

"Sounds good!"

"It's at someone's house—I can't remember his name."

"Okay!"

I hear a click as my father suddenly picks up the extension. "Hi, cutie! Having a good time? Everything okay?"

"Everything's fine," says my mother. "She's just going to some parties."

"Okay! Have a good time!"

There is another click as my father hangs up.

"I don't think anyone will be able to bring me back until the morning," I tell her. *"I'll be gone all night."*

"Well, I guess we'll see you tomorrow then!"

"Okay—"

"Oh, honey, one thing," she broke in.

I sighed. Here came the storm. *Are you out of your fucking mind? Has everyone around you been tested for AIDS?* "Yes?" I asked.

"Go ahead and use the credit card if you need anything. And have fun!"

Liz expertly caught the cell phone before it fell to the pavement and switched it off. "Told you." She smiled. "Let's get out of here."

It was at this party that I drank my first, second, third, and fourth beers. It was also at this party that Jacob Plotkin, pouty-lipped and still two years away from morbid obesity, Jacob Plotkin who used to pick the dead flies off the glue trap at Sunday school and put them in his M&M's, Jacob Plotkin who had once called the rabbi "dickmunch," became the first person to touch my breasts. I had a kissed a boy once, during the end credits of *In the Army Now* starring Pauly Shore; I had explored the fascinating mystery of my vagina regularly since I was four; but it was Jacob Plotkin who put his fingers in my underwear that night and said, "Gross! It's wet!"

It was also on this night that young Katie Sussman entered this selfsame room a mortal, a mortal who wore her skirts a little too short and her eyeliner a little too thick but a mortal nonetheless, and exited a legend.[N]

When I wriggled free from the drunken embrace of Plotkin and rejoined the party, Liz pulled me, stormily, into the laundry room. I had done a bad thing, a very bad thing indeed. I had broken protocol and I had shamed her; indeed, through her association with me, I had put her own reputation on the line.

[N] And now, a Great Moment in Nebraska History, although not one you are likely to find in anyone's social studies book: *l'affaire* Sussman. There is some debate as to whether the lady in question orally pleasured each young gentleman involved in turn while the other watched, or if she in fact somehow accommodated both appendages in her mouth, pleasuring them simultaneously. A conclusive answer had never been reached; for reasons of my own, and mostly out of the deepest respect for the extraordinary tenacity and skill of Ms. Sussman, I prefer to believe the latter.

"I *believed* in you," she said angrily. "How do you think this looks?"

"But what about Katie Sussman?" I asked.

"Katie Sussman is a whore," said Liz. "And Katie Sussman is from Council Bluffs."

I hung my head. Acceptance, popularity, an unlimited supply of cheap beer—they had nestled in the palm of my hand like a trio of sun-warmed pebbles, pebbles that might have turned out to be jewels, and what had I done? Flung them recklessly at the first passing car that stuck its tongue in my mouth. Except that cars didn't have tongues; they had exhaust pipes. Was an exhaust pipe to a car what a tongue was to a human? And was the carburetor the heart? It was getting awfully hard to think. And stand. Was this being drunk? Was I drunk?

"I don't feel so good," I mumbled. "I think I might have a brain tumor."

"Don't you dare," Liz whispered furiously. "Don't you dare throw up. Is that what you want? You want to be a slut *and* a light-weight?"

I didn't. I wanted to go home where my not-angry mommy would tuck me in and pet my head.

"Then pull yourself the *fuck* together. Go sit on the couch. And whatever you do, *do not speak to Jacob Plotkin. Do you understand me?*"

There was a large crack in the cement floor, encrusted thickly with pink glitter from some long-ago craft disaster. If I concentrated very hard, I could inch along its length, slowly but reassuringly upright. I imagined the flecks of ancient glitter underfoot were an army of Lilliputian but maternal drag queens, spurring me on my way with salty affirmations. "Looking fierce, baby," they crowed. "You work it out, girl, with your soggy pussy. Approval neither de-sired nor required!" And finally I stumbled, the contents of my stomach still in place, into a welcoming corner of the L-shaped couch.

Catching my eye, Liz nodded in tacit approval. Jacob Plotkin, a cigarette tucked ostentatiously behind one ear, waddled through the sliding door from the outside patio, a phalanx of smirking underclassmen in tow.

I didn't speak to him again until we had graduated from high school.

The sexual etiquette of youth-group society was full of unspoken regulations and hierarchies, labyrinthine and implacable as anything out of Edith Wharton—or even the court of Louis XIV at Versailles. There were some basic rules of conduct, applying mainly, as usual, to females: one was expected to drink but not to become visibly drunk. One must not smoke a cigarette unless others were around to notice you smoking it. If one was known to be rather . . . ahem . . . *injudicious* with her favors, one must compensate by appearing in public dressed in loose flannel pajama bottoms and oversized sweatshirts from a decidedly unsexy educational institution such as Colgate or the University of Colorado. But the overriding principle, the unbreakable rule, was this: one did not hook up at after-parties with the local Jewry. It was too close to home, easily verifiable and distastefully public. Not only might a nosy or prurient mother notice the hickeys on your neck after a dance and think you were a slut or, worse, part of a couple, but in a Jewish community as small and interconnected as Omaha's, you could never be 100 percent sure who was or was not a distant cousin.

Luckily, there was another place where one could indulge one's appetites, free from the inhibiting lens of adult supervision and the latent disapproval of chaste, churchy public-school classmates with their promise rings and Christian rock concerts and vacant grins for Jesus that made them look at once deliriously happy and deliriously constipated. A place where one could reinvent oneself, in safety and anonymity, and discover that cheating on your Gentile boyfriend isn't cheating if it's with a Jew. A place so sacred that we spoke of it in private with the hushed, almost mystical tones generally reserved for the films of Ethan Hawke and the state of Israel.

I refer, of course, to the mythical Valhalla of Yiddishkeit[†] called "Convention."

Convention. The word itself, as it must for every dentist who ever lured a drunk hygienist into a Holiday Inn hot tub, every mortgage broker who woke up with a splitting headache, naked and bound to the ice machine with his own patterned suspenders, still sends a dreamy shiver down my back. *Convention*—that heady weekend every fall and every spring when all the members of our proud fellowship, the Jewish teens of St. Louis: Gateway to the West; of Kansas City: City of Fountains and BBQ Capital of the World; and of Omaha: The City Where We Don't Have a Nickname, but If We Did It Would Probably Also Have Something to Do with Meat[N] gathered for three days in a suburban Marriott to "explore our Jewish identity."

And so many identities to explore! As far as the eye could see, circling the lobby gift shop, spilling into the conference rooms, lounging in every deck chair, at every banquet table, an infinite smorgasbord providing a variety of toothsome delights from every walk of male teenage life.

[†] A term meaning, literally, "Jewishness," but more accurately, the "pride one takes in said Jewishness." Can be measured by the number of Jewish-themed knickknacks around the house—for example, decorative dreidels, figurines of Orthodox rabbis, or bears wearing yarmulkes—the frequency with which one verbally notes the Jewish heritage of various celebrities, and the depth of the mistrust directed toward other cultures.

[N] Actually, we did get one later, coined at great expense by a professional branding firm: "O! What a City!" and for business "Buy the Big O!" O, you see, stands for Omaha. Also, for *ostrich, octagonal,* and *oblivious.*

1. THE BEAUTIFUL ONES: Broad chests clad in faded Grateful Dead shirts of competing age and provenance, they slip their feet from their perfectly worn Birkenstock Boston clogs and dangle them lazily over the arms of the overstuffed chairs in the lobby, running a large, finely made hand over a flat belly, diffidently rubbing a muscular shoulder, running their hands through their thick shining hair, fragrant with the scent of American Spirits and organic shampoo and good pot, which they smoked a lot of without ever talking too much about it. They were always touching themselves, these calm, beautiful boys, stroking their arms and stomachs, embracing each other with masculine tenderness; the only hope of them touching you with similar affection was if you were equally beautiful—one of those fair, faraway girls who made silence seem profound and could wear a peasant blouse without looking like a waitress in a Greek restaurant, which probably meant at least one of your parents was a convert.[†] If you were not so dainty a flower, built with the thick limbs and barrel chest of the Pale of Settlement, you might hope that one of these lovely tall boys (they were always tall, unusually tall for Jews, sometimes even topping six feet), these Jewish Brad Pitts, might bum a cigarette one day and reward you with a brief conversation about their magical Gentile girlfriend back home and the way their love—not to mention their lovemaking—moved them toward a higher spiritual plane and how your energy reminded him of her, a little, except, you know, like more nervous, and so you'd go to the bathroom, allow yourself three slow tears, and resign yourself to taking off your bra for:

2. THE SHORTISH HIPPIES: Similar in dress, taste, and manner, but lacking that je ne sais quoi of languid grace with a hint of vague intellectualism—despite being much, much smarter—that made the Beautiful Ones the Beautiful Ones and the Shortish

[†] Please see footnote, page 59.

Hippies, well . . . Shortish Hippies. In stature and aspiration, they were always coming up short: their Phish shirts were too new, their haircuts too fresh. They treated their mothers like mothers, not like girlfriends; they might wait for hours to score some weed in the parking lot of a suburban Kinko's and tell everyone about it. A Beautiful One might indolently strum a guitar while gazing soulfully into the eyes of some impassive half-Swede named Rhi-anna, but it was the Shortish Hippie who schlepped the guitar there on the bus. The Shortish Hippies were generally liked and for the most part were nice, bright, interesting guys with good grades who would ultimately do very well in life, so you can imagine how appealing they were to a pretentious fifteen-year-old.

3. THE PUNKS, THE SKATERS, THOSE WHO LIKE SKA AND THOSE WHO WISH TO: It's irresponsible to spend one's weekend at a youth group convention when there are bands to see, ollies to master, racists to harass, and Lexuses (Lexii?) to vandalize, so there were always rather few members of this cate-gory present. Those who did show up were usually somewhat shy, with possible skin problems, and tended to stick together, as if numbers could ward off the contagion of lingering patchouli oil. As they were the most like the people I went to school with, I tended to seek them out for commiseration and friendship; how-ever, when it came to choosing a lucky lady, they generally over-looked me, going instead for maternal preppy girls with large breasts who were "social smokers" and said things like "I think it's cool how you're, like, eclectic."

4. FUTURE FRAT BOYS OF AMERICA GROUP A: Guys in white baseball caps who listen to the Dave Matthews Band, Bob Marley (because no place in America identifies with the black man's struggle like Leawood, Kansas), and the Beastie Boys. Often hold positions of leadership and are reflexively respectful to women, at least in public. Wear Ralph Lauren aftershave. Drink fairly often but can tell you the exact number of times they have

smoked pot, which they have obtained at great cost from their sometime friend, the Shortish Hippie. In situations of an intimate nature, tends to ask politely, "Will you please give me head?"

FUTURE FRAT BOYS OF AMERICA GROUP B: Guys in white baseball caps who listen to Dr. Dre, Tupac, Snoop Dogg, and the Beastie Boys. Sometimes hold positions of leadership and say dirty things to women. Wear Tommy Hilfiger aftershave. Drink occasionally and very often smoke pot, which they obtain from a cousin of the black kid they sit next to in algebra. In situations of an intimate nature, tend to push their partner's head down forcibly before ordering her to "give me head."

5. THE ONES WHOSE MOTHERS WORRY ABOUT THEM: Unusually obese or unusually scrawny, and silent except at mealtimes, when they gather together at an isolated corner table to discuss weaponry, marksmanship, hand-to-hand combat, and how to best combine all three with the ultimate goal of world domination. Occasionally will choose a hapless girl with whom to become obsessed, usually one who has shown them some form of politeness such as nodding or answering a simple question such as "Where is the bathroom?"—*best to avoid entirely.*

By the time the orientation dinner had ended, an enterprising girl would have identified her top ten picks from the first *four* categories (see warning at end of #5), made her choice according to availability, accessibility, and inclination, compared and negotiated with her friends and accomplices (while a little overlap was expected, and healthily competitive, too much was impractical and indulgent). Once dessert was served, she was ready for action.

During the day, we attended workshops and discussions on various topics thought by the adult leadership to be of interest, and the gossip would begin to trickle in. I attended a lecture on the sanctity and struggle of Israel, besieged by hardship from its inception yet an inspiration to us all, and found out that Todd Hirsch and Jennifer Golden had been discovered having honest-to-God intercourse (which was generally frowned upon, unless you were a senior) by a hapless maid. In the midst of an earnest discussion on the dangers of intermarriage (or benefits! ventured Adrienne Christensen-Yeager breathily, while my beautiful Brian Schiffman—oh! *Brian Schiffman!* Is it acceptable to masturbate to the memory of a teenage boy into your late twenties? Brian Schiffman, if you're reading this, know I love you still—stroked her straight Scandinavian hair), Missy Paskowitz told me breathlessly that Stephanie Rakoff and Joshua Neiman had engaged in three separate acts of reciprocal oral sex after meeting at the hamburger station the night before, a development that was furtively and disgustedly seconded by the Silent Gellman. While struggling to produce impressive-looking tears during a seminar entitled "Auschwitz: When It Happens Again," I found an intricately folded note tucked into the pocket of my regulation binder. It was from my friend Liz, and it smugly informed me that a circle jerk had taken place that afternoon in room 516, possibly led by my own Jacob Plotkin.

"Don't wear a bra that hooks in the front—he'll never get it off," we advised one another during evening free time as we shaved our legs and perfumed our bodies, preparing ourselves for assignations in neighboring hotel rooms, like call girls at a business convention. "And don't eat meat at dinner; it makes your pussy taste bad."

Years later, I often wonder about the gay kids. We didn't hear about them much, but the seeds were certainly there; the girls who rubbed each other's backs with suspicious tenderness, the boys who knew all the songs from *Les Miz* and after manfully, if reluctantly, slipping a tongue in your mouth could scarcely hide their relief when you didn't want to go any further. I hope they found one another, but if they did, it was a secret; not a secret like Stacy Mendelson's genital warts, but a *real* secret, the kind you don't tell anyone.

I also wonder why. Why? Besides being teenagers brought together in a hotel for a weekend with very little adult supervision (and the supervision, such as it was, provided mostly by people in college), were we rebellious sex-gods, postfeminist bohemians unafraid to love as we saw fit? Were we celebrating being Jews together, no longer outsiders in our overwhelmingly Christian high schools? Don't forget, this was the Midwest, where the Christians are fucking serious—the church lock-ins and conclaves of our Gentile counterparts, with their perplexing concept of sin, must have made us look like something out of *Caligula*. Or was my initial assumption when confronted with my mother's almost irrational insistence that I make some nice Jewish friends correct? Weakened by centuries of pogroms, expulsions, assimilation, were we acting out a subconscious, primordial urge to (for lack of a less loaded terms) proliferate—even purify—our race? But if that was the case, would we have given so many hand jobs?

A few weeks after Convention, I received a letter in the mail from the son of a cantor in Missouri. Enclosed was his school photograph. It was a good picture, his eyes very blue against the gray background, his olive-colored T-shirt and deep olive skin making him look just the teeniest bit like a member of the IDF.

Amazed and overjoyed (we'd exchanged addresses and phone numbers of course, with a promise to KIT, but who ever bothers to actually KIT?), I showed them proudly to my mother, forgetting for the moment that I "fucking hated" her and that "as far as I was fucking concerned I was no longer her fucking daughter." We hadn't been getting along so well.

"Let me look at him." Taking the little picture between her thumb and forefinger, she held it up in the light and gasped. I had heard the same expulsion of air before, a combination of shock and pain, when her acid reflux seized up.

"Are you okay?"

"Am I okay? Honey, he's gorgeous!"

"Do you think so?"

"He looks just like a young Paul Newman. In *Exodus.*"

Paul Newman in *Exodus.* Those were some strong words.

My father padded into the room, sucking on one of his special low-calorie Fudgsicles that were always in the freezer. "Who's
that?" he asked, peering at the photograph.

"A boy who likes Rachel!" bubbled my mother.

"Mom!" I cried.

"Very nice," said my father.

"Don't you think he's cute?" my mother pressed on. "I think
he's very cute. And he *must* like you if he sent you his picture! Oh,
sweetie, that's great!"

"Very nice," my father repeated, disappearing upstairs with
his frozen snack for several hours of battle with his desktop. My
mother just beamed.

I felt it unnecessary to tell her that I had orally pleasured
young Ari Ben Canaan under a banquet table in the Grand Ballroom, a pool of watery semen dribbling down my Nine Inch Nails
T-shirt onto the floor. Not that it would have dampened her
mood. She was thrilled, happier than I'd seen her in months, and
in spite of myself, I was thrilled that she was thrilled, proud that I
had made my mother so happy. Proud and happy. I was no longer
an "ungrateful little bitch who thinks the sun rises and sets in her
own ass" but a nice, well-behaved Jewish daughter, who would
one day give her a nice, well-behaved Jewish son-in-law. She
would have nice Jewish in-laws, with whom she could swap
recipes and argue with over the White House's Middle East policy.
She would come to our home for holidays, laden with noodle
puddings and books with titles like *Matzoh Ball and Mrs.
Moskowitz* or *The Littlest Afikomen* for her nice Jewish grandchildren; what did it matter that genetic material related to said
grandchildren was currently being power-vacuumed from a soiled

carpet panel by a Mexican janitor in the St. Louis Marriott? There would be more where that came from. After all, I had three more years of high school.

"Why don't we go out to dinner tonight, huh?" she asked, stroking my hair. "Someplace special. Just you and me."

So that's why we did it. It was for our parents.

Seven

A Lot of People Are Virgins

Rachel Shukert
P.O. Box _____
Omaha, NE 681___

February 28, 1998

Rep. Newt Gingrich
Speaker of the House
U.S. House of Representatives
Capitol Building
Capitol Hill
Washington, DC 20001

Dear Mr. Speaker,

Hello. My name is Rachel Shukert. I am a high school senior in Omaha, Nebraska (a staunchly conservative state, as you know). I hope this letter finds you well.

As you and your colleagues in Washington proceed with your investigation of improper conduct on the part of President Clinton, I am sure that you have been deluged with letters of late. Processing this mountain of correspondence can be no small task, and I have no desire to keep you from the important business of guaranteeing the right of every American to the full disclosure of all pertinent identifying marks found on the presidential genitalia. However, I wish to bring a small matter to your attention.

I will begin, if I may, with a story.

Last Sunday, as is my custom, I paid an afternoon visit to my grandparents' house. My grandmother served me an afternoon snack of cashews, Swiss cheese, and hard candy retrieved from the hollow body of a wooden clown. As I savored this motley repast, she suggested that we look through some old family photos together. Obviously, I had no choice but to agree.

We settled onto the yellow couch in the living room, facing the pair of three-foot porcelain cockatoos perching above the unused fireplace, and gave ourselves over to the gossamer veil of memory.

"That's your cousin Ida," said my grandmother, pointing at a youngish woman, reclining on a lawn chair, her pudgy torso encased in a plaid one-piece swimsuit. "Boy, did she think she was hot stuff. You know, she never got married."

The screen door leading to the downstairs garage slammed shut as my grandfather climbed the stairs, his golf clothes damp and rich with the scent of sweat and Aramis.

"Do you believe this shit?" He brandished a copy of *Newsweek,* with Monica Lewinsky's eager, oblivious face grinning from the cover. "These jackasses, the second they get someone in there who knows what the *goddamn hell* he's doing, and they have to tear him down."

Mr. Gingrich, my grandparents are Democrats. Rabidly, reflexively liberal on every issue, and in a manner that is charmingly antique; my grandmother regularly brings herself to tears lamenting the misery of the "poor little colored children starving to death" and the people discriminated against because of their "alternative" lifestyles.

"What's it my business?" she says with grand magnanimity.

"Who is it hurting? It's not what I want to do, but hey, I'm not the one who has to go to bed with them. I have to go to bed with your grandfather every night. What's it to anyone?"

My grandmother sighed now. "It's a *shande*.[†] And just think how poor Hillary must feel."

I may have neglected to mention that my grandmother and Mrs. Clinton are on a first-name basis. They shook hands at a re-election benefit in 1996, and ever since, my grandmother has sent cards and offers of knitwear to the White House for major holidays.

"A *shande*, a *shande*," my grandfather spat. "And for what? A little blow job?" He turned to me. "Let me ask you, honey. Do you know what a blow job is?"

Mr. Speaker, I have known what a blow job is since my first time at sleepaway camp the summer before fourth grade when Amy Kleinman explained the term to me during one of our many forced marches through the Nebraskan outback. Naturally, I was scandalized. Agog.

"Did your mom tell you that?" I asked.

Amy poked a rock with the end of her muddy stick. "No."

"Then how did you know?"

"I saw a movie one time where Shelley Long did that to her boyfriend."

I'm not sure which film it was—I think *Outrageous Fortune*, co-starring Bette Midler? Anyway, I believe Amy Kleinman has since become quite religious. But I digress.

Not one to take a hint, my grandfather decided I hadn't heard him properly. "Rachel, honey, I asked you a question. Do you know what a blow job is?"

"Yes," I replied. "I believe I do."

[†] *Shande* is Yiddish for "outrageous shame." In this case, the *shande* is the "great right-wing conspiracy," not the sexual act itself, although the ethnic heritage of Ms. Lewinsky is both a *shande* and a point of pride.

"So, do you think it's a big deal that Bill had some little intern back in there in the office with him? You think they don't all do it? Oh boy. I could tell you stories about Kennedy, Roosevelt even."

"Roosevelt was a saint," my grandmother snapped. "He couldn't help it if his wife was a . . . what do you call it. A—le—a leprechaun. You know, with the other women."

"I believe the word you are looking for is *lesbian*," I offered.

"That's right," my grandmother said. "I understand she had a secretary she was very close to."

Chortling, my grandfather shoved a handful of cashews into his mouth. "I'll say. Old Franklin had a secretary he got pretty close with too."

"Well, listen, honey, a man has needs, even if he is a cripple."

I cleared my throat. "Daddy said it isn't so much about whether Clinton did it, it's about the obstruction of—"

"Never mind what your dad said." Small bits of cashew were propelled from his lips, landing daintily in my lap. "Let me tell you something. All your dad knows about blowing is when a tire goes out."

Mr. Speaker, I have no idea what my grandfather intended by this statement, nor do I have any wish to examine its ramifications. What I do know is that in the course of one afternoon I was interrogated over my knowledge of sexual practices, heard my father's masculinity insulted by a man wearing yellow Bermuda shorts, and was forced to admire photographs of cousin Irving's bon voyage party from 1942.

Mr. Speaker, for this egregious assault on my senses, psyche, and youth, I do not blame Bill Clinton.

I blame you.

Time and time again I have heard your colleagues in the House and Senate decry the effect a presidential sex scandal is having on younger Americans. "What are we to tell the children? What are we to tell the children?"

Mr. Speaker, the children already know. They get it. They understand what Monica did to Clinton, and what Clinton did to Monica. They understand why it felt good, and why they felt compelled, despite all sense, to do it again and again.

"Forget the sex," cry the moralists. "He's a married man! Think of the sanctity of the family! Think of his poor wife!"

Newt (do you mind if I call you Newt?), I think you of all people know that Hillary Clinton needs no pity.

"Forget the sex and the family!" cry the very naïve. "It's the perjury! The obstruction of justice! The president, the Leader of the Free World, who is meant to be a symbol, a beacon of all that is Good and Noble and Pure—God, Superman, and Tom Hanks all rolled into one—lied to us! He said, 'I did not have sexual relations with that woman [Miss Lewinsky].' And he did! He did have sexual relations with that woman (Miss Lewinsky.) *He's a liar!*"

And then there are the pragmatists, who say, "Okay, so big deal. He got a blow job from an intern. Big deal. My intern gave me a blow job in the limo on the way back from serving divorce papers to my cancer-ridden wife in the hospital (*ahem*). But how will it look to the rest of the world, none of whom have ever in their life received a blow job from someone to whom they were not married, should we fail in our patriotic efforts to make an enormous, humiliating, and ruinously expensive circus out of this when we have the chance?"

Well, Newt, here's the good news. I can help you resolve this constitutional crisis that threatens to imperil our way of life and rend the very fabric of our nation, a fabric that for more than two hundred years has remained as clean and unstained as the day Betsy Ross first threaded her needle. That is, until some fat, spoiled Jewess wiped her fat, Jewish, DNA-smeared lips all over it.

Here is my proposal:

First, stop lamenting about what you're going to tell the

children, particularly the impressionable teenagers among them, who are sure to become pregnant and HIV-infected now that the president, *their one and only role model,* has shown them how to lie about a blow job.

It's a lesson that hardly needed learning, Newt. In fact, I believe teenage boys lying to their friends about blow jobs are pictured in the magnificent hieroglyphs excavated at Abydos dating back from the Naqada IIIa period of the thirty-third century B.C. It's true that they may be a bit taken aback at the idea of lying about the occurrence of a blow job that they *actually received,* unless bestowed experimentally by a fellow member of the wrestling team. But should denying the occurrence of such acts be a trend they choose to emulate, I think I speak for the reputations of young women everywhere when I say that along with balancing the budget, reinstating peace talks in the Middle East, and bringing a much needed dash of decadent glamour back to the White House, Bill Clinton has once again made the world a better place.

Which brings me to my second point.

Now, we're all lawyers here. Except you, I guess. You were a history professor before your rise to power, and you know what? I like that about you. It's refreshing. Quick, summarize the events leading up to the papal schism of 1378! Hah! Don't worry. I'm just playing with you. You must hear that sort of thing all the time in chambers. The rest of the Georgia delegation look like big history buffs.

But I'm digressing.

You're not a lawyer; neither—and this may surprise you—am I. However, I am a teenager. And who better to point out this simple and finite definition that every teenager knows: *Sexual relations* (i.e., what the president did not engage in with that woman [Ms. Lewinsky]) = fully penetrative vaginal intercourse, lasting more than thirty seconds or until ejaculation, whichever comes first.

I'm sure that you, like many of your colleagues in Congress who champion abstinence-only sex education, are familiar with the concept of "everything but." "Everything but," as it has been explained to me by a variety of gym teachers posing as sex educators over the years, asserts the basic truth of the following statement:

"It's natural to feel sexual at your age, but sexual intercourse (that is, the aforementioned penetrative vaginal kind that must last at least thirty seconds or until ejaculation, whichever comes first) can have serious moral and physical repercussions. Luckily, there are all sorts of other fun activities one can engage in to feel closer to one's partner, such as hand-holding, kissing, tonguing, taking long walks, heavy petting, *mutual masturbation,* sexually explicit talk, finding an activity you both enjoy such as volleyball or bowling, or *genital stimulation with hands, mouth, or tongue.*" (Italics mine.) I believe we can add the insertion of a smoking implement into the vaginal cavity to this titillating and thoroughly God-friendly list.

As a result of this creative view of human sexuality, the only member of my peer group who counts oral sex as real sex is my friend Richard, who engages in it regularly with fifty-year-old men he meets at the bowling alley, a place that offers the bonus of another fun activity they both enjoy.

But your constituents would be no fans of Richard, an astigmatic but otherwise well-adjusted young homosexual. Richard has inscribed the entire text of *De Profundis* (the Oscar Wilde one) on his bedroom walls with a Sharpie and therefore can hardly be trusted by the Moral Majority. So permit me to present you with another case study of teenage sexuality.

Me.

Like the hapless Ms. Lewinsky, I am not a Christian and therefore can hardly be expected to conform to any decent standards of behavior. However, unlike her, I was raised not in the iniquitous squalor of Beverly Hills but deep in the God-fearing state of Nebraska, and more than a little of that flat land of college football, corn subsidies, and constant disapproval has rubbed off on me. Mr. Gingrich, I have given a hell of a lot of blow jobs in my two-and-a-half-year career. And still, I have it on good authority that I remain a virgin.

Don't believe me? I offer up the following testimony for the good of my country.

Ah! Show me a girl without memory of her first blow job, and I'll show you a woman with no romance in her soul. The dull scent of stale beer, the hiked-up bra cutting off the circulation of her shoulders, the pressure on the back of the head—firm yet gentle. She resists at first, as she's done so many times before, until finally she thinks, *Fuck it, how bad can it be?* And so the zipper comes down, and he says, "Wait a second" and pulls the entire pants apparatus down over his hips, belt, chain wallet, and all, so that his bare ass is *actually touching the seat of the car*, and the warm little bundle she has only prodded demurely through that convenient hole in the boxer briefs is actually in her mouth and if she is lucky she can taste along with the salty, meaty sweat on surprisingly soft skin, the sweet and unmistakable flavor of power.

Imagine that the warm little bundle in question is attached to the Leader of the Free World.

The feeling doesn't last. After a few more moments, the thing jerks violently, almost choking her, and her mouth fills with a thick and not-unpleasant liquid vaguely reminiscent of her grandma's chicken soup.

She looks into the flushed face of her beau, cheeks full like a hamster hoarding food, and spits out the window into the parking lot, spattering the tires of the empty car in the next space.

"Was that okay?"

"Yes, it was okay," he says.

Emboldened by success, she stares at her swollen lips in the side mirror as he drives her home and decides to offer up her maidenhead (or whatever tattered bits remain of it after years of bicycling, horseback riding, and masturbation) to this youth, callow, spotty, and indifferently attired as he may be.

What else is she to do? Cary Grant is dead. She can hardly expect to be considered for any kind of royal appointment (Princess of Wales, marriage to a Saudi oil baron) that would require some sort of virginity board certification. She is *fifteen,* after all, the same age Madonna was when she lost it, and besides, it's summer, and she likes the idea of returning to the familiar corridors of her high school a new person, a *sexy* person, who has only to turn her smoky gaze on any man, woman, or child to draw them instantly to her side, speechless and unbidden.

But mostly she just wants to know what it's like.

You know?

Newt Gingrich, do you remember when your mom (or maybe it was your dad, I don't know how it is for boys) summoned you up to her bedroom and sat you down and got out this book with watercolors of naked people with lots of pubic hair and explained to you where babies came from?

It's possible this didn't happen to you—you're a lot older than me. My grandmother says no one ever told her—only that when she reached a certain age, her mother told her she'd better not kiss any boys. But the point is this: however you may have discovered that when a man and a woman love each other very much, and they both want to, the man puts his penis inside the woman's vagina (just how this is accomplished is not fully explained), when you do, it's like you're part of the club all of a sudden, in on the big secret. All those jokes on TV, all the things you overhear your parents' friends say to one another when they've had a few glasses of wine and think that because you're building a castle with your fish sticks you aren't paying attention—they suddenly make sense. *Oh,* you think. *That's what* schwing *means.*

It's like a whole new world.

The way they talk about it in school and in all those public announcements where Arsenio Hall tells you to wear a condom (or Dennis Rodman, my personal favorite, who's all, "It's okay to party, but it's okay to play safe too," and then, like, throws a basketball at your face), it sounds like it's so easy to have sex. Not emotionally or whatever, but, like, you could just be at a pool party and whoops! Like a woman must employ every ounce of her cunning to ensure sure that, like a volley of arrows, penises do not bombard her from every rampart, entering her parts most delicate with the ease of a gnat flying into an open mouth.

And so we lit some candles that sultry August night, the summer before the tenth grade, and watched the first seven or so hours of *Braveheart*, sharing cans of Milwaukee's Best pilfered from the fridge before we ascended, undressed, and began.

Several hours, eight condoms, and an entire tub of Vaseline later, we return downstairs, slicked in August sweat. I will be unable to pee without discomfort for days. My pudenda is swollen, red, and bruised from the battery it has received.

My hymen, on the other hand, is appallingly intact.

Shirtless, he flops onto the sagging, flowered sofa, takes a long pull of the now-warm beer, and turns on the TV. Mel Gibson, his wide eyes stretched heavenward, is being castrated to the amusement of guffawing Englishmen.

"I'm sorry," I say.

"I'm sorry," I'd said when first he rammed himself against my unyielding pubic bone, grinding my coccyx against an errant bedspring. "I'm sorry," I'd said, when he cried in pain, snapping the latex of a fourth condom against his skin. "I'm sorry," I'd said, on my hands and knees, my entire groin slathered in Vaseline, saliva, hair gel—any emollient we had handy.

"Quit saying you're fucking sorry!" he'd said, as he pulled his underwear back on and disappeared into the bathroom.

"Free—*dom*!" croaked Mel Gibson weakly, as the British slit open his stomach and rip his steaming entrails from his body.

"Don't worry about it," he says now, not unkindly. "A lot of people are virgins."

I don't know if you're aware of this, Newt, but being a virgin puts a major damper on your sex life, particularly if you would like your sex life to include sex with other people. You see, it turns out that most guys are not leering spiders desperate to violate the untouched maiden who strays too close to their webs.

"Are you breaking up with me because I've never had sex before?" I asked Dan.

"Well, no, not completely," said Mike.

"Though that's a big part of it," said Chris.

"But I want to have sex! Please!" I cried.

"I just don't want that kind of responsibility," said Andrew, zipping up his hoodie.

"I mean, girls are weird about the guy who takes it," said Mark, buckling his belt.

"They, like, fall in *love* with him," said Jason, picking up his skateboard and tucking a joint behind his ear for the road.

"I won't fall in love with you! I promise!" I cried after him. "I just want to get it over with! Just fuck me, please!"

"Don't you want it to mean something? What's wrong with you?" asked Ryan.

I didn't chase after him. It was cold outside and I couldn't find my bra.

Finally, after years of searching and with my self-esteem still reasonably intact, I found someone willing and able to perform the repugnant task of deflowering an attractive seventeen-year-old brunette with large breasts and a desperate nature.

"It's a hard job, but I guess somebody's got to do it," said the gentleman in question.

"So, that's a yes?" I said, all business. Should I have some sort of contract ready? Would there be collateral?

"It's a yes."

With arrangements made, prophylactics purchased, and parents carefully lied to, I arrived at his house a few days later with an overnight bag, clad in a red velvet cocktail dress and specially purchased undergarments. He was a couple of years older and lived on his own, so there was no rush: no curfews to make, nobody arriving home unexpectedly, no mothers coming up the stairs saying, "I'm just coming in to put away some laundry—OH MY GOD!" We would have all night, even the following morning if necessary, to consummate our—not love, exactly, but abiding *fondness* for each another.

The following morning, I drove home, immaculately intact as ever in my red velvet cocktail dress, singing along sadly with Morrissey. *Last night I dreamt . . . soombody luvved me.* Well, at least somebody tried.

Oh, Morrissey. Where are you? Why aren't we together? You may be celibate/ambiguously oriented and my vagina is fused shut, but we're perfectly suited: two of a kind, both of us delicate flowers, frustrated and lonely and too smart for all these people and their bullshit. Why must we suffer so? Why? Why?

"Why?" I moan when he calls a couple of days later to tell me he has gotten back together with his old girlfriend.

Why?

Why is the pope Catholic? Answer: Because the pope is the head of the Catholic Church. Why is the sky blue? Because it is the color of the sky. WHY AM I A VIRGIN? BECAUSE I AM A

MUTANT. SERIOUSLY. IF I WAS ONE OF THE X-MEN,
THAT'S WHAT MY SECRET MUTANT POWER WOULD
BE. MY MUTANT NAME WOULD BE VIRGO, AND I
WOULD HAVE A VAGINA IMPENETRABLE BY ANY SUB-
STANCE, HUMAN, ANIMAL, OR MINERAL. "GOOD MU-
TANT POWER," PROFESSOR XAVIER WOULD SAY,
WHEN I ARRIVED AT THE XAVIER INSTITUTE FOR
HIGHER LEARNING. "IT WOULD BE ESPECIALLY USE-
FUL AS A SAFE FOR PRECIOUS OBJECTS OR BITS OF
CODED INFORMATION—*IF WE COULD GET ANY-
THING IN THERE!!!!!*"

Surprising myself, I started to cry.

"I don't see why you're so upset," he continued. "I mean, it's
not like we even had sex."

I shot a furtive glance into the family room, where my sister
seemed fully immersed in a rerun of *Full House.* "But I gave you
. . . *head.* Lots of times."

He laughed uncomfortably. "Yeah, but . . . that doesn't count."

"I know," I said miserably. "It doesn't."

You see, Newt? *It doesn't count.*

It doesn't count. The emperor has no clothes.

And so it comes full circle, the entire point of this rambling
letter in which I have revealed my deepest, darkest secrets and im-
molated myself before the Republican leadership. I sent a copy to
Trent Lott as well, so you guys can read it out loud together during your slumber parties on K Street. Just don't prank call my
house, okay? My dad is kind of an asshole after about ten o'clock.
But now you see, President Clinton did not have sexual relations
with that woman (Miss Lewinsky). He didn't lie, not technically,
and he's a politician. That's the best you can ask for. So let it drop.
You're humiliating the country. They're laughing at us in places
where they have a healthier attitude toward human sexuality—
you know, places like *Iran.*

If you keep on with this retarded charade, proceed at your peril. You're playing a dangerous game, Newt, setting a precedent where the bedroom activities of politicians are fair game. It's like doing DNA testing in royal families. I don't think that's something that you want once the shoe is on the other foot. And it will be. It always is.

In the meantime, feel free to enter this letter as any kind of evidence you wish. Print it in *The Washington* fucking *Post* for all I care. A desperate nation, its citizens forced against their will to discuss oral sex with their grandparents, beseeches you.

Please, Mr. Speaker. Think of the children.

Sincerely,
Rachel Shukert

Eight

On the Question of My Obscurity

Integrity. Innovation. Beauty. Strength. Vulnerability. Masterful. Virtuoso. Empress. God. These are just some of the words our readers submitted when asked to describe the subject of this interview. To them, I would like to add a few more.

Honesty. Courage. Dignity. Inspiration.

This past decade has been the most imaginative, fulfilling, artistically ambitious period the stages of this city have ever seen; a Golden Age, if you will, of Omaha Theater. Incidentally, this period is almost completely congruent with the spectacular career of the artist with whom I am about to speak.

Coincidence? I think not.

Heads swivel as she enters the room, all eyes drawn to this magical creature like iron filings to a glorious, long-legged magnet. Onstage she appears, regal, queenly even, an imperious goddess issuing pronouncements from on high, but in person she is all rosy cheeks, impish smile, a luxurious tumble of dark curls gathered in a careless bunch at the back of her head. Though her body is sleek and undulating as the mahogany haunches of an Arabian stallion, she is surprisingly delicate, childlike even, if not for those extraordinary eyes. Far greater men than I have written of those eyes, been felled by those eyes, driven mad by those eyes, eyes like a pair of Persian almonds sculpted from the clearest jade, eyes that seem to hold the knowledge of a thousand lifetimes, eyes that refract the viewer's own essence back to him like an emerald arrow through the heart. Rachel Shukert's eyes are that of the greatest kind of artist: an artist of the—

"*Fuck!*" Rising slightly in my chair, I plunge two fingers into my ass crack to dislodge the bit of sweaty tulle that had worked itself all the way inside. Again.

My boyfriend smirks. It was his idea for me to go without underwear to the ceremony. He thought it would be hot. Afflicted with the clueless wantonness of those who have just had sex for the first time, I agreed, and now am faced with the horrible eventuality of having to face my mother's dry cleaner with a skid mark on the crinoline of my old prom dress. "Is it your category yet?" he asks.

"I hate you," I say.

Onstage, a blowsy middle-aged woman in a sparkling teal pantsuit is about to announce the winner for Best Musical Direction in a Musical and is laughing hysterically at some uncomfortably flirtatious quip of her co-presenter's. "I swear!" she cackles. "Stop right now, or I'll leave my husband for you. Oh, wait," she deadpans, mugging wildly to the audience. "You *are* my husband!"

It amuses me when women who have spent their lives singing in the First Lutheran Memorial Church Choir act all Borscht Belt and caustic, as if appearing in a dinner-theater production of *Mame* has transformed them into Bea Arthur. Right. Like a Jewish woman over the age of thirty would appear drunk in public. Shouting, yes, with lipstick on her teeth and hardened cream cheese encrusting her diamonds, but drunk? Never.

"What do you say, boys?" the husband asks, scanning the crowd. "Anyone want to take her off my hands?"

Every marriage needs its little shtick, I guess, especially an emphatically childless one to a man wearing Gucci loafers (mail order, since you couldn't buy those *here*) and a crystal-studded AIDS-ribbon lapel pin; the kind of AIDS ribbon you *invest* in. My own AIDS ribbon, collected from the public basket, is thrust rakishly through the jet beadwork of my mother's evening bag. Oh, how she glared when she saw that as we left the house!

"What?" I snapped. "You hate AIDS now?"

"Enough!" The woman in teal squeals like a tipsy pig being led to the slaughter, her stomach quivering like a Christmas Jell-O mold as her gay husband tickles her in front of two hundred people.

"But I just can't keep my *hands* off you!" he lies desperately. *Silly man,* I think. *Don't you know that every time you tell a lie, the Baby Jesus cries?* That's what they told me at Methodist preschool.

The five nominees for Best Musical Direction in a Musical include two men nominated twice in the category for their work, as well as the music directors of two rival productions of *Annie.* My boyfriend retrieves the small silver flask tucked into his sock and tips the contents down his throat.

At my other side sits my good friend and fellow nominee Max Sparber, clad in a pristine smoking jacket of red brocade, his tasseled cap resting on his knees. "If we don't win tonight, this whole thing is a farce," he mutters. "A total farce." Max's brilliant play, *Minstrel Show,* a fearless and innovative exploration of the terrifying 1919 lynching in Omaha of William Brown, a crippled and clearly innocent black man accused of sexually assaulting a white woman, had enjoyed a rapturous critical reception, a sold-out six-week run, even a call for boycott from Omaha's answer to Al Sharpton (not having seen or read the play, he objected to the word *minstrel* in the title), and had landed Max his first Theater

Arts Guild nomination in the scantly populated Best Original Script category, where he was competing with two loosely termed musicals in which poodle-skirted bobby-soxers at the soda fountain sang doo-wop ballads about the good old days to a paunchy middle-aged insurance salesman dressed like Elvis.

Naturally, he doesn't stand a chance.

"A farce," he declares minutes later as we watch a fifty-year-old woman in a poodle skirt accept his award from a man in a waistcoat printed with treble clefs. "A complete and utter fucking farce. I'm going to the liquor store. Good luck."

This was my last chance to win the coveted Omaha Metropolitan Area Theater Arts Guild Award for Best Youth Actress. Next year I would no longer be a youth, having exceeded the age limit, and would be up against a much tougher pool of seasoned actress/realtors (the Omaha equivalent of actress/model) capable of turning in layered, feral performances in such classics as *Brigadoon, Bus Stop,* and *The Best Little Whorehouse in Texas.* Besides, God willing, I might not live here anymore. The acceptance letter hadn't come yet, but it would, I could feel it. It had to.

> Acceptance letter?
> *Yes, I've applied to the extremely prestigious theater program at New York University.*
> The big city, huh? Rachel, what will we do without you?
> *Well, I haven't gotten in yet!*
> You will. How could you not?
> *That's so sweet of you to say. But now, I just want to focus on getting through tonight!*
> Well, if anyone deserves a TAG Award, it's you. Why, you're the greatest talent to come out of Nebraska since Mr. Henry Fonda!

I had first heard of the Theater Arts Guild early in my stage career as long-seasoned veterans in the shabby communal dressing rooms of Omaha's theaters would apply contour shadow in front of cracked mirrors and whisper about "the TAG meeting" or "the TAG board" as if discussing a secret society like Skull and Bones, the Ku Klux Klan, or homosexuality. Despite the secrecy, I assumed they referred to some uninteresting grown-up thing, like tax season or hospice care. The idea that said Theater Arts Guild was a body that might one day honor me with some kind of award (in a ceremony televised by Nebraska Public Television, no less!) did not enter my consciousness until I appeared in an annual Christmastime musical with an enormous cast, including more than twenty child actors. Unlike most of the children, who were simply trotted out silently to lend an atmosphere of carefree holiday gaiety, I had been given a line—"It just can't feel like Christmas without snow!" While this utterance, delivered in the final scene of the play before we were presented with gift-wrapped blocks of wood which we were instructed *not under* ANY *circumstances* to unwrap, placed me in a slightly higher theatrical caste and earned me the resentment of my peers (or so I liked to think), it did not exempt me from that dark afternoon when every cast member under the age of eighteen was instructed to arrive at the theater early, get into costume, and assemble onstage. My costume was an ill-fitting dress of plaid taffeta, a hand-me-down from Ballet Omaha's recently retired production of *The Nutcracker*. Stiff with seventeen years' worth of the sweat of young dancers, and redolent of their young-dancer odor, it also had a large, scratchy label sewn inside the collar. After I'd worn it a few days, an angry rash had broken out on my neck, so I took a pair of my mother's nail scissors to the theater and cut out the label. Now the rash had moved to the strip of bare flesh between my undershirt and the waistband of my tights. The itching was so intense I had trouble getting to sleep. I considered asking my mother to take the costume to the dry cleaner to be disinfected, but we had been warned that to leave the premises with any prop or costume item would be considered by the producers an act of theft, punishable by dismissal and, possibly, death.

Our musical director stood before us. The crusty remnants of a meatball sub dotting his battered Huskers windbreaker, he narrowed his pale, lashless eyes as he regaled us with a litany of our sins. We were hyper. We were noisy. Our footsteps backstage were audible during the show, which was completely disrespectful to the real performers onstage, acting and singing their hearts out. "Presents" had been found unwrapped, despite repeated warning. Some of the tiniest children had been nodding off backstage during the second act and missing their entrance cues.

"I play the damn entrance music for the Snow Fairies, and *there're no goddamn Snow Fairies!*"

Several of the Snow Fairies, including my sister, began to cry. I pulled her onto my lap and kissed her wet cheek.

"No goddamn Snow Fairies!" he continued, in disbelief. "And it makes me look like a goddamn idiot!"

In the magical North Pole from which they hailed, the Snow Fairies were known to have magical, transformative powers. They turned a pile of ice into a pile of toys, a group of unruly elves into a team of prancing reindeer. However, in the case of our musical director transforming into a goddamn idiot, I didn't think he needed a lot of help from the Snow Fairies.

"Also, some of you," he shouted, the insults of the Snow Fairies having driven him to a fury, "have *defaced* your costumes!" To this accusation there was a general feeling of guilt. I wasn't the only one scratching uncontrollably. We often compared rashes backstage, and I knew I wasn't the only one to have done something about it. "Don't think we can't tell who you are, or that your *parents won't be charged for repairs.*" His lack of colored irises made his icy stare all the more chilling. "If I was your father, I'd make you pay for every penny of the damage yourselves."

"Goodthgyrntmyfather," muttered Derek Ziederbeck, a stocky nine-year-old boy wearing a candy-pink sailor suit with short pants and a creeping brown stain at the groin. In Derek's defense, the stain was there when he got the costume.

"What did you say?"

Cornered, humiliatingly dressed, with twenty-odd sets of eyes gleaming with schadenfreude upon him, Derek had no choice but to kneel at the edge of the hole he had dug for himself. "I said, GOOD THING YOU'RE NOT MY FATHER!"

"Right," said the musical director. "Right. Derek, go to the lobby and call your mother."

"For what?"

"Tell her to come pick you up. You're out of the show."

"Tonight?"

"Every night."

Bang! Oozing blood, the metaphoric Derek jerked headfirst into his grave, his dead eyes gazing blankly at the light grid, the pale brown stain on his pink shorts growing dark and foul. The real Derek violently ripped the plaid bow from his neck and threw it, overturning several chairs as he stamped out.

"Good riddance," said the musical director. "Jonathan, do you know his solo?"

Jonathan, an awkward boy in lavender who willingly studied tap, looked up, delighted. "Yes, of course."

"It's yours." A palpable current of envy rippled through the group as Jonathan clenched his fists in victory. "You see, kids. Accountability. Discipline. Respect. That's what you need if you want a career in the Theater. If you don't have those, well, I don't care how talented you are, you're never going to make it." I could see his rashy knees through the holes of his green sweatpants. Was he wearing our costumes too?

"You know," he continued, "I was talking to DeeDee this morning"—DeeDee, an odd, pop-eyed woman who would not look out of place pushing a shopping cart across the Central Park Mall with two bright slashes of rouge across her cheeks and the

Omaha World-Herald's Living section thrust between her but-
tocks, was a veteran of the theater community who played the
wicked witch/mother figure (the details of the plot are as fuzzy to
me now as they were at the time)—"and she said that for her, the
gold standard for child actors was really set when Happi Holliday
played the title role in *Annie* at the DTC."

"Happy Holiday?" I whispered to my friend Abby.

"Be quiet!" Abby whispered. *"Happi Holliday. It's a stage
name."*

"She must have been about twelve then," the musical director
rhapsodized.

"Twelve and she had a stage name?"

"Shut up!" snapped Abby in a loud whisper. Unlike my
mother, who was deeply skeptical about any activity that would
not result in my eventual acceptance in a competitive university
and membership on the board of an affluent Conservative congregation, Abby's mother took her daughter's showbiz career seriously. Abby had headshots, a private dance instructor, and was
registered with WhizKidz, the child talent agency in town. Today
I believe she is a twice-divorced pharmaceutical rep in Wisconsin.

"Happi Holliday did a four-month run and a Nebraska/Iowa
road tour of *Annie*. She left school and did her homework in cars
and motel rooms. She made them laugh, she made them cry, and
she did it every night. And one week, she got sick. Strep throat, a
temperature of a hundred and four degrees. And did she com-
plain? Did she ask someone to drive her home from Pawnee City
and tell them to give the audience their money back? No. She
went on. Nearly delirious with fever, dehydrated; man, I don't
know how she did it, but she did. And she was incredible. She was
better than she'd ever been, and that audience gave her a standing
ovation that night and every night." He paused, lost for a moment
in the power, the glory, the fire and ice of Happi Holliday. "She
won a TAG Award for that performance, didn't she, DeeDee?"

"She sure did," shouted DeeDee from the back of the house where she had been sitting all the time. "She sure did. And she's the reason why I have a *pretty* hard time dealing with people who try to make excuses for themselves, just because they happen to be *children.*"

I had a feeling DeeDee had been behind this from the beginning. Sure, you thought she would be cuddly and grandmotherly, because she was old and fat and crazy-looking, but she wasn't a grandma. She was a bitch.

Thus shamed, we were dismissed. "Quietly!" shouted the music director.

"What's a TAG Award?" I asked Abby backstage, waiting for our cue. The actor would say, "It was elves, Mama! Elves that came and ate all the sweetmeats!" and then we would run across the stage, covering our mouths and giggling.

"Shhh."

"No, really, what is it?"

She sighed. "It's like a Tony."

". . . came and ate all the sweetmeats!"

"But in Omaha? Like an Omaha Tony? An OmaTony?"

There was a small fad at the time of melding *Omaha* with another word to create a new word that honored the modifier and diminished the subject, such as *Omahomie, Omaterial,* and *Omasexual,* a verbal gesture that encompassed hometown pride and deep self-loathing.

"Yes. But *really important.*"

"IT WAS ELVES, MAMA!!!!"

"Shit. Go. *Go!*"

During a performance later in the two-month run, a large area of heavy, ancient shelving in the attic supply closet that served as the children's dressing room collapsed during intermission and trapped me underneath for ten minutes until the stage manager came upstairs to call places. I was badly bruised and shaken, my ribs seemed quite possibly broken, and a nail had punctured my wrist, leaving a rust-rimmed stigmata, but the show must go on. If Happi Holliday could do it, so could I.

"What the fuck were you thinking?" exclaimed my mother. She had picked me up after the performance and, shocked, driven me straight to the emergency room, where I received a tetanus shot and had X-rays done. "Why didn't you have them call me?" she asked while we waited for the X-rays to come back.

"The show must go on. They couldn't have done it without me."

"Without you? You have *one fucking line*. One of the other hundred little girls couldn't have said 'It isn't Christmas if there isn't snow'?"

"I believe you'll find the line is, 'It *just can't feel like* Christmas without snow.' And no, they could not. It's *my* line." *You think I was going to let Abby have my line? Think again, lady.* "I'm a professional," I added haughtily. "I fulfill my professional obligations. In fact, I think it's time for me to start working with a stage name."

"What's wrong with your real name?"

"I need something perkier. Something with a little more pep. Like Brandi. Or Cherry, or Starla. Rachel—I don't know, it just sounds too . . . too . . ."

"Too unlike a prostitute?"

I twisted the knife. "Too Jewish."

The doctor returned. My wrist was sprained and a rib was cracked. He put me on a round of antibiotics. "Just in case," he said. "Also, you'll need to limit your movement for a few days. If you can get out of the next few performances, I would."

"Absolutely not," I said. "I want to win a TAG Award."

"That's my Brandi," said my mother. "What a little trouper."

Still, it took two more years of solid work for me to receive the postcard festooned with clip-art comedy-and-tragedy masks, informing me that the Theater Arts Guild had selected my stellar and critically acclaimed performance (*Omaha World-Herald,* June 15, 1992: "Rachel Shukert is particularly fine") as Brigitta von Trapp in the Rodgers and Hammerstein classic *The Sound of Music.*

"Why don't you call Kalico's,"[N] I instructed my mother. "See if they're interested in sponsoring my gown for the event."

"I've got a better idea," she said. "Why don't you call your grandmother and see if *she's* interested in sponsoring your gown for the event. She hasn't got much of a nose for bullshit."

"Why can't you be more supportive?"

"Sweetheart," she said. "I'm very proud of you. You want more support, take five dollars and go buy some pantyhose."

Luckily, it was summer, and I could devote a great deal of time to preparations. Like most people in the First World, I have practiced giving acceptance speeches almost from the moment I was able to talk; now, faced with the imminent possibility of delivering one, I practiced for hours standing in front of the full-length mirror in my parents' bedroom, clutching against my heart a small plastic Oscar they had received as a favor at an office Christmas party.

"Oh my God, this is so overwhelming! I just don't know what to say." Here I heave, as though forcing back a flood of tears, turn away for a moment, pinching my sinus at the bridge of my nose between my eyebrows, and look up again. "I just can't express how grateful I am to have had the chance to tell this incredible story of triumph, of family, of courage, of . . . (*voice breaks*) of *hope,* at a time when a darkness had truly descended over humankind. And before anything else, I want to thank those two extraordinary men

---

[N] The day a girl first went to Kalico's was a Great Nebraska Moment indeed. A one-store, family-owned boutique specializing in girls ages seven to seventeen, it was *the* place for Omaha's little princesses to buy their formal wear, sportswear, and formal sportswear. My own Bat Mitzvah dress and suit, as well as every dress for a wedding, a dance, and the High Holidays, came from Kalico's until hormones did something to me and I began to do things like shoplift and cut my own hair with a knife. I believe the store is now a Pottery Barn.

of the theater, Richard Rodgers and Oscar Hammerstein, for their bravery in telling that story. Because *The Sound of Music* is an extraordinary masterpiece, one that dives headfirst into the gritty realities of life, the twisted, rotten soul of bigotry and hatred, and finds that salvation lies in the beauty of a mountain, a pure white flower, the laugh of a brook as it trips and falls over stones on its way, *to sing through the night,* LIKE A LARK WHO IS LEARNING TO PRAAAAAAAAAAAY!!!!!!"

"You woke me up!" My sister appeared, pink and crumpled from her afternoon nap, her curly head pressed against the doorjamb.

"I'm practicing!"

"What are you practicing?"

"My *acceptance* speech!"

Her small eyebrows creased in confusion. "How come you were singing?"

"I wasn't!"

"Yes, you were. You were singing really loud."

"I was *experimenting*. Figuring out different way to make my speech memorable. You have to do something a little different. Like the greatest Oscar speeches, you know, you remember them. Like 'You like me, you really like me!' Or when Marlon Brando sent that Indian lady. Or Vanessa Redgrave with the PLO."

"What's the PLO?"

"You know, the bad guys. In Israel."

"There are bad guys in Israel?" Her chin quivered. "But everybody's Jewish there."

I sighed. "Not Jewish people. Arabs."

"Oh. How come you aren't wearing any pants?"

Recently, I had noticed for the first time that there was a problem with my thighs. My thighs, it seemed, were fat. This realization had taken me somewhat by surprise. I had assumed that when I grew up I would be five feet ten inches tall and 110 pounds, like Princess Diana; it had never occurred to me that my legs would one day resemble a pair of smoked hams standing upright, their upper sections curved and swollen like the prow of a ship. As I stood in front of the mirror, it made sense to be pantless—all the better to poke them, slap them, gaze at them in a variety of angles and positions, and attempt to ascertain if this sudden gigantism was a trick of the light or an inherent flaw in my own person that would need to be dealt with at the earliest opportunity.

"Mommy wouldn't want you in her room without pants."

"Well, until Mommy buys me a full-length mirror for my own room, she'll have to deal with it."

She pouted. "Mommy's *nice*. Can I stay and watch?"

"I guess. If you're quiet."

Happily, she ran into the room and flung herself onto the bed, as I thanked the cast, the crew, the members of the Academy, my sixth-grade teacher, the costume designer and carpenters, the *Omaha World-Herald*, my father, my mother, my grandparents, my friends, my hairdresser, my voice teacher, my pediatrician, my mother's obstetrician—"Mine was a difficult birth, and without his gentle, knowing hands manning the forceps that fateful day, the artistic achievement you honor today might never have been"—and of course, my public.

My sister removed the tail of her shirt from her mouth. "How come you didn't thank me?"

"You're included with the cast." My cherubic sister, she of the golden curls and enormous eyes, had played Gretl, the littlest von Trapp, uttering the immortal lyrics "The sun / Has gone / To bed and so must I-I!" To which we older, uglier von Trapps echoed with "So long / Farewell / Auf Wiedersehen / Good-bye!"

"How come I'm not winning an award?" she asked, frowning.

"Well," I said as kindly as I could, "this isn't really your calling."

"I've been in lots of plays! I was Janey Popper in *Mr. Popper's Penguins* and Zuzu in *It's a Wonderful Life.* You weren't even in those!"

This was a point of tension between us.

"But think of it this way," I said. "It's the difference between Meryl Streep and, like, Jennie Garth. Jennie Garth may be younger and cuter and blonder, but she's never going to win an Oscar."

Wrenching as her sobs were, something in them told me she knew I was right.

There's a lot of crying in the Theater, and most of it isn't on-stage. The long hours, the constant frustration, and, week after week, the arbitrary, unpredictable, crushing rejection; and most of us are tender, sensitive souls—as regards our own feelings, at least. After my first audition, when I failed to be cast in a lavish production of *Fiddler on the Roof* at the newly refurbished Jewish Community Center Theater, I prostrated myself on the heated cement of our back patio, smearing ashes from the grill on my face and hair in the manner of the ancient Romans, until our next-door neighbor appeared to tell me that my unbridled screams of anguish were spooking the terriers. But I'd learned my lesson. Rejection was par for the course in this business, and if you wanted to survive, you'd better learn how to deal with it.

"Don't worry about me," I said, as my parents clucked over me at the reception, after I'd lost. "I'll be all right. I've got a skin as thick and shiny as an advanced scleroderma patient."

My parents exchanged a look.

"What? Bob Saget's sister has it. They gave us a brochure in Hebrew school. Do you know that it tends to affect Ashkenazi Jews, and that eventually your organs harden and you die? They think the first cases of it might have been in ancient Greece, and that's where the Medusa myth comes from."

"Good," said my father. "I'm glad you're taking this well."

"It's an honor just to be nominated," I continued. "But everyone knows they only gave it to the girl that won because she's eighteen and she's never going to have another chance in the youth category. Like when they gave the Oscar to Jessica Tandy. You know, because she was probably going to die soon?"

"I see," my mother said.

"Don't worry," I reassured them. "I have lots of time left to win."

But I was a junior in high school by the time my second nomination came, for my performance in a maudlin little play called *Anne Frank and Me*, written in that time-honored conceit of young adult literature: girl meets boy, girl expresses indifference/skepticism re the Horrors of the Holocaust, girl suffers minor head injury and wakes up Dorothy-like in the magical land of Occupied Europe, where neighbor turns against neighbor and Jews are hunted like the Most Dangerous Game. The project appealed to me for a few reasons.

ONE: I was pleased to be offered not the role of the hapless Jewess but that of her Gentile protector, a coquettish Parisienne. This would afford me a showcase for my finely honed French accent, perfected after countless screenings of *Gigi*. I would be costumed not in the usual limp rags with the enormous yellow Star of David obscuring my entire left breast (they had to make them especially big to read onstage) but in a chic day dress of navy crêpe de chine with rose silk facing, vintage ankle-strap heels, and a Rita Hayworth pompadour topping the arched eyebrows and strong mouth. It also meant that of all the girls who had auditioned at the JCC that day, I was the one the director looked at and thought, *There! There's one who can walk onstage without us thinking "Jew, Jew, Jewy McJew"!* After a lifetime spent in Omaha among apple-cheeked Scandinavians and hulking Slavs, I found this notion extremely flattering. I attributed this good fortune to my nose.

TWO: The production would reunite me with the ambiguously oriented (but gorgeous!) young actor with whom I had begun a passionate and tormented affair earlier that year during a teen production of *Cat on a Hot Tin Roof*. He had been cast as my twin brother, lending a deliciously sordid psychosexual element to our already thorny relationship. Just the thought of it made my insides quiver in expectation; nothing is catnip to the libido of a certain kind of sixteen-year-old girl more than the promise of impending emotional torture.

THREE: The play included a scene set in an actual gas chamber. Oh yes.

My character, sent to Auschwitz along with the Jews she had bravely protected, was among the victims. Now, actors will tell you about their favorite kind of death scenes—gunshot, disemboweling, stroke, hanging, poison—but no one knows what death looked like inside a gas chamber at Birkenau, except for a very few people who, for legal reasons, aren't telling. It left a lot of room for artistic license. I could gag. I could choke. I could throw myself to the ground and writhe in spastic agony. I could squeeze tears of despair and terror out from under my eyelids, cradle another agonized, screaming victim in my arms (usually my sister, as an adorable, doomed child), and die in anguish, my fingernails scraping, heartbreakingly, futilely, against the imaginary iron door that separated me from life. And as I was playing a wealthy Gentile whose personal comfort had not been meaningfully affected by the German occupation, I could do it all in a *divine* full-length silver mink I had ordered the wardrobe assistant to fetch from the costume archives for me.

"It's essential to my character," I said. "It really makes me understand where this woman is coming from. And just think about the stage picture it creates! Tell me, what could be more effective than seeing this proud, elegant *aristocrat* die in the gas like an animal, like a Jew? It *rips* your fucking *guts* out." The mink wasn't for me. It was for art. And every night, after I slipped it off and the dressers packed it into its garment bag, I crept into the scene shop and, illuminated by the blinding glow of the clip lights, engaged in an agonized make-out session with my ambiguously oriented boyfriend.

"No," he said, as I wrapped his hand in mine and attempted to force it onto my clitoris. "I'm just not comfortable with this."

Our audience was scant, culled mainly from the local Talmud Torah's fifth-graders (the first year the Holocaust became a full-time part of the curriculum) and a motley assortment of catatonics and dementia patients wheeled over from the Rose Blumkin Home for the Jewish Aged, many of whom began to weep or laugh uncontrollably and had to be wheeled back out again, so the nomination was quite a surprise.

"Congratulations!" squealed my sister when the notice came in the mail. "Maybe you'll win this time."

"I don't think so," I replied. I may have been flunking trig, physics, and aerobics, but I knew my award shows. Unless you are British, you can't win for something nobody saw.

"Just don't forget to thank me," she said. "If you win, it's mostly because of my work in the gas-chamber scene."

I didn't put a lot of effort into the ceremony that year. I prepared no speech, did nothing particular with my hair; I don't even think my parents came. The lack of interest matched my general attitude toward life. I had dropped my ambiguously oriented boyfriend for one less physically repulsed by my private parts, and he then dumped *me,* plunging me into an ugly and desperate cycle of wailing, sleeplessness, and late-night drive-bys, listening to the single mix tape he had made me until I couldn't stand it anymore, at which time I would replace it with the Smiths and drove to the nearest Village Inn, where despite being too depressed to eat, I would polish off a double-decker grilled cheese with tomato and an extra order of French fries before getting back into the car and turning on the windshield wipers to

make it look like it was raining as I wept, pretending to be in a
British music video from 1984.

> That sounds like a terrible time for you.
>
> *It was. Oh, it was!* (chuckles)
>
> How did you ever find the strength to go on?
>
> *Well, I think Diana Ross said it best: "Everybody has some pain in*
> *their life, and if I have a lot of pain, well, I'll just use it sometime in a role*
> *when I have to show pain."*
>
> Brava! You're the greatest talent to come out of Nebraska since . . .
>
> *Montgomery Clift?*
>
> Montgomery Clift!

Speaking of Monty Clift, my friend Richard agreed to be my
date to the awards, held that year in the ballroom of Harrah's
Casino in Council Bluffs.

"Classy," said Richard.

He was speaking to me again, now that I was no longer abus-
ing what he called "the vaginal tyranny of heterosexual preroga-
tive" by withholding a valuable member of the already limited
teenage gay Nebraskan dating pool. We sat in the parking lot
smoking bowls until it was time to go inside.

"I'll meet you in there," I said as we reached the lobby. "Just
got to—"

"You're not going to yak, are you?" he asked. "That weed was
fucking strong."

"No, I'm fine. I just have to go to the . . . *you know.* The
head." I started to giggle. "I have to go to the HEAD!"

"HEAD? You want the HEAD? Honey, don't look at me!"
Richard shrieked with laughter, drawing the ire of the gamblers in
the next room. Two very large women, one strapped to the kind
of motorized cart used to transport airline luggage, rattled their
jugs of quarters disapprovingly in our direction.

Designed to accommodate patrons with particular spatial

requirements, the empty ladies' room was huge. Each stall could comfortably park a compact automobile, and at the end of the row was a cubicle outfitted with safety railings and a helpful step-stool of no-slip rubber along with a sink, a counter, and a changing station lined with a thick mat covered in plastic. The toilet seat was clearly intended for a race of giants. I am not short, but my feet dangled over the floor as if I was a small child, and it was a long way down. A very long way. Like, such a long way that the TelePrompTer in my head that conveys my sentient thoughts to me read: *It's a loooooooooooooooooooooooooooooooong way down from this toilet seat.*

Thank God for the step. What kind and thoughtful casino owners to assist their patrons in such a tender fashion. Truly they had only our best interests at heart. I loved them. And I had so much love in my heart to give. So much love. Look at that face in that mirror. That face was loving. That face was shining. That face was . . . blue.

Blue? No, yellow. Yellow and blue. And red. And vibrating. My face was blue, yellow, red, and vibrating, as though I was watching a 3-D movie without 3-D glasses.

"I'm dying," I said out loud. "I'm dying."

There must be a gas leak somewhere in the casino, and gas is seeping through this enormous toilet and poisoning me. With my skewed sensory perception, the vibrating, abstract images in the mirror, it seemed obvious that my neurological functions were shutting down. My organs would soon follow. I could leave the bathroom, run away, but it was too late. I had already ingested too much of the gas to live, and to open the door now would only expose others to certain death. The lonely gamblers outside, stuffing their slots with nickels and their mouths with bacon, might not have much to live for; but I would not bring their doom, not this day. No, the burden was mine to bear, and bear it I would; stretched upon the plasticized mattress of the baby-changing station, I would die of asphyxiation from poison gas, as my ancestors had done before me. There was an upside to this: as the last gasps of life slipped from my body, I would be able to gauge the accuracy of my gas-chamber histrionics. In my final moments on earth I would know at last if I was really a good actress.

"Where the fuck have you been?" Richard snarled, when I staggered into the ballroom. "They just did your category!"

"What? Did I win?"

"No," he said. "Too bad. I was all set to go up and refuse on your behalf in protest of Nebraska's partial-birth abortion ban.[N] You know, because you have them all the time."

Rachel—may I call you Rachel?

Of course!

Can you put into words how much this night—this honor—means to you? Now that it's your last chance?

Well, certainly, it would be nice to win! But honestly, I don't understand how you can compare one performance to another, as if artistic accomplishment is some kind of quantitative thing. I absolutely admire every single one of the actresses in my category. I mean, they may have played plucky singing orphans or plucky singing Austrians or plucky singing orphans in a different musical about orphans, and I may have turned in a critically lauded performance as the young washerwoman who strikes up a deeply complex psychosexual relationship with the Marquis de Sade in Quills, *Doug Wright's Obie Award–winning exploration of censorship, violence, and religious and sexual taboos, but really, it's apples and oranges. They may have executed difficult tap maneuvers, and I may have writhed*

[N] Truly a Great Moment in Nebraska History when the state legislature passed that one, using the phrase "partial-birth abortion" in legal terms for the first time and providing no exception for the health of the mother, the grounds by which it was found unconstitutional in 2000 by the Supreme Court, with the much missed Sandra Day O'Connor casting the deciding vote for the majority. Of course, the antiabortion people had much better luck on their second fishing expedition, as you may have heard, ensuring once and for all that desperately ill or impoverished women will no longer callously murder their babies for the amusement of the godless liberal elite. Hallelujah!

atop a stone crypt, a reborn succubus detailing my forced triple penetration by the three-pronged phallus of Satan, striking lust and terror into the heart of the tormented priest who secretly loved me, but is one really more diffi-cult, or more praiseworthy, than the other? I don't know—I'm not much of a tapper! But to be nominated against a group of such incredibly talented nine-year-olds is such an honor, and I really do wish them all the best of luck.

"Good luck," my boyfriend said, squeezing my knees as the previous year's recepient mounted the box behind the podium to announce the new winner. "I really hope you win."

"Me too," I said. "Me too."

I didn't want to make a big deal about it or anything. When my mother took the star-shaped TAG Award off the shelf and began to fold it in bubble wrap as we packed up my room, I shook my head. "Keep it here," I said. "I don't want the other kids to think I'm a show-off."

"Are you sure?" asked my mother.

"I'm sure." I didn't want people to be intimidated, or worse, *awed.* If they were going to be my friends, I wanted them to like me for me, not because I was the 1998 winner of Omaha's Theater Arts Guild Award. All summer long, in fact, since I'd gotten the letter welcoming me to NYU's Tisch School of the Arts, it had been the same thing: "Keep in touch! Don't forget me when you're famous!" Frankly, it was getting a little tiring. Sure, so I was meant for bigger and better things than the rest of my high school gradu-ating class. Was that not apparent all along? I was still a normal person. I just wanted to be treated like anyone else. My huge talent would be apparent soon enough when we started class—better to deal with the fallout then. I'd sift through the resentment, the flat-tery, the petty jealousies, and I'd know who my real friends were. And truthfully, I hadn't felt quite the same about the statuette since they gave it to me and I noticed they'd misspelled my first name. R-A-C-H-A-E-L. It just looks stupid. The awards chairman had offered to send it out to be reengraved (at my own expense, naturally), but I told him not to bother. A mistake is a mistake. You can't take it back.

"You keep it, Mom," I said. "You're the one who drove me to all those rehearsals over the years."

Her eyes filled with tears. "I'm really touched."

"Can I have the bubble wrap?" my sister piped up. "I like the sound." She grabbed the sheet from my mother's hand and began popping happily. She would be starting high school that fall.

"Mom," I said, watching as my sister rocked meditatively, soothed by the symphony of the bubble wrap exploding and deflating beneath her fingers. "Has it ever occurred to you that she might be autistic?"

"Shut *up*!"

"Nah," said my mother. "If she was autistic, she'd *hate* that sound."

The first few nights of college started off promisingly. Beer was drunk. Pot was smoked. I borrowed a hammer from the musical-theater major next door and engaged in an impromptu sing-along of songs from *Into the Woods*. New acquaintances were plentiful; yet as the days passed, I couldn't seem to turn any of those acquaintances into friends. They all seemed to know one another already. The New York kids hung out with the New York kids, the New Jersey kids with the New Jersey kids, the L.A. kids . . . well, you get the idea. No one else was from Nebraska—a theme I sensed would persist for the rest of my adult life. The more I tried to engage people in conversations, reaching for common ground on something, anything, the more they pulled away.

"Your last name is Friedman? You're Jewish?"

"Um . . . yeah . . ."

"Oh wow! So am I."

"Oh," said young Friedman. "You're not from, like, the Chabad[†] people, are you? Because I'm really not interested."

My new roommate, an obscenely well-groomed redhead from Bel Air, was kinder. "You know, when I got the thing saying you were from Nebraska, I thought you were going to be, like, a hayseed. Like overalls and tractors and shit."

"And I'm not?"

"No," she said. "I mean, I wouldn't say you're like, *sophisticated*"—to her great amusement, I had sworn in shock earlier over a fourteen-dollar entrée—"but you're not a total hick."

"Thanks."

"Don't get me wrong," she said. "I *like* you. I feel, like, you know, *protective* of you."

Classes, when they started, offered little respite. I had imagined wowing my peers with my skillful scene work and impressive ease with heightened text, but we seemed to spend most of the day barefoot, making strange and unpleasant noises with our tongues stretched to the sky, forcing our bodies into a series of squats, lunges, and contortions, or walking around in circles for what seemed like hours until the teacher told us we could stop.

"Interesting," the teacher said. "Now, what did you learn

[†] Gentiles, depending on what you look like—for example, if you are Italian— you may have walked through a large urban center and been approached by a black-hatted, bearded man holding a ritual object of some sort who asks you, "Are you Jewish?" Obviously, being a Gentile, you reply in the negative, but if you say yes, he will usher you with great delight into a waiting caravan, where you will be encouraged to say whatever blessing it is he wants you to say (depending on the time of year) and rewarded with a paper cup of flat 7-Up and a cookie. This man is a member of the Chabad-Lubavitch sect, a group devoted to getting secular Jews more involved in Judaism; they are in some ways like Jewish Hare Krishnas, except that most Hare Krishnas are also Jewish and the Chabad people only want you to give up small donations here and there, not all your worldly goods.

from that?" We were expected to have an answer, and it could not be "I once thought I would never again attain the stratospheric level of boredom induced by a concert of liturgical music at Temple Israel in 1987. Today, however, I have learned that this is not the case." As we lay on our backs with our legs thrust over our head after one particularly grueling and pointless exercise, the girl beside me caught my eye and grimaced playfully, indicating that she was in as much physical and mental discomfort as I. Sensing an ally, I approached her shyly after class.

"Wasn't that horrible?"

"I know," she grimaced. "This is kicking my ass!"

"And it's so pointless!" I exclaimed, wild with excitement. "I mean, how is all this rolling around on the floor trying to feel our livers move going to make us good actors? It's so indulgent . . . not even indulgent, it's just stupid! I don't know about you, but I've done a lot of *real* work, and this kind of thing is completely—"

She was grimacing again, only this time without a hint of playful conspiracy. Just disgust. "They're trying to get us into our bodies. I'll see you tomorrow, I guess."

Into our bodies? Were we ever outside our bodies? What does that even mean? Why did no one want to be my friend?

Days seem very long when you are lonely. Even with several hours of class each day, it was a struggle to think of enough things to occupy my time. I invented errands for myself, buying useless and unneeded items: wall hooks that remained in the package, picture frames, a humidifier. I went uptown to the museums several afternoons a week, skipping the subway and choosing instead to walk the eighty blocks to fill up the time. Long after I had finished my food, I sat for hours in the dining hall, hoping that someone, anyone, who I recognized would come in alone and have no choice but to sit with me. My expectations were steadily shrinking. Thirty, fifteen, ten minutes not alone, that's all I wanted.

When a conversation I had started with a classmate, a soft-spoken boy from California, continued down the steps from the studio and out into the street, I was delighted. He showed no inclination of fleeing; we even joked about classes and teachers as we trudged toward our dormitories. *We're walking home together,* I thought; *my friend is walking me home.* Just two friends laughing and joking as they walk home together. I could have wept with joy.

"So," I said. "Did you do a lot of acting back in California?"

"Oh, you know," he said. "School plays and stuff."

"Yeah," I replied. "Me too. We did *Fiddler on the Roof* and *Hello, Dolly!* last year—you know, stuff like that. I did the leads. How about you?"

"Oh, we did some Ionesco. Some Beckett. This one girl, her mom's an actress, and she came and did *American Buffalo* with us."

"Yeah, I know about all that stuff. There's a lot of really good theater in Omaha. Like, more experimental stuff, you know? I did that play *Quills,* you know, *Quills* by Doug Wright? About the Marquis de Sade? It won an Obie when it came out in New York, I think. Anyway, this was, like, the Midwestern première, and it takes place in an insane asylum in eighteenth-century France, so we did it in this abandoned train station that was really creepy inside and it didn't have any heat, and when the run finished I had a fever of a hundred and four, and Matthew Broderick came to see it because he was in town shooting a movie, but I wasn't nervous, because work's work, you know? And I actually won an award for it, a TAG Award, which is sort of like a Tony Award but for theater in Omaha, but not just Omaha; Council Bluffs too, and Ralston and Bellevue. You know, the whole greater Omaha area too, which includes parts of Iowa . . . anyway, they have this whole awards show and they broadcast it on TV and it's exciting."

"Wow." He sounded genuinely impressed. Finally! "That's cool."

"Yeah, whatever," I said, flushing slightly. "I miss it. You know. Real acting."

"Well, we'll get to do some soon, I think," he said.

"What about you?" I asked. "Did you do any acting outside of school?"

"Um . . . a little. My mom works in . . . um . . . TV, so I did a couple of little TV things . . . I don't know. Nothing big."

"TV, that's huge!" I said kindly. "I'm sure you were great."

"Thanks. Hey, listen, what are you doing later?"

Sitting in my dorm room. Weighing myself. Crying and keeping my mother on the phone for three hours, just to have someone to talk to. When even your mother is begging to hang up on you, it's quite a blow.

"Um . . ." I bit my lip. "I'm not sure. I was maybe going to hang out with some people . . ." Some Hare Krishnas had approached me and invited me to a free vegan dinner at their sacred squat in the East Village. "You look lost," they said. "Let us show you the way." I just wanted someone to eat dinner with.

"Well, if you're not busy," he said, "why don't you come by later? A bunch of my friends that go here from home are coming over to watch *Waiting for Guffman*. Have you seen it?"

Wasn't that the movie about two sad old men, one black, one white, meeting on a park bench and teaching each other about life, laughter, and love? The acting must be phenomenal.

"Okay," I said. "Maybe I'll stop by."

I knocked on my new friend's door around nine, after circling his building several times to keep from getting there too early. I didn't want to look overeager.

"You made it!" he exclaimed. "We were just about to start watching! You want a beer?"

The room was full of kids. He introduced me around. They

were all from L.A. I sat at his desk, Heineken in hand, and noticed a few framed photographs propped up against the shelf. It seemed his mother not only worked in television, his mother *was* television, the star of a classic sitcom still in syndication. Several of my new acquaintances also had·last names I recognized, and now, looking at them, I found their features eerily familiar, as though I'd seen them all, in a slightly different arrangement, somewhere before.

"I can't wait to see this movie," said a girl. "My dad just wrapped a project with Chris Guest and said he was the *nicest* guy."

"Oh, he is," said another. "And Jamie Lee is such a sweetheart! You know she's Jake's godmother?"

"That's right!" squealed her friend. "I heard that! And Jake's got something big coming out. Do you want to fly home for the première? I told him I thought we might have midterms that week, but fuck it, right?"

Another girl closed her eyes. "I miss L.A. *so* much."

"Me too."

"I miss the fucking *food,* motherfucker," said a boy in an artfully faded Ramones T-shirt. He looked at me meaningfully. "I need some fucking In-N-Out, right fucking now."

This was not, I learned later, a proposition of intercourse, but rather a reference to the local burger chain preferred by the young scions of the Hollywood Dream Factory, particularly when drunk and about to go for a 3 A.M. dip in Dustin Hoffman's hot tub.

Nor was *Waiting for Guffman* a sentimental film about two crotchety oldsters and an unlikely friendship; I had confused the stodginess of its title with *I'm Not Rappaport.* No, *Waiting for Guffman,* as I'm sure you know, is one of Christopher Guest's typically skillful send-ups of outrageously easy targets—in this case, a deluded community theater troupe in a small Midwestern town.

Omaha is no Blaine, Missouri. We have more than one Chinese restaurant, and not only are our dentists Jewish, so are our endocrinologists and our tax attorneys. To my knowledge, no rouged and tempestuous impresario has ever prevailed upon the city fathers for $100,000 to immortalize Omaha in song and pageantry (although there is no doubt in my mind they would give it to him if he did). Still, the similarities were unavoidable. Soft-fleshed fusspot outfitted in jewelry and colorful vests who nevertheless asserts the existence of a beloved and cherished wife? Check. Boozy husband-and-wife duo in matching jogging suits who pepper their speech with the self-conscious lingo of stage veterans, particularly when it is neither necessary nor accurate? Check. Gum-smacking dim bulb with dreams of stardom? Check. Deeply unnatural stage makeup causing males and females alike to resemble the syphilitic prostitutes of an Otto Dix painting? Check. And the heartfelt, almost desperate adoration of the hometown crowd, as though they were cheering on a doomed but beloved sports team? Check. I'm not sure which one I was supposed to be. Probably Corky St. Clair, the flamboyant director with delusions of grandeur.

Rachel, how do you feel when faced with colleagues who grew up in the business? People who by the sheer power of their connections will never have to worry about getting an agent or manager, seeing casting directors or attracting press coverage for their work—not to mention the sheer advantage of knowing how the system works; what to look like and how to behave and what kind of person the business is looking for? Don't they have a huge head start?

Yes, I guess so. But ultimately, I have faith that it all comes down to talent. They may be a little bit ahead, but it's the talent and the commitment that really push you to the next level. Basically, it's the work that's important to me—not the trappings of it, the money and the fame and the calling of Spielberg and Geffen by their first names. The work is all that matters.

But how do you feel about them? Be honest.

Honestly? I hate them.

"Dude!" My new friend turned to me when the film had ended. "Is it really like that?" There was no malice in his question. He really wanted to know. He wasn't unkind, this friendly boy with a SAG card and an agent that he'd had from the age of six, who had spent his childhood diving for Emmys in his Beverly Hills pool. He hadn't meant to embarrass me. Inviting me over to watch this movie was a small act of friendship, and God knows I needed a friend.

"A little, yes," I said.

He laughed. "That's hilarious. Isn't that movie hilarious?"

"Yes," I replied. "I laughed until I cried."

Nine

The Anorexic's Cookbook

Note: The following is excerpted from *The Anorexic's Cookbook: A Cornucopia of Deprivation,* the landmark yet-to-be-published tome from lifestyle guru Rachel Shukert.

Introduction: ALL ABOUT YOU!

Take off your clothes and go to the mirror. Run your eyes over every part of your body—your arms, your waist, your thighs. Look at your stomach—really look at it. Poke your finger in the fat. Gather it up in your hands and feel it. Now let it drop back into place, and listen to the noise it makes. Is there a dull squish, like the sound of your lip knocking hard against your teeth? Or is it a thud, like a big burlap bag of lard sliding around in the back of a truck?

Look at your wrists. Can you encircle one wrist with your thumb and forefinger and still have room to spare? What about your hands—are they slim and delicate, or thick and meaty, like they might have just garroted someone named Vito in the back room of a strip club? Look at your chest, your shoulders, your neck, and then, very slowly, raise your head and look yourself in the face.

It's hard, isn't it?

Were you happy with what you saw? Did you look at the un-sightly ripples, the wobbling folds of sweaty flesh, the revolting, pock-flecked lumps of tumescent blubber and think, *Well, I'm just lucky to have my health*? Are you someone who thinks, *Gee, it's an honor just to be nominated*?

Or are you the kind of person who looks at that pasty, quiv-ering blob in the mirror and thinks, *I can do better!*

If so, this is the book for you.

Because you *can* do better. The question is: Do you have the guts? I mean, I know you have *a* gut, but do you have *the* guts? The guts to stand up to all the jealous naysayers who will try to keep you in your place to make themselves feel better about their own pathetic, fat, miserable little lives? The guts to keep on going, even when it gets painful, even when the doctors try to stuff your head full of "symptoms" and "statistics" the way they fill their own disgusting mouths with bacon cheeseburgers?

They'll say it's a prison. Well, I've got news for them. Prison isn't voluntary, unless it's one of those nonviolent-offender prisons in Finland. And as long we're playing word games, let's look at another term for prison: *corrections facility*. Corrections—as in "making right." If something's wrong, a responsible member of society fixes it.

Maybe most of the world is content to be the way they are, mediocre peasants eating cheese balls in the dirt, but remember, the middle of *anorexic* is *rex*. Not just a dog or the sophisticated British star of stage and screen, but Latin for "king." Anorexic: you are *royalty.*

Jump in the air and feel that gut move with you. You can still see it move even when you land, can't you? That's disgusting. Look at all that fat wobbling and rippling on your body, shaking as you move up and down. Listen to yourself as you hit the floor—it's like an elephant is trying to dance. How does that make you feel?

Some people deserve to be in prison.

Chapter One: BREAKFAST

You know what most cookbook authors have to say about breakfast. They'll write about mornings at their grandmother's sprawling old farmhouse, waking up to the smell of bacon frying and coffee perking, of buttermilk biscuits fresh from the oven and thick slices of country ham and sausages made out in the smokehouse, of cheese grits and hash browns and hand-cut oatmeal with sweet cream and strawberries and Grandma herself in the middle of it all, a faded apron tied about her ample middle, flipping flapjacks at the old woodstove. They'll write about how every time they make the Best Blueberry Pancakes or Pastor Steven's Sausage Loaf they think about the lost world of their dead grandmother and her hand-embroidered linen napkins that would be worth a fortune today.

ENOUGH! Go ahead and scream. ENOUGH!

They say breakfast is the most important meal of the day. It's also the most difficult meal to skip, particularly if you wake up having eaten very little the night before. But here are a couple of quick and easy recipes to start the day off right.

Easy Chocolate-Vanilla Fiber Bowl

Remember that old *Saturday Night Live* sketch with the commercial for the fake breakfast cereal Colon Blow? Too bad it wasn't real. The trick to this recipe is using the highest-fiber cereal you can find on the market—something with a name like Fiber Max or Kleenios. Remember, fiber is our friend—seven out of every ten fibrous calories consumed are burned just digesting it! This decadent, dessert-inspired breakfast doesn't just take care of those pesky morning hunger pains, it totally cleans you out. You'll feel light as a feather in no time.

>   *Ingredients*
>   ½ cup high-fiber cereal (60 calories)
>   3 tablespoons fat-free vanilla yogurt or vanilla soy milk (30–40 calories)
>   1 packet diet Swiss Miss instant hot chocolate mix (20 calories)
>
>   *Combine the cereal and the yogurt or soy milk in a small bowl. Sprinkle with the hot chocolate mix and stir to taste. If desired, garnish with 1 packet Sweet'n Low (add 5 calories), or drizzle lightly with fat-free, sugar-free chocolate sauce (10 calories). If still hungry, supplement with coffee, water, or diet soda until full. Wait for bowel movement before leaving house (approximately 10 minutes).*

I guess it looked weird to other people, but I didn't really mind the lanugo so much. There were other symptoms a little harder to deal with: the migraines, the mottled skin, the bradycardia that left me swooning when I stood up from a chair; but the wispy, pale hairs that had rapidly begun to sprout all over my skin in my body's desperate attempt to warm itself in the absence of an insulating layer of fat fascinated me. Every morning I would admire them in the mirror, patting the silky down like a teenage boy admiring the first evidence of a beard, basking in the miracle of evolution, the resourcefulness of the body.

As a child, I had spent many happy hours poring over my father's big medical dictionary, memorizing symptom profiles and presentation sequences, hoping to convince my teacher/school nurse/mother of an acute case of bronchitis/carpal tunnel syndrome/pancreatic cancer necessitating my immediately being sent home from school.

"You don't have cholera," my mother says, placing my *Star Wars* lunch box firmly in my hand.

"I have back pain," I protest. "I feel like I might have diarrhea soon. Those are both classic symptoms of cholera onset."

"You don't have cholera," she repeats, zipping up my sister's *Little Mermaid* backpack.

"Thank you, Mommy! I love you!" she chimes. Outside, the car-pool mother honks the horn.

"Mommy, listen," I cry, frantic now. "The average life span of a cholera victim, if left untreated, from the moment of symptom onset can be as little as six hours. I could be dead by this afternoon. Wouldn't you rather we spent that time together, instead of living with the knowledge that I spent my final moments on earth being tested on words I already know how to spell?"

"You don't have cholera!"

The car-pool horn blares again, louder and longer.

"Mommy, please." My eyes begin to water, prettily, I think. "My stomach hurts real bad. I'm scared, Mommy. I don't want to die."

BEEEEEEEEEEEEEEEEEEP!!

My sister looks stricken. "Is Rachy going to die?"

"No!"

"Am I going to die?"

"NO!" my mother shouts. "Neither of you is going to die!"

I glance out the window to see the car-pool mother, swathed in several yards of zebra-print cotton, waddling up the walk. She doesn't look happy. Shoving my sister outside, my mother turns to me. "Rachel, look at me. You get cholera by drinking other people's shit. Have you been drinking other people's shit?"

"You don't know what goes on at that school," I say darkly. "It's a *dirty* place."

"And you," says my mother, bringing her face inches from mine, "are a weird fucking little girl."

Once I was a failure. It had always been all in my head. But I now had an honest-to-God, indisputable physiological symptom of my very own, settling over my body soft as a snowdrift, and I had made it all by myself. Little old me, from Omaha.

I couldn't help but be a little proud.

Chapter Two: LUNCH

Lunch—who needs it? Not you! After all, you're a busy girl on the go! There are deals to make, papers to write, worlds to conquer—not to mention spinning class, step class, and power yoga. Whew! But sometimes, even super-skinny superwomen need a little mid-day pick-me-up. Don't feel any guiltier than you need to with these great lunchtime fixes!

Hard-Boiled Surprise for Hard-Boiled Dames

You know the type. You see them in the movies, usually with a cigarette in one hand and a man in the other. They're fast-talking and fast-living, slim, trim, and in control; nothing gets past these dames. There's no surprising them, except for this lunch, guaranteed to make anyone feel like a lovely leading lady.

Ingredients
1 egg (75 calories)
Mustard
Salt (to taste)
Pepper (to taste)
Tabasco or other hot sauce

Hard-boil and shell the egg. Cut in half lengthwise. Carefully remove all trace of yolk and discard. Squeeze mustard along the cut edge of each half of the egg white. Season with salt, pepper, and plenty of Tabasco (hot sauce can speed metabolic functions by as much as 30 percent, so be generous). Stick the halves back together to form a whole egg, with the mustard acting as glue. Take a big bite. Without the yolk, that formerly fattening egg now costs you only 15 calories! Surprise!

Pick-Me-Up Power Lunch

Frothy, fizzy, and fun to eat, this great lunch can't be beat! A real treat as exciting to the taste buds as it is to your waist. Only one thing to worry about: what are you going to do with all that extra energy?

Ingredients
2 cans Diet Coke or Diet Pepsi (according to preference)
1 Twizzler (30 calories)

Bite the ends off the Twizzler and reserve. Open the first can of soda and drink the entire can, using the Twizzler as a straw. Repeat with the second can. Eat the Twizzler and the reserved ends. For a fun twist, experiment with different-flavored Twizzlers—chocolate, watermelon, even grape!

For an extra kick:

Pepped-Up Pick-Me-Up Power Lunch

Follow the direction for Pick-Me-Up Power Lunch, but when you open the second can of soda, empty out one third, and refill it with vodka. Drink, using the Twizzler as a straw. Eat half of the Twizzler, and use the other half to snort one line of cocaine. Eat the cocaine-encrusted half of the Twizzler. Repeat as needed.
Note: On scoring cocaine—this should not be a problem if you live in an urban area and have regular access to an ATM card; in rural areas, feel free to substitute with homemade methamphetamine (recipe page 367). Enjoy!

Perhaps no animals are as bizarrely overrepresented on the walls of medical facilities as cats, which is strange when one considers their notorious indifference to the well-being of humans. Cats don't give a shit how you feel. You could be moaning on the sofa after a brutal round of chemotherapy, and a cat will still walk over your face on its way to destroy the houseplants. Yet for some reason feline images are everywhere in the world of health care, smirking as you submit to a root canal or reenact childhood molestation with finger puppets, urging you to "Hang In There" and "Keep On Truckin'!"

I stared at one now: a puckish Siamese inching dangerously close to a large, elaborately frosted slice of cake, training its implacable blue stare on the viewer as if to say: "That's right, I'm about to park myself on your dessert and start licking my own asshole. Hang with that, motherfucker." Encased in a layer of shiny laminate intended to shield it from the salivary assaults of unbalanced patients, it hung just above the bent head of my doctor-appointed nutritionist, as she arranged the brightly colored plastic food in groups on the table.

"And . . . there!" She laughed delightedly, adding a plastic clump of peas to the plastic banana, the plastic apple, the plastic hamburger with its plastic lettuce, plastic cheese, plastic tomato, and plastic bacon.

I picked up a plastic drumstick and turned it over in my hands. "My sister had a ton of this when we were kids. She liked to play food bank in the basement."

The nutritionist laughed, or rather she made the shape of laughter, tossing her head so that her silver-and-turquoise arrowhead earrings slapped against her neck, though no sound came out. "Isn't that a riot? How adorable!"

There are numerous things a person can do to earn my mistrust. Fake laughter and the wearing of Native American jewelry when one is not recognizably Native American are high on the list, along with thumb rings, a fixation with college athletics, and the frequent invocation of God outside of a place of worship. But also I hated her because she was trying to make me fat.

"These are to help us estimate serving sizes," she said, briskly removing the drumstick from my hands and returning it to the table with the rest of the meat group. "For optimum health, you need to eat a certain number of servings from each of the four food groups each day. Now, a good rule of thumb"—here she held up one of hers, adorned with a grotesquely thick band of silver etched with tribal markings—"is to think of your fist."

I shuddered. "My fist?"

"A single serving of fruit or vegetables, like an apple, a bunch of grapes, or a helping of cooked veggies, is about the size of your fist."

I made a fist. It was reassuringly small. "What about people with really big fists? Do they get to eat more food?"

She ignored me. "A serving of protein—like fish, steak, or chicken, is about the size of your palm. Now, most of us eat more than that—"

"Not me!"

"*Most* of us eat two or three servings at a time. Now, the food group we want to eat the most of is breads and cereals, or the carbohydrate group. You want to have six to eleven servings from that group per day."

"Never," I said. *"Never!"*

"I understand that carbohydrates have gotten a bad name," she went on calmly, "but that's not really a lot. For example, one serving is a single slice of bread. If you eat a sandwich, that's two servings right there."

"I cannot," I said with what I imagined to be great dignity, "remember the last time I ate a sandwich."

Pursing her coral-painted lips slightly, she took in all ninety-eight pounds of me—the bony wrists, the protruding clavicle, the sallow face beginning to sprout soft, thin hairs. "Would you like to eat a sandwich?"

I started to cry.

"Listen to me." She reached across the table and took my hand, still balled in a single-serving fist, in hers. "One day, in the not-so-distant future, you are going to eat a sandwich. I promise."

Guilt-Free Sandwich à la Nan Kempner

Borrowed from the late, great, Nan Kempner, socialite and fashion doyenne extraordinaire, who famously said, "I think most people in the world look so disgusting. I loathe fat people." We're with you, dahling.

Ingredients
2 large lettuce leaves (10 calories)
1 slice fat-free American cheese (30 calories)
1 slice fat-free turkey (30 calories)
1 slice tomato (5 calories)
Mustard, Tabasco or other hot sauce, or vinegar

Place cheese, turkey, and tomato between lettuce leaves, as though they were slices of bread. Add mustard, Tabasco sauce, or vinegar as desired. Bon appétit!

Chapter Three: DINING A DEUX

All sorts of unkind things are said about our kind of girls in today's dating market. We're "afraid of our sexuality." We're "damaged goods" or "high-maintenance." Men "don't want a stick figure." That's the biggest lie of all, mostly perpetuated by disgusting fat girls without boyfriends to make themselves feel better as they shovel down the Ben & Jerry's on Saturday night. That's right, Porky. Men want a woman with meat on her bones. Now go watch *Bridget Jones's Diary* for the seventy-third time and cry yourself to sleep.

I'll tell you what, ladies. The next time you see George Clooney with a woman bigger than a size four, go eat a sundae.

Men might talk a good game when they're being quoted, like in *Cosmopolitan* surveys, saying things like "I just want a woman who's comfortable with her body and herself" or "If a woman eats like a pig, that really turns me on, because I know she's going to be hot in the sack," but let's remember, *Cosmo* has also recommended putting a doughnut on your boyfriend's dick and eating it off.

If your boyfriend has a dick that can fit through the hole of a doughnut, it might be time to get another boyfriend.

As you lose weight and become more desirable, you are going to get more male attention than ever before. Hot guys will be falling all over themselves to get to you. But with guys come dates, and with dates come food. However, there are a few foolproof ways to control the damage:

SHARE: Take *Lady and the Tramp* as your inspiration: nothing can be more romantic than gazing into each other's eyes over a shared plate of pasta, and nothing is easier than keeping him from noticing how little of it is passing your lips. Take one bite to his seven, and the food will be gone in no time—and he won't want to stick around for dessert!

COOK: The way to a man's heart is through his stomach, but you don't have to fill yours. Rail passionately about the outrages committed against animals by the meat industry, then cook him a great big steak. He'll be genuinely touched by your hypocrisy and won't think twice about you sticking to salad.

COME CLEAN: If there's anything a man finds more appealing in a woman than extreme thinness, then it's the inward manifestation of it: extreme vulnerability. Give up your power and he won't be able to resist. Confess it all to him: your issues with food, your emotional fragility and self-doubt. Begin to cry, daintily at first, then with more conviction, and just as he takes you in his big, strong arms, suggest engaging in some comforting oral sex. The food issue won't come up again, but something else will!

It wasn't long before I was on a first-name basis with most of the third-floor staff at the Student Health Center: Desmond, the Jamaican security guard, Santos, the friendly maintenance guy, and the ray of sunshine that was Danita, the part-time receptionist, a stickler for rules who felt little compunction about openly displaying her contempt for the overprivileged college kids who thronged her lobby, seeking to correct the mistakes of an ill-considered weekend.

"Where your ID at?" she would bellow at an unfortunate student.

"Um . . . I don't have it."

"Well, go get it and come back."

"I can't. I think I lost it."

"You ain't got no ID?"

"No."

"Well, I need your ID card to enter you in the system. How I'm supposed to enter you in the system if you ain't got no ID number?"

"I can tell you my ID number, I just don't have the card."

Danita raked the girl up and down with disdainful eyes. "What you here for?"

"I need the morning-after pill."

"The morning . . . after . . . *pill.*" Danita repeated the phrase as though it was a concept so foreign each word required its own separate thought. *"The morning-after pill,"* she said again, this time loudly enough that the rest of us waiting in the lobby could look up from our eight-month-old copies of *Time* and turn our gaze to the wanton who dared brazenly to stand among us. This treatment was not reserved just for females—I once had the pleasure of witnessing her dealing with a boy who had come to the clinic for treatment of an intimate nature: "You have a *what* on your personal area?"

"A *wart,*" the boy said furtively.

"That's what I'm asking you," pressed Danita. "A *what?*"

It's not every receptionist who can make an Abbott and Costello routine out of a teenager's first outbreak of genital herpes, and those with the talent and motivation should be properly commended. But it wasn't all comedy with Danita. She could be caring and sympathetic when the occasion called for it. For example, as I waited in the lobby one day, she said to me: "You too skinny. What's wrong with you? You got cancer or something?"

"No," I said. "I have been diagnosed with anorexia nervosa."

"Anorex-a . . . that be that thing where you can't eat?"

"That's right."

"So why you don't just get some McDonald's? Just go get you a Big Mac or something."

"I can't," I said. "It's a very serious psychological problem."

Danita threw her head back and laughed. "Problem? Girl, you come back when you got five kids and they go and shut the power off, then we talk problems. Till then, baby, you ain't got no motherfucking problems."

In this she reminded me of my beloved seventh-grade choir teacher, an imperious woman who would sniff us as we entered her classroom and send anyone she deemed overripe to the locker-room showers. One afternoon she came upon me, clearly worked up over some conundrum or other, and paused in her inspection. "What's matter with you?"

Tearfully, it all spilled out; whatever it was—a rotten test score, a scheduling conflict—clearly spelled the very end of the world for me. "What am I to do?" I said, sobbing. "What, oh, what is to become of me?"

She sighed a sigh that had seen ten lifetimes of suffering. "Child," she said, "one day you're going to be grown up and you'll have forgotten this day ever happened."

These words have stayed with me during times of hardship for the rest of my life. I loved her for it. I loved Danita too. But I was glad it was not she who was at the desk that afternoon when I came in but Gladys, a small, stout woman who lived with her elderly mother in the Bronx and was fond of wearing accessories

specific to whatever holiday or season was closest at hand—
a predilection that in my opinion showed an endearing willingness
to make the best of things.

"Hi, Gladys," I said.

"Hi, baby," Gladys said, smiling. "Where you going? You
going to see Dr. Gupta today?"

"No, Gladys, not today," I said grandly. "Today I shall be visiting the Office of Sexual and Reproductive Health."

Thank God Danita wasn't there. Thank God. I could almost
hear her—*Repro—what? What you got going on down there? Something nasty?* Gladys just nodded, handed me a clipboard, and told
me to wait, she'd see who was available.

I was, quite frankly, expecting the worst. About a week earlier,
I had begun to experience severe vaginal itching. I experimented
with a variety of creams and suppositories, but this only seemed to
exacerbate the discomfort, which was quickly joined by the near-
constant discharge of an oddly colored fluid with the consistency
of dishwashing detergent and the stench of, in a word, *death*. It
smelled so fucking bad. It smelled like the inside of a garbage
truck. It smelled like a meat locker after a long power outage in
August. It smelled like that smell that hits you sometimes in the
subway, so fetid, rotten, and overwhelming that you know that
you're in a place where the body of an enormous rodent is currently decomposing, or a homeless person has very recently been
naked. There was a demon in my vagina, one that threatened to
make me ill each time its putrescence hit my nostrils, and when
my boyfriend—if that is what one can call someone with whom
one is in love but who refuses to call you his girlfriend while you
both occasionally sleep with other people—came back into town
to announce he was in love with someone else and would no
longer be interested in sexual intercourse with me, I was so relieved I let him sleep over anyway. He had nowhere else to go that
night, having given up his apartment for the summer to a couple

from Delaware, and as the couch was already occupied by an acquaintance who had arrived three months earlier from Arizona and showed no sign of leaving, I tucked a bar of scented soap into my underpants to mask the stench and hoped for the best. He left in the morning before I woke, leaving me to spend the next three days in my bedroom, happily immersed in a case of Scotch whiskey. When the Scotch ran out, I realized that I had a splitting headache; I also realized that the smell was worse than ever, so I put myself in a taxi (the only place I could be sure that somebody else's body odor would be more overpowering than mine) and came to the place that had provided me with care and solace for nearly two years.

"Well, I have your charts here," said the nurse, a man in periwinkle scrubs I had never seen before. The Office of Sexual and Reproductive Health was not one I visited often. "It says you're being treated for anorexia? By Dr. Gupta? How's that going?"

"Fine," I said.

"It seems to be," he said. "Dr. Gupta's noted here that you've gained a little weight, which she must be pleased about."

I had gained eleven pounds, to be exact, and when I had last seen Dr. Gupta four weeks ago she was overjoyed.

"You're out of the danger zone!" she said, clapping her hands in delight.

"Yes," I said.

"How do you feel about that?" she asked me hastily.

"I am delighted that I am no longer in danger of sudden cardiac arrest," I said.

"It's terrific," she replied. "Really. You should be very proud of yourself. And you know what?" She lowered her voice excitedly, as though she was about to reveal what Santa was bringing me for Christmas. "A few more pounds, and you might even start to menstruate again!"

I didn't tell her that while I had indeed allowed myself to

teeter on the brink of health, at least 75 percent of my increased caloric intake was alcohol. She was so happy, and it seemed cruel to spoil the moment.

After endless stories from credentialed health care professionals about the likelihood of starvation-induced complications; after watching *Superstar: The Karen Carpenter Story* while enjoying a hit of acid with my friend Bj one night, my dread of death had finally overcome my dread of food, but just barely. I still didn't think I was really that thin, but booze seemed like a good compromise. It was highly caloric but in the best way—its calories didn't just feed your body, they fed your soul. I also found that when I did attempt normal food, the alcohol's inhibition-lowering properties helped. A couple of shots of vodka with breakfast, and I could choke down a container of yogurt and a slice or two of dry toast. Another quick shot midmorning and I tackled a banana. A nice glass of Scotch at lunchtime, and I might even manage the yolk from an egg.

"So," said the man-nurse. "What seems to be the trouble?"

"I believe I have a urinary tract infection," I lied.

"What are your symptoms?"

I listed them. After thirty or so seconds of extremely unprofessional silence, he regained his composure. Pussy, I thought.

"That doesn't sound like a urinary tract infection."

"Oh," I said innocently. "Does it not?"

He paused to draw a small circle in the corner of my chart before asking, "Have you been sexually active in the last few months?"

While the alcohol I had been consuming pushed me further each day from the reach of congestive heart failure, it was also causing me to black out, sometimes for hours at a time. For months I had been waking up in my bed at home with no memory of how I'd made it there, but lately, things had become a bit more complicated. I might be enjoying an afternoon cocktail at a sunny café in the Village only to find myself hours later having a late supper in Chinatown with a raucous groups of total strangers, or holding hands with a Senegalese watch vendor in a Duane Reade, waiting in line to buy hair dye. There were vague flashes of memories of men at parties—a hand there, a mouth here, a laundry room—and I couldn't be sure how far things had gone. But given my demographic—a perpetually drunk twenty-year-old student of experimental theater with self-esteem issues and no particular religious or moral convictions living in New York City—a gambler would have no trouble calling the odds.

"I think so," I said.

Given my fuzzy recollection of which pilgrims had of late been admitted through the sacred portal of our Mother Goddess, the he-nurse asked if I would be willing to submit my reproductive organs to a few simple tests. I agreed. He informed me it was possible I had fallen prey to an opportunistic infection, transmitted by unprotected sexual contact. I confessed that this had crossed my mind. Having signed the necessary consent forms, I followed him down the hallway to a small examining room, where he presented me with a paper gown and gallantly took his leave.

"Good luck," he said.

"Thank you," I said. "You've borne up admirably."

He blushed at that. "Oh, well, just part of the job."

I undressed and sat on the examining table, the smooth paper cool against my bare bottom. The Smell filled the room, and I clamped my legs shut, hoping to contain it, when the door swung open.

She didn't remember me, but I knew her at once. At a university health center, each staff member needs to be something of a jack-of-all-trades, ready to set a broken bone, perform a urethral swab, or administer an IV at the drop of a hat, and it was this very woman who had treated me when I came to the clinic in the first semester of my freshman year, ill from severe dehydration brought on by a particularly virulent (and untreated) strep infection. Over the protests of the senior staff, she had found me a bed and sat with me, stroking my sweaty brow as I forced apple juice down my swollen throat. She had telephoned my mother and held the cell phone to my ear so I could hear her voice. She brought me tissues when I wept with homesickness and exclaimed over my age—"You're just a baby!" she had said—and told me I was a very brave girl. And here I was, back in her care two years later, being treated as an outpatient for a serious psychiatric disorder, having purposefully ruined the good health she had labored to restore, and now itching and stinking—*stinking!*—from a disease I had caught from one of the countless, faceless men to whom I had wantonly given myself. Oh, and I was probably an alcoholic. I hung my head with shame.

"Okay!" she said brightly, flipping through my chart. "So we're screening for STDs today?"

I paused from hanging my head in shame to nod.

"Would you mind lying down for me so I can take a look?"

I scooted to the edge of the table and positioned my feet in the stirrups, lowered myself onto my back, and spread my knees, watching her face all the while for the first flinch of repulsion when the stench hit.

There was nothing. Just the cold, familiar unpleasantness of the speculum.

Oh, doctors! To have mastered your revulsion at the disgusting functions of other people's bodies, that coolly medical poker face that allows your patients to think their repugnant discharge and hideous lesions are really not so bad, to have conquered your own fears of death and decay and the possibility of catching something all in the interest of science, to bring hope, to save lives; Oh, the glory, the wonder of it! What a noble, unthinkable, impossible thing to be a doctor!

"Well, here's your problem." My doctor (later I would find

out she was really a physician's assistant) was suddenly sounding like an auto mechanic. Leaving the speculum in place, she stood up to change her surgical gloves. "When was your last period?"

"I don't get my period," I said, as haughtily as I could manage naked from the waist with a metal clamp affixed to my parts most delicate. "I am an anorexic."

"Be that as it may," said the PA, "you've got a tampon stuck up in there. Been there for two, maybe three weeks, from the look of it."

?

??

????

"I . . . didn't know that could happen," I whispered.

"Neither did I," she said. "But there's some blood, so it looks like you definitely had your period. Did you just forget you had it in?"

"I've been drinking a lot lately," I said.

"I'll have to take it out in pieces," she said. "Frankly, I'm surprised you're not dead."

"Maybe all the alcohol kept me from going septic," I said, laughing weakly. "Like you know how they use it to sterilize things, like in the movies?"

Surgical scissors in hand, she regarded me for a long moment. "That's doubtful," she said finally.

Was it possible? Had I been drinking that much? So much that I failed to remember getting my first period in more than eight months? As I watched the long instruments flashing back and forth between my legs, bearing on each return trip a tuft of soiled white cotton, I tried in vain to capture an inkling of what had happened—a stained pair of panties, a knee hoisted on the edge of the sink for easy insertion. Could I have dismissed PMS symptoms, a headache, cramps, as a bad hangover? Had it been tampons, and not hair dye, I was trying to purchase with the

Senegalese watch vendor? Eventually, in the interest of science, I was forced to conclude that, yes, I had been drinking that much.

The PA had finished. "Okay! You can get dressed. Go home, take a shower, and you'll be fine. I'm going to tell Dr. Gupta that you're menstruating again. She'll be so pleased!"

"Thank you," I said. "Are you sure I don't need any medicine or . . . anything?"

She looked at me for a moment, her face suddenly warmer, and I imagined I saw a flicker of recognition in her eyes.

"You might really want not to drink so much," she said softly. She smiled a little. "You're just a baby."

A few weeks later, the baby woke up at 7:34 A.M. hooked to an IV on a stretcher in a downtown New York City hospital, having been delivered by ambulance a few hours earlier, with facial lacerations, three stitches in her knee, and a severe headache. The attending physician was unsure of the circumstances of the baby's accident; he did, however, mention that the vigilant ER attendants had performed a rape kit on the semiconscious baby, and finding no evidence of assault, they proceeded to pump her stomach, treat her wounds, and administer intravenous hydration. The consensus among the attendants was that the baby, in a state of extreme inebriation, had collapsed in the street and injured herself, and that a well-meaning but anonymous third party had come upon her and phoned the ambulance. At 9:12 A.M., the baby was disconnected from her IV and discharged on her own recognizance, along with a prescription for a mild antibiotic, a topical soothing cream, and a hospital bill for emergency services rendered. The bill for the ambulance, she was informed, would arrive in the mail.

Ten

A Nice Girl Like You

I had three serious career ambitions when I was very small. One: to be a professional toy player. Two: to be a professional nose picker.

"I don't understand," said my mother. "You mean you would be paid to pick your own nose, or other people's noses?"

"Both," I said.

"Well," she reasoned, "it's good to do something you love."

The third was to own a restaurant in which each dish would be created from the base ingredients of poop or pee. Poop Steak with Pee Sauce. Pee-za. Spaghetti Poopagnese. Pee soup with Pooptzah Balls. And for dessert, a choice: Pee Ice Cream, Poop Pie, or Chocolate Pooping (like pudding, but thicker and more filling). I made a menu out of construction paper, carefully crayoning a picture of each dish, but when I asked my teacher for help writing out the names of my creations, she called my mother.

"What?" my mother asked angrily. "Does every little girl have to want to be Barbie when she grows up?"

As I got older and more easily shamed, the list of possible occupations evolved into more conventional choices. I wanted to be a princess. A bride. An astronaut. An archeologist like Indiana Jones. A Nazi hunter like Simon Wiesenthal. Around the age of ten, I settled on the rather quotidian aspiration of being a movie star and, to the horror of all who cared for my well-being, failed to outgrow it. Twelve years later, after I'd graduated from college with a bachelor of fine arts in acting, with no agent, no manager, no offers, and no marketable skills, my list of potential jobs looked like this:

1. Stage actress
2. Film actress
3. TV actress
4. Star
5. Film star
6. TV star

Be realistic, warned the career self-help book my friend Bj had shoplifted for me from Barnes & Noble.

7. Cynic
8. Raconteur
9. Wit

But don't be afraid of a challenge!

10. Cynic, raconteur, *and* wit!

Think about your hobbies, the things you love to do. What are some careers that incorporate these elements?

11. Wino
12. Prostitute for broke, nocturnal singer/songwriter types in South Williamsburg
13. Cocaine dealer

And don't be afraid to dream big!

14. Olympic bronze medalist, ladies' figure skating, singles event
15. HRH the Princess of Wales
16. President of the United States

"Go fuck yourself," said my mother. The list of job options had been her idea. My mother is very big on lists: shopping lists, to-do lists, lists of things to obsess about in descending order of rationality, lists of people who skimped on the sweets table at their *Oneg Shabbat*.[†] "Do you know your sister is in her first year of college and she's already making all her spending money babysitting?"

"You don't understand what it's like in New York right now," I protested. "There's nothing."

"I'm putting your father on."

My father got on the phone. Together, we waited several moments in silence, until my mother got the message and hung up the receiver on the extension.

"Just pretend," he said helplessly. "At least act like you're trying to find some way to make money." He sighed. "It would really help me out a lot around here."

My graduating class was the first to come out of the university after what was still sometimes termed "recent events." We had begun our senior year optimistic, giddy, full of plans, and then one beautiful morning, as we sat lingering over coffee on our

---

[†] For the Gentiles! May you live in peace! An *Oneg Shabbat* is a reception after Friday-night or Saturday-morning services, usually held in the synagogue social hall and sponsored by someone with something to celebrate: a Bar Mitzvah, an anniversary, or an engagement. Allow me to put it to you in these terms:

  Floral Arrangement: $300
  Egg Salad for 250: $150
  18 Noodle Kugels: $214
  Giving your friends and family the chance to guess your annual income based on whether you serve sliced lox or whole smoked salmon: Priceless

rooftops, wondering if we could skip our morning anthropology lecture even though we'd only been to one class so far, a plane crashed into the World Trade Center. We gaped in shock, and had just gotten out our cameras to capture this unthinkable, freak accident, an image that seemed artfully doctored like a piece of conceptual photography in the Whitney Biennial, when out of the blue, blue sky a second plane hit the second tower. A rooftop chorus of *"What the fuck?"* echoed over Brooklyn, and we realized this was no accident. We ran downstairs and turned on the TV and the radio and computer and learned that the world was ending. So we called our parents, but we couldn't get through, so we finished our coffee and watched the news, full of people screaming and running and covered in ash, and we cried, and then we went back up to the roof just in time to see the motherfucking Twin Towers collapse, crumble into dust like something out of the Old Testament, and there was fluttering paper, decades' worth of facts and figures and seasonal reports and bank statements littering the sky, and we felt thankful that our roof wasn't close enough to the water that we could see the bodies falling, even though we knew they were there. And suddenly we realized it had been three hours—*three hours*—since it happened and we were definitely not going to anthropology, so we went back inside and called our mothers and fathers again, this time from the land line, and we got through, and they were crying and hysterical and thanking God we were all right, thanking God we weren't down there, and we said, "Mom, the only time I've ever been to the World Trade Center was that time my friend's dad came in from Maryland and took us to Windows on the World and got wasted on Glenlivet and tried to sleep with me," and our dad asked us if we wanted to come home, because even though all the flights were grounded, he would drive to New York, through the night if he had to, and pick us up, all we had to do was say so, and against our better judgment but with some pride we said, "No thanks, I think I'll try to tough it out." And then our sister called, and she had run out of her high school algebra class sobbing with terror and hidden in the bathroom for an hour calling and calling on her cell phone until she finally got through and we calmed her down and told her we were fine, go back to class, but if it was us we might just take the day off. And then the phone still seemed to be working so we called the boy we slept with sometimes who we liked much better than he liked us and offered to marry him to keep him out of the army if they reinstated the draft and he said, "I don't think that's how it works anymore, but thanks for the offer," and we sat for a moment and thought, *What does he mean by that?* But people were dying outside and we might be incinerated by a nuclear bomb any minute, so we picked up the phone again and called our grandparents, and our grandma said that our grandpa was at physical therapy, but it was just awful what was happening, and how were we? And we said we were fine, but you know, scared, and she said: "Don't worry, dolly. It's just like when they attacked Pearl Harbor and that all turned out fine!"

Armed with those fortifying words, we pressed on. We hauled out sleeping bags and air mattresses and opened our apartments to friends who had lost theirs, and we watched as others said they were going to New Hampshire for a few days, just until this all blows over, and never came back. We went to class and talked about our feelings for several weeks and read about a man named Osama bin Laden, whom nobody seemed to have heard of before but whom we now knew was an outlandishly tall Arab with a heart condition who lived in a cave and hated our freedom, and we also learned that the president's idiocy was not just laughable but legitimately terrifying, and Giuliani, whom we hated, whose notorious police force had once given us a hundred-dollar ticket for peeing on the sidewalk outside at 3 A.M., wasn't going anywhere for the time being, even though his term was up, and we wondered about the political ramifications of this kind of temporary totalitarianism but not too hard because mostly we were afraid, and numb. Or we were numb until that afternoon a few weeks after it happened, when we were walking down Sixth Avenue and the signs were everywhere, the photocopied signs with the pictures—"Have you seen my husband?" "Have you seen our mom?" "Have you seen my sister Michelle?" And it was just too much all of a sudden, so we sat on the sidewalk outside the bagel place, sat directly on the New York City pavement that everyone knows can give you hepatitis[†] if you touch it with your bare skin, and cried. And this kid waiting for the bus, this thug kid who usually, if he got on the elevator and you were alone, you got off (even though you felt guilty about it), reached out and touched our shaking shoulders very, very gently and said, "I know how you feel."

And then there was the anthrax, and the Orange Alert, and the *Post* headlines with the French dressed as weasels and calls to genocide. We got the fliers in the mail warning us to have plastic wrap and duct tape handy in the case of bioterrorism, and then it was Christmas, and we went home to our small towns where they cooed over us like we'd been in a war, and we liked the attention but were glad to get back, even though we were about to be vaporized or infected with smallpox. Then it was spring, and we took our final exams, and we had our commencement, where the keynote speaker was not Adam Sandler, as in past years, or Alec Baldwin or Martin Scorsese, but one more appropriately suited for these troubled times, the police commissioner, who delivered a measured and sober address about the "new and arduous challenges that would besiege us as we made our way in this changed world," meaning not only were we much more likely to be incinerated in the subway or blown up at a Mets game, but there would also be no jobs. No jobs for any of us. And such jobs as there were would be competed for by not just the drama school graduates

---

[†] Like shellfish, New York City sidewalks are nonkosher.

already accustomed to the idea of a life of menial labor, but the MBAs and law students, who last year would have been hired straight out of school at an annual salary of eighty thousand dollars but who would now be killing themselves for receptionist jobs and bartending gigs like the lowliest performance studies major.

"Too bad there's no job that pays you to feel sorry for yourself," my mother said uncharitably.

Oh, but there is, Mommy! You're reading it!

"I like feeling sorry for myself," I said. "It gives me a sense of purpose in a hostile world."

"Fine," she said. "You can always come back to Omaha for a while. Plenty of jobs around here. After all, we are the telemarketing capital of the world."

Chastened, and freshly showered for the first time in a disturbingly long while, I arrived at the temp agency the next day and was greeted by my liaison, a cheerful woman with enormous hair named Tina. Think Melanie Griffith in *Working Girl,* if Melanie Griffith had actually sounded like she was from Staten Island.

"We're *so* glad you thought of us!" she exclaimed, as though I had just asked her to cater my million-dollar wedding. "Thank you so much!"

"Um . . . you're welcome."

"Now, let's see." She paused, scanning the clipboard with my filled-in questionnaire. "You just graduated from college—congratulations! But such a terrible time to be entering the workforce. There's nothing out there, just nothing."

"I was hoping you could help me with that."

She rewarded me with a grimace of false apology. "Well, we'll try! All we can do is try!"

Tina ushered me into a small, featureless room, empty apart from a tiny Indian man clicking away at a computer keyboard. "That's Mohan, our tech support," whispered Tina dramatically.

"Hi, Mohan!" she sang. Mohan didn't look up. "He's a little shy," she said. "Most of them are."

I took two examinations, designed to test my proficiency in the English language and on a computer keyboard, and signed an affidavit saying I was neither a felon nor, to my knowledge, criminally insane. Whether this would be held against me as false witness if I were found to be criminally insane at a later date was unclear. Tina returned to score my tests and gave me the good news: I was fluent in English and able to type. I told her this made me very happy. She gave me another form to fill out, this one detailing my work experience.

"New York only," she said, wrinkling her nose again in fake apology. "And please give as much detail as you can."

Even in my halfhearted, Eeyore-ish job search, I was finding this common: New York employment history was all that mattered for potential employers. You might have ten years' experience waiting tables in four-star restaurants in Chicago; you might have single-handedly founded a real estate empire in Pittsburgh, but the Starbucks at Astor Place had no use for you, as no previous social interaction, no matter how advanced, could prepare you for the supreme challenge of delivering a Mocha Frappuccino to a resident of Manhattan. The intimation, of course, was that New Yorkers were so discriminating in taste, so exacting in standards, and so utterly unconcerned with any semblance of human decency, that upon being confronted with their demands, a feebler being—especially one from what were sneeringly termed "the flyover states"—would collapse into a blubbering puddle of goo before blowing her brains out in the staff bathroom, causing nasty water damage and legal problems.

In fact, I did have a brief period of New York City employment, although wholly undocumented and impossible to verify. My mother and I were wandering the streets, having fled from the threatening hurricane of my father assembling shelves in my new freshman dorm about a week before I started college, when we discovered the Dream Factory. It was a large shop in the West Village, specializing in vintage clothing and accessories, particularly items with some connection, however tenuous, to a Golden Age Hollywood star. The walls of the store were lined with film stills and glass cabinets, like museum cases, displaying platform heels that belonged to Joan Crawford, a monogrammed handkerchief of Lana Turner's, a dress worn by Ann-Margret at the 1967 Golden Globes. Such priceless items were not for sale but meant to ascribe meaning to those items that were—the pencil skirt that looked very much like one that Anita Ekberg once wore while disembarking a jet in Gstaad, or a handbag emblazoned with a *K* that you could pretend had belonged to Kim Novak—and the proximity of such merchandise to the sacred talismans encased in glass above affected their pricing accordingly.

"Two hundred dollars for a sweater with a hole in it?" my mother exclaimed, pulling her hand away as if the mohair had burned her.

"Yes," piped up a large man in a Hawaiian shirt, "but it's an original Bobbie Brooks, almost identical to the one Shirley Temple wore in *The Bachelor and the Bobby-Soxer.*"

We left, but not before I pressed my phone number on the man, asking him to call me if ever they were hiring.

"What do you want a job for?" my mother asked. "You don't need the money. College is the last time you have before you have to work."

"It'll be fun!" I said breezily. "It's such a cool place! Besides, I'll be good at it. I love gay men and they love me!"

"Yes," said my mother, "and with you starting drama school in New York and all, I can see how you'd need to really seek them out."

A couple of weeks later, after my parents had left and I had begun, shakily, to realize they were not coming back, I received a phone call from Charles, the large man in the Hawaiian shirt from the shop. It seemed they could use me.

"Maybe it'll be good to have some new blood around here," Charles said doubtfully, and instructed me to report to the shop the next Saturday at 10 A.M., at which time I would be trained and introduced to the owner, Mel.

Also present among the Detritus of the Stars was a large collection of memorabilia involving Mel himself, harkening back to his younger days as the host of a kiddie TV show in the Baltimore area. Mel was now a dapper man in his late sixties, fluttering about the showroom and murmuring to his dresses as though they still encased the fabulous women who had once worn them. When he met me, his eyes lit up.

"Fabulous. You know who you look like? I mean, really look exactly like?"

"Who?" I purred.

"Monica Lewinsky," he said. "Really. Exactly like her. I mean, it's uncanny. Aren't you some sort of actress? Tell your agent or whoever, if they ever make a TV movie or something about all this, to send you out for it. You're a shoo-in."

"I don't have an agent," I said through gritted teeth.

His eyes flickered over me. "No, you wouldn't, would you?'

My duties were fairly simple. I was to troll the racks of clothes, making sure they remained sorted by color and style, and examine them, looking for pieces with small imperfections—a broken zipper, a jagged hem, some loosened beadwork. I brought those that needed repair into the back room, where a seamstress sat, charged with small repairs and alterations. When a customer entered the shop, particularly if said customer was younger than sixty, dressed in loose clothing, or carrying a bag, I was to follow at an inconspicuous distance through the racks to make sure she or he didn't take anything. Mel had a horror of shoplifters; when customers wanted to try something on, I was to enter the dressing room with them, to zip and unzip and keep them from thieving.

"What if they don't want a stranger in there while they're changing their clothes?" I asked.

"If they won't have you in there with them, then you tell them you're sorry, but you're not comfortable allowing them to continue to shop here," said Mel darkly. "If they don't want you in there, they are clearly up to no good."

"Right," I said.

"And don't forget," said Mel. "While you're in there, you have to sell! Sell, sell, sell! And always check out the handbag and the size of the diamonds. That way you'll know how much they'll spend."

"Fabulous," proclaimed a slim man as I zipped him into a tangerine Pucci minidress. "Bet you've never helped a gentleman into his cocktail frock before."

"No," I said truthfully.

He smoothed the fabric over his taut hips, swiveling to face me. "Well, girlfriend, welcome to Chelsea!"

I didn't point out that we were in the Village.

For this job of Rack Patroller and Dressing Room Voyeur/ Appraiser, I was to be paid six dollars an hour, off the books. My co-workers, apart from Mel and the ever watchful Charles, were Janine, a spare, sallow woman who kept silent watch over the priceless collection of costume jewelry at the cash register, and Rita, a cheerful Ruth Gordon clone who brightened up the shift with colorful and wildly conflicting stories from her life as a Rockette, a hat model for Hattie Carnegie, a Mississippi sharecropper, and a bootlegger's moll. "Of course, all of that was before I married the baron," said Rita, "but that ended when he turned out to be a Nazi sympathizer. Here, have a date. I brought them from home." Rita was 117 years old.

"Customer!" hissed Charles, appearing out of thin air. "And she's wearing *overalls*. Make her uncomfortable so she'll leave."

"Don't mind about him," whispered Rita when he was out of earshot. "His blood-pressure medicine makes him grumpy."

A woman came in one day looking for a gown to wear to a benefit in Florida. "Fat," she spat disgustedly as I struggled to close the zipper around her upper back. "Fat, fat, fat."

"You're not fat . . ." I began.

"Oh, save it," she snapped. "I don't need to be patronized by you. I know what I've got. I've got a pretty face, and nice tits, but the rest of me is so disgusting my husband can't even keep an erection anymore when he looks at me. He said that. He can't keep it up, because his wife's a fat, disgusting pig. Oh God." She dissolved into tears. "What am I going to do? What am I going to do?"

What was *I* going to do? I felt bad for her, but she was also dripping mascara all over an Yves Saint Laurent coral evening caftan priced at $785. Legend had it that it had once been breathed on by none other than Elizabeth Taylor. "Um, maybe you should talk to your husband . . . I mean, if he loves you—"

"Oh, shut up!" the woman snarled. "What are you, twenty-two?"

"Eighteen."

"*Eighteen?* Eighteen!!!!!!!"

Her wail of despair ripped Mel away from where he was communing with a rack of bathing costumes worn by Sally Field. "What is going *on* back here?" he demanded, a pink gingham bra top draped around his neck like a tape measure.

"She just . . . I don't know . . ."

"My husband won't fuck me!" the woman sobbed. "He says it's like fucking a Jell-O mold!"

"I'm sorry," I started, but Mel cut me off.

"I'll handle this," he said sharply. "You've done enough." He watched as I slunk back onto the floor, and called out after me:

"And darling, so good to see you wearing something form-fitting for a change! Be proud of that womanly shape!"

I began to be more honest with customers, offering opinions like "It's not so flattering from the back," "That color makes you look nauseous," or "You're right, four hundred dollars does seem like an awful lot to pay for a housedress, even if it does look just like the one Shelley Winters wore in *A Place in the Sun*." When customers asked why I was following them around the store and into the dressing room, I replied truthfully: "My boss thinks you look like a criminal." After an incident in which a miscommunication as to the placement of a rack of fifties circle skirts led to a screaming fight between Mel and Charles, I fled to the back room, where Rita was packing a hefty girl into a spangled teal Balenciaga with faint stains under the arms.

"Why did they get so mad?" I said, weeping. "Charles told me to move the skirts and then Mel said to move them back, and I was only trying to do what they said and I'm tired and lonely and I want to go home!"

Rita patted my shoulder absently. "There, there. Did I ever tell you about belly dancing for the shah of Iran?

It suddenly occurred to me that Rita was crazy. They were all crazy. I was working in a shop full of crazies, and if I didn't get out of there soon, I would be ninety years old, telling the next unsuspecting young thing who stumbled into the dusty web about the time Prince Faisal raped me just minutes before I won the Olympic gold medal in women's downhill skiing. I left for lunch and called from a pay phone an hour later to tell Janine I wasn't feeling well.

"Mmm," said Janine.

The next day, Charles called my dorm room to inform me that the Dream Factory would be manufacturing its dreams without me. Somehow, I didn't think being fired after five weeks of illegal employment in a fashion mausoleum run by cruel and delusional senior citizens would be a valuable addition to my résumé.

"No previous New York work history?" asked Tina now, frowning at the clipboard that held my blank questionnaire.

"I just got out of school," I said. "Is that a problem?"

"Well," she said brightly, "it just means we'll have to knock your rate down to ten dollars an hour. But don't worry. You'll do just fine, a nice girl like you!"

That night, my grandmother called me, eager to hear tales of triumph and glamour in the big city. Normally, I would have made up something for her to brag to her friends about, an invented meeting with a mythical agent, a nonexistent medical student I met at the Jewish singles event I didn't go to, a fictional audition for an unplanned Spielberg picture. Tonight however, tired, hungry, and very shortly to be a temp, a position held back home mainly by alcoholic divorcées fighting with their exes over custody of the pit bull and the hunting rifles, I didn't have the energy.

"I don't understand why you won't just go on *Regis and Kelly*," my grandmother said, as though my failure to appear on the program was due to an unreasonable obstinacy on my part. "Now, I know it's not real artsy-fartsy or anything, but some of these young kids, they go on *Regis and Kelly* and then *boom,* they're everywhere. The TV programs, the pictures, everything."

"They're on *Regis and Kelly* because they're promoting TV shows and movies."

"But these young kids, they go on *Regis and Kelly* and—"

"Grandma," I said, and sighed. "It's not going on *Regis and Kelly* that makes them rich and famous. They go on *Regis and Kelly* because they are already rich and famous."

"Oh," said my grandmother in that special way she has, as if she has just opened a gift-wrapped box from Tiffany's and found an empty bottle of drain cleaner inside. "And you don't want to be rich and famous, is that it?"

"No, Grandma. I went to drama school because I want to be poor and unknown."

She changed the subject. "I'm going to get a box together and send it this week. I'll send you some of the most marvelous instant soup. Do you have that good instant soup over in New York?"

"We used to," I replied. "But it's getting pretty scarce since the Philadelphian warlords have had the city under siege."

"Don't tease your grandma," she said. "I'm the only one you've got."

It was several weeks before Tina the Temporary Employment Liaison called me.

"Things have been slow," she apologized. "Honestly, you couldn't have picked a worse time to graduate."

I confessed that this had occurred to me. However, since I had finished all my requirements for my degree, the school refused to keep me. Perhaps the blame went to my parents, for choosing the unlucky year of my birth. No one could have predicted an airplane slamming into the World Trade Center? Please. I didn't buy it from Condoleezza Rice, and I didn't buy it from them.

"Anyway," chirped Tina. "The good news is I have something for you! It's ten dollars an hour, and it should last for a couple of weeks, at least!"

Excellent. Figuring for taxes and agency commission, after working two forty-hour weeks I would be able to pay one eighth of my rent, and still have $7.50 left over!

"You want the job or not?" Tina asked huffily.

I wanted it.

"Great! You'll be doing data entry at a publishing house. And please"—she switched rapidly from her perkily businesslike tone to one of maternal concern—"don't hesitate to call me if there are any problems. Really."

Data entry, it turned out, meant sorting file folders pertaining to long-out-of-print textbooks into hundreds of ancient file cabinets crowded in rows in an enormous underground antechamber that had not seen the touch of a broom since Peter Stuyvesant ruled lower Manhattan with a fist of iron and a leg of oak. A piece of crumbling drywall cordoned off a section of the room my supervisor informed me was off-limits. I could only assume it held the crumbling remains of unlucky temps before me, unable to bear up under the strain. The job was excruciating: tedious, filthy, and cruelly Sisyphean. Every time I emptied a cardboard box of folders, another, bigger one appeared in its place, as if by magic. By eleven-thirty I was checking my pulse regularly, wondering if I was, in fact, dead, trapped in some kind of hellish netherworld of repentance, forced to process one thousand folders for each time in life I had hit my sister or had sex without a condom. By three o'clock, I had twice slammed my finger in the rusty door of a file cabinet, drawing blood, broken the heel of my shoe, and begun to think of ways to take my own life. When my supervisor appeared to tell me I was dismissed for the day, I had almost forgotten about the existence of the world outside, a happy place full of smiling people who sat eating grapes in parks or fondling one another in movie theaters. Blinking bewilderedly in the sun, like a soldier emerging from a bunker to find the battle ended, I called Tina.

"I can't do this," I said. "I feel like I'm in prison. I feel like every minute I spend in there is crushing another piece of my soul in its pincers, like a walnut, but the walnut is alive, and it screams."

"Try to tough it out another day," she said soothingly, as if I were a small child. "Can you do that for me? Can you just make it through one more day?"

The next day my co-worker Carlos arrived.

"Hi!" he exclaimed, playfully hoisting a box of folders in the air as I trudged through the door, battling tears. "Boy, do we have our work cut out for us!"

It was clear to me almost immediately that Carlos was not quite of this world, but he was friendly and cheerful, and his presence had a mitigating effect on some of my more morbid tendencies. It's difficult to fling oneself in a heap, sobbing hysterically, or search the dirty floor for a glass shard sharp enough to open a vein, with another person in the room. Left together for hours at a stretch, we began to talk.

Carlos enjoyed his work as a temp, but his true passion was his cable-access program, a nighttime talk show hosted by Carlos's alter ego, a prurient sock puppet with a dirty mouth named Fredo. Proudly, he showed me the photos of Fredo he kept in his wallet, or read out loud from the newspaper in Fredo's voice, a cross between Triumph the Insult Comic Dog and Ricky Ricardo.

"Saddam Hussein eez eemportin' u-ranium from Ni-jer," said Fredo. "Well, Saddam Hussein can leek my balls."

I should come on the show sometime and be interviewed by Fredo, Carlos thought. I was just the sort of person Fredo was looking for. I could help Fredo and Fredo could help me. "You'd be great on TV," said Carlos. "A nice girl like you?"

We began to eat lunch together, and Carlos began to open up more. He spoke to me of his girlfriend, Linda, who lived in Connecticut and was sexually frigid. Linda refused to stay overnight at his apartment in Manhattan. Still worse, she refused to watch porn with him. Her reticence in the area was a particularly bitter pill for Carlos to swallow. He had accepted her constant denials of intercourse, but why could they not simply sit together and watch some of his favorite films? This seemed to him deeply unfair.

"I do everything she wants," complained Carlos. "It's like I'm pussy-whipped, and I'm not even getting any pussy!"

I began to seriously wonder if Linda existed.

Despite all signs to the contrary, the job at the publishing house eventually ended, and I received a phone call from Carlos. Carelessly, I had given him my number at work when he suggested it might be useful to be able to get in touch should one of us be running late one morning. He wondered when I might be free to be interviewed by Fredo the Sock.

"I'm not sure," I said. "I'll let you know."

Undeterred, Carlos began to call several times a day, until one morning I walked into the lobby of my new assignment, doing payroll for Major League Baseball, and found him already there, nestled in a huge armchair shaped like a catcher's mitt.

"*Yess!*" he exclaimed when he saw me, pumping his arm in triumph. "This is awesome! I told Tina to always put us together because we get along so well."

"Did you ask Tina how long this assignment was going to last?" I asked thinly.

"She told me about seven weeks," he replied. "So, do you want to get interviewed by Fredo tomorrow, or . . ."

One can only outrun one's fate for so long before one at last is trapped in its fetid claws. At least I'd be able to tell my grandma I was going to be on a talk show.

My friend Neal, who has the highest tolerance for total weirdos of anyone I know, accompanied me to Carlos's apartment on the grounds that I feared for my personal safety. "I'm sure it'll be fine," Neal said reassuringly. "It just sounds like this guy has a little crush on you."

"That's what I'm afraid of."

It seemed that the building Carlos lived in required its tenants to pay by the week. On the stoop, two men lay semiconscious while their toothless companion muttered softly to himself surrounded by creased Radio Shack bags, lovingly fingering a vial of meth.

"Let's leave," said Neal.

"We can't," I said. "I have to work with him tomorrow."

"So quit."

I closed my eyes for a moment, savoring the possibility. Could such a thing be done? "Even if I quit, he'll keep calling me, and calling me. I'll have to change my number and my name and have reconstructive surgery and move to Fort Lauderdale."

"Well," said Neal reasonably, "at least you'll be near the beach."

Carlos appeared and took us upstairs to his room. "The bathroom's down that way if you need it," he said, pointing down a dark hallway outside his door. "You might have to wait though. I share it with the fifteen other guys on this floor." His room, stinking of incense, was decorated with pictures torn from *Penthouse* and the Kama Sutra, and lighters littered the floor, clustered on the table, covering nearly every available surface. It's not a good sign when someone owns that many lighters. The video camera was too large for the room, so Carlos set up in the hallway, facing a makeshift platform upon which rested a sock with large, immobile eyes. I looked behind me. *Where the fuck is Neal?*

"I just called Ada," Neal whispered, reappearing at my shoulder. "I told her exactly where we are. If she doesn't hear from us in one hour, she's going to call the police."

When the last seven-figure checks to retired shortstops in Boca Raton had been issued and the baseball job ended, I called Tina.

"Listen, the next time you give me an assignment, could you make sure Carlos isn't placed there?"

"He's one of our best workers," she replied. "Has he threatened you in any way?"

"No . . . he's just . . ."

"What?"

"He's just . . . *weird*," I said helplessly.

"I see," said Tina. "Well, we'll certainly try our best to *accommodate* you."

I didn't hear from her for a while, but I could hardly blame her. Given the choice, who would you rather send out as a representative of your company: a cheerful, positive, and tenacious young man who happens to spend his evenings watching porn in a flophouse with a talking sock, or a disgruntled postadolescent who shows up late and hungover and oozing hostility? Still, when she finally called after several weeks to offer me a brief position in the administrative offices at a company I'll call MTV, I began: "Will—"

"Oh no, *please* don't worry," she cooed, solicitous as ever. "We're not sending anyone else on this assignment. You'll be totally alone."

There was a time when I might have found it quite exciting to go the MTV offices, imagining a workspace that looked like a cross between the backstage area at Glastonbury and an exhibition of conceptual art—rockers in leather pants and clever eyewear lolling and sniffing cocaine on plush loungers in front of a bank of television screens alternating white noise and found images from cutely retro shampoo commercials. However, months of constant disappointment had conditioned me to expect the worst, and when I was seated in front of a blank computer screen at a gray metal desk in yet another windowless, featureless room, I didn't even blink. It's best not to use your imagination in the corporate world. You'll just try to kill yourself that much sooner.

Carolyn, the woman charged with my care, put a box of folders on the desk in front of me. "Here," she said. "You'll need to alphabetize these." She pointed to a small man in a Rocawear jersey at a neighboring desk. "This is Lester."

Lester smiled, revealing several spectacular golden teeth.

"He'll answer any questions you might have," she continued.

"Do you want me to answer the phone or anything?" I asked.

"Oh, no, that's Lester's job."

"What do I do when I've finished alphabetizing these?"

She frowned. "*If* you finish alphabetizing, I guess you can come find me and I'll give you something else to do."

As I was always in the very highest reading group in my class all through elementary school, I finished alphabetizing the folders in less than half an hour. I stared at my hands for another half hour, looking for paper cuts and blinking back tears before I decided to go find Carolyn. She looked up from her crossword puzzle with a shocked expression as I entered, as if she had no recollection of ever allowing me into the building. "Can I help you?"

"Um . . . I finished alphabetizing . . . so . . ."

"All of them?"

"Yes. There weren't so many of them."

"Oh. Well, go through them again and make sure it's done correctly, please. I don't have time to deal with mistakes."

Fuck you, Carolyn. I scored a 780 on my verbal SATs. When I was in preschool, they had to order a whole new set of advanced reading books for me. "I didn't make any mistakes."

She glared at me. "Look, I'm in the middle of something. Go back to your desk and check your work. I'll be out in a minute with further instructions."

An hour later, there was still nothing. I looked at Lester for help, but he was on the phone, so I tiptoed back into Carolyn's office. She hadn't made much progress with her puzzle. I thought of giving her some help, but she probably wouldn't be too keen on such an offer from someone who has so much *trouble* with the alphabet.

"What *is* it, Rebecca?" she hissed.

"It's Rachel, actually."

"What is it that you *want*?"

I stammered, "Well, I just thought, if you don't have anything for me to do, could you maybe tell me the network password so I can get on the computer?"

She put down her pencil. "Is there a reason you need to get on the computer? Has somebody given you a task that requires access to the computer?"

"No . . . I just thought . . . if there's nothing else for me to do . . ."

"There's absolutely no reason for you to have that information." She sounded offended, as if I had just asked her to tell me the details of her father's affair or why her boyfriend shouts "Arthur!" when he comes. "Now go back to your desk, please, and when I need to speak to you I will *come and find you*." Picking up her pencil, she turned her attention back to her puzzle. *Refuged,* I thought. 61 Across, "Sought sanctuary, old style," is *refuged,* you *stupid, stupid cunt.*

Lester was still on the phone when I got back. For a horrible moment, I missed Carlos, until I started to listen to the conversation Lester was having. "Ooooh," he moaned into the receiver. "Baby girl. Now I'm rubbing that oil all over your fine brown skin. Aw yeah. Now I got you all smooth and lotioned up, I'm gonna lie you down and I'm gonna get out the whipped cream, and I'm gonna spread that sweet cream all over your sweet brown body. That's right." He spoke at a normal volume in a conversational tone, the same way one might say, "Paul, I need to see the MacNeil report," or "Crack whore, I have Sumner on line two." Several co-workers passed his desk throughout his recitative and seemed unfazed; one or two of them even nodded in friendly greeting. It occurred to me that having phone sex at work is like reading *The 120 Days of Sodom* out loud to a baby; it doesn't matter what you say; what matters is how you say it. Filled with new respect for Lester, I decided to follow his example and salvage the day by returning a few phone calls of my own.

TO MY MOTHER: . . . the lymph node behind my left ear is definitely swollen. No, I don't feel like I have a cold. It's been like this for a couple of days. . . . No, it's not too big, you kind of have to dig to really feel the swelling. I mean, maybe it's just the muscle behind my jaw, but I really don't think so, not unless the right side of my jaw is much less developed than the left. . . . Yes, I'm taking vitamin C, but given my age, I really don't think we can rule out Hodgkin's. . . . It's the most common form of cancer in my age group. . . . Don't! Just because you don't care about my health . . . I hate you.

TO MY FATHER: . . . I know, I think the war is inevitable too, but it is *such* a bad idea. I mean, what are these assholes thinking? They don't honestly think the Arabs . . . I know! Liberators! Who do they think they're dealing with? . . . Well, it's all about oil. . . . Yes, it is. It's all about the oil. Have you been reading *The Nation*? . . . No, I know they're anti-Israel, but they're completely right about this. . . . Yes, and then Bush and his fucking Oedipal complex . . .

TO MY BEST FRIEND: Lauren, if you know anything, you have to tell me. . . . Well, you're the one that's friends with him, so . . . No! I didn't say you were lying! But the other night he was all, "I think we should get tested for STDs," and I was like, "Why? Do you have any symptoms?" and he was like, "No, but I just think it's a good idea, just because," and I was like, "You're the only person I've been with lately," and he was like, "I know," and then he just sort of stared off into space and why would he say that if he wasn't fucking somebody else? I mean, what guy would go and have a Q-tip shoved up his . . . Are *you* drunk? . . . Whatever.

TO MY GRANDMA: No, Grandma, a casting director is who actually gives you the part. An agent just sort of sends you out on auditions. . . . Because you can't get into any auditions without one. . . . Yes, I'm sure Erica Kane has an agent, she'd . . . Yes, I'm pretty sure Natalie Portman has one too. . . . I did know she's Jewish, but thanks for the heads-up. . . . Yes, everything's fine, can't talk anymore, I'm at work. . . . Work! . . . Okay, bye.

Once I was cheered by the company of family and friends, the rest of the day flew by. I left MTV that day feeling pretty proud of myself. Talk about resourceful! I'd taken a bad situation and made it better. In this uncertain age, surely no skill could be more valuable to a modern employer than that. The next day, as I waited in line in the lobby of Viacom to be identified, photographed, fingerprinted, and approved to go upstairs to work, my phone rang. It was Tina.

"You're not to report upstairs today. In fact, I think you'd better come straight here, to our offices."

Half an hour later, face-to-face, Tina informed me that MTV had registered a formal complaint about me. It seemed they found my behavior disruptive, uncooperative, and hostile. I had made repeated attempts to hack into their highly classified computer system and, when foiled, had spent several hours making personal phone calls. Was that true?

"I didn't try to hack into their computer system! What do they think I am, some kind of corporate-espionage person? I barely know how to send an e-mail attachment."

"Oh, please." Tina held her hand up to my face, displaying the curled backs of her long orange nails. "You scored very high on your Microsoft Word aptitude test, so we both know that isn't true. Did you make personal phone calls?"

"I—"

"It's a simple question. Did you or did you not spend company time making personal phone calls on a company phone?"

There was no way to lie. "I did . . . make a few phone calls." Tina smirked, folding her braceleted arms across her cleavage as she sat back in the desk chair. "But you don't understand," I continued helplessly. "She had *nothing* for me to do. *Nothing.* Is this some kind of endurance test, like the Vietcong did to prisoners of war? Am I really just supposed to sit staring at the floor for seven hours until it's time to go home? Is that what's expected?"

Yes.

With considerable pleasure, Tina told me that I had not only been banned from ever again setting foot in the MTV offices, I had been banned from all of Viacom. Nickelodeon, Comedy Central, VH1—none of them would have anything to do with me. Like Mel Karmazin, Howard Stern, and the Toms Cruise and Freston, I had earned myself a spot on Sumner Redstone's Enemies List. How this would affect my future career prospects, Tina couldn't say, but one thing was for certain; given that 95 percent of the clients the agency provided staff for were Viacom subsidiaries, there was no way they could continue working with me. She could refer me to another temp service, of course, but as a colleague, she would feel compelled to warn them about my problematic behavior. "It's a shame," she said, wagging her tower of stiffened hair in regret. "I thought you'd do so well. A nice girl like you."

I had been fired from my temp agency. Until today, I had not imagined such a thing was possible. My firing a few years before still filled me with shame, but that at least I could chalk up to the inexperience of youth and the capricious whims of bitter old show queens. But fired, banned from a temp agency, the last refuge of the chronically unemployable? How could this have happened? How could I live with the shame? Where was I to go? What would become of me?

Dejectedly, I wandered the streets, ignoring the daily morning phone calls from my mother. As you may have already deduced, I am not particularly adept at withholding information; in fact, the more shameful and humiliating the secret, the more people I am likely to tell. It would be the first thing out of my mouth. And I just couldn't hear her shit. I just couldn't.

"You got fired from a temp agency? *Who gets fired from a temp agency?* The last temp they sent my office had Down syndrome, for Christ's sake. Down syndrome! What the hell is the matter with you?"

Believe me, Mom. I've been asking myself the same question my whole life.

I'm not sure how long I walked, but it must have been quite a while, because I found myself all the way downtown, standing in front of a bakery I had passed many times, the kind of old-fashioned place you walk by and wonder how they stay open. In this brave new world of designer baked goods, of size-zero women lining up for four-dollar cupcakes, the window display was defiantly anachronistic and unchanging: thick, buttery babkas, piles of rugelach, stacks of hamantaschen big as a large man's hand, and, taped inside a corner of the window, something I had never noticed before, a small, hand-lettered sign. HELP WANTED.

Perhaps this sign was more than a sign. Perhaps it was an actual *sign*. I imagined myself, the recovering anorexic—irony of ironies!—ruddy, chubby-cheeked, and smiling, scooping challahs and rum cakes and slabs of strudel into crisp white bakery boxes, fastening them deftly with string twisted around my rosy fingers, and presenting them to the assembled throng of smiling Jews to take home to their families for the holidays. "*Gut Shabbos,* Mrs. Weinstock! My love to the children!" "*L'Shana Tova,* Mrs. Nachman! Something sweet for a sweet new year!" The Jews would be happy, their eyes shining in anticipation of something delicious to eat. They'd ask for samples and tastes and we'd haggle about the prices and I'd always add a little something extra, a piece of halvah, a little mandelbrot, a surprise for when they got home and cut the string on the boxes, so they'd know they were valued customers. Like family.

A cluster of bells jingled as I pushed open the door, but no one greeted me. The shop seemed empty.

"Hello?" I called.

There was a rustle in the back, and after a moment a tall Hasid appeared, his black frock coat lightly dusted with flour. His eyes raked over me in my poorly chosen business casual attire, the fitted, button-down blouse, a hideous flowered skirt my grandmother had bought for me at The Limited in 1996.

"Can I help you?" He spoke with the odd, garbled accent that so many Hasidim have, as if they are talking through a mouthful of hot soup that threatens at any moment to spill out, burning their chins. I dropped my gaze.

"I saw your sign in the window that says you're looking for help and I thought, well, I wanted to help."

I think he might have smiled at this, although it was hard to tell with the beard. "What's your name?"

"Rachel," I said.

"Tell me something, Rachel," he said. "Are you Jewish?"

I nodded. This time even the beard couldn't hide his smile. "So it's Ruchele, then?"

"I guess so. At Hebrew School they called me Rahel."

"Of course, Rahel, she was one of the matriarchs of the Jewish people. She was a beautiful woman, Rahel."

"Yes, I know. Jacob worked fourteen years for her."

He chuckled his hot-soup chuckle. "A scholar, as well as a beauty! Tell me, Ruchele, are you hungry?"

"A little," I confessed.

"Come with me to the back and I'll give you something nice. Something sweet. And we'll talk a little more."

"About the job?"

"About you, about the job. Come."

I followed him into the back room. The linoleum was smudged and cracked, but it smelled like heaven—of cinnamon, butter, baking apples. From a large metal tray on a rolling rack he chose a puffy golden biscuit, gleaming with egg yolk and dusted with powdered sugar, and handed it to me.

"Kichlach," he said. "For *Shavuos*. You know kichlach?"

"My grandmother makes them," I said.

"Try this. The best you ever had."

He sat down as I bit into the cookie. It was soft and yielding, the butter crumbling delicately in my mouth, rich yet indescribably light. I sighed with pleasure.

"You like it?" he asked. "The best. Here, have another." I've noticed that when some people watch another person chew, their mouths move as well, even if they're empty. He watched intently as I licked the last buttery crumbs from the corners of my lips, and when he spoke again, his tone was almost fatherly. "Tell me, Ruchele. Do you have a boyfriend?"

"I did," I said.

"So, *nu,* what happened?"

"I don't know. He didn't like me that much. I don't think he ever really liked me that much. But I liked him a lot, so I kind of ignored it."

"And tell me something else, Ruchele, this boyfriend, the meshuggener, he's a Yid, a Jew?"

"No," I said. "He sure isn't."

He clucked in disapproval, as I knew he would. "Ruchele, Ruchele. You need to find a Jewish man. A Jewish man, and make for him a Jewish home. Marry. Have children. This is what life is about. Your mama, she would want that you marry a Jewish man."

"Yes," I whispered. "She would want that."

"Your mama," he continued. "She is living?"

"Yes," I said, surprised. "Of course. Both my parents. They live in Nebraska. That's where I'm from," I added lamely. "Nebraska!"

"Nebraska!" he exclaimed. "I hear Nebraska, I think cowboys and Indians. In Nebraska there's Jews?"

"Some Jews, yes," I said. "Not many."

"Tell me, does it bother your mama and papa, you so far away from home? They don't worry about you?" He brushed my hand. Surely this was a mistake, an inadvertent slip. He didn't mean to. Everyone knew that a Hasid couldn't touch a woman who wasn't his wife. When they came to our house in Omaha every fall to put up the sukkah, they wouldn't even take the water my mother offered them from her hand. She had to put it on the counter for them, in Dixie cups purchased specially for the occasion.

"I think they worried at first," I said. "But I've been gone almost five years now. They're used to it."

Very slowly, the Hasid placed one of his hands on each of my hips, pulling my body closer to his knees. I was too surprised to react, too surprised to breathe. "Ruchele," he said softly. "I'll tell you something. If you want to work, of course, you'll work, but why don't you come here sometimes to see me. We'll sit, we'll talk, I'll give you nice things to eat. Sweet things. And then maybe, after a while, you'll learn a little bit what it means to be Jewish." Barely moving, his hand inched along my hip, giving it a single, tremulous stroke. "What do you think?"

I have done a lot of things. I have forced insecure old women to strip to their underwear in front of me and endured constant comparisons of my physical appearance to the giver of the world's most famous and ridiculed act of fellatio. Under pressure from parents and health professionals, I have regained thirty pounds, effectively ending any prospect I had for a career in the field to which I am accredited. I have spent hours filing in a windowless prison listening to the bizarre fixations of an omnipresent coworker, allowed myself to be questioned on camera about my sex life by a sock with eyes, and been fired unfairly from the establishment that employs the master of said sock, along with assorted meth addicts, layabouts, and aspiring singer/songwriter types, by a woman whose GED is framed and displayed on the wall next to a picture of a frog wearing a bow tie. And while I may have freely given my body to hundreds, probably thousands of caddish non-Jews who didn't like me that much, I was not going to prostitute myself to a Hasid in the back room of a dirty storefront for baked goods.

What do I think? "I don't think that's such a good idea," I said hotly.

"Good-bye then, Ruchele." He didn't seem surprised, and somehow I sensed this had happened before. "But *nu,* so you'll take my number. You'll call if you need anything. I insist. It's a big city, you know? It's lonesome. And it's not good for you to be so alone all the time, a nice girl like you."

Eleven

Have You No Shame?

On the evening of February 1, 2007, my grandmother took a shower before bed. She and my grandfather, wary of the minor household accidents that could send an octogenarian prematurely to the glue factory, had increasingly complex precautions in place for such an event. Both of them had to be home, both of them had to be awake, both of them had to be on the same floor of the house. As a result, the simple act of bathing had become quite a production. I imagine her moving into the bathroom, taking off her faded housecoat, and lowering her body onto her special bath chair with excruciating slowness. She had never moved quickly, but lately, everything seemed to take forever. You could bring a pregnancy to term in the time it took her to get out of the car; by the time she had made it up the walk to the front door, the kid would be taking his LSATs. My sister and I had begun to joke on our visits home that the Grandma we saw, inching down the hallway at a snail's pace, was actually the refracted image of the real Grandma, who was moving at the speed of light.

"Don't tease Grandma," said my grandmother, speaking of herself as she often did in the third person, like Jesus Christ or Kanye West. "Grandma's old. Someday you'll be old too."

Shortly after she had turned on the water and started to wash, my grandmother began to slip out of her chair. She grabbed the faucet handle, a single lever controlling both temperature functions, to break her fall, jerking it all the way to the left as she tumbled to the floor of the tub. With the bath chair blocking her way out, she was unable to move and remained trapped under the heavy spray of scalding water for close to three minutes. My grandfather heard her screaming over the TV in the next room. He rushed into the bathroom, although after a life spent on his feet butchering sides of beef and several rounds of arthroscopic surgery, he wasn't exactly Speedy Gonzalez himself; with great effort he managed to turn off the water and heave his naked wife out of the steaming tub. As she lay on the blue bath mat, screaming in pain and terror, he did what any thinking person would do in an emergency: he called my mother.

"I almost went to a movie that night," my mother said later. "I would have had my phone off when they called." She paused. "Of course, your father was out of town."

She ran several red lights and made it to their house in ten minutes flat, took one look at my grandmother, and suggested calling an ambulance. My grandmother said she didn't want to make any trouble for the paramedics. Refusing to argue, my mother wrapped my grandmother in a blanket, carried her down the steps, and placed her in the backseat of the car. My mother suggested driving straight to Clarkson Hospital, where they had recently installed a state-of-the-art burn unit, but my grandparents were adamant. Bergen Mercy was where their primary-care physician was on staff; Bergen Mercy was where my grandfather had had his most successful knee surgery (the one that didn't al-most kill him); Bergen Mercy it would be.

Several minutes later, in the Bergen Mercy emergency room, a nurse took one look at my grandmother and sent her in an am-bulance to the burn unit at Clarkson.

"I don't want . . . to make any trouble for anyone," my grand-mother said weakly.

She had second-degree burns on nearly a third of her body, including her right leg, her torso, and most of her back, with a few small sections on her arms and hands. While her vitals were checked, her wounds dressed, her blood flushed with morphine, my mother and grandfather stole a few minutes of sleep on the couches of the waiting area. At about 4 A.M., she was finally stable. My mother went home, tried vainly to sleep for an hour or so, and called me.

"Is she going to be okay?" I mumbled sleepily.

Ben rolled over in bed, pulling his pillow over his face. "Who is that?"

"My mother."

He expelled a great gust of exasperation. "It's so early. What does she *want*?"

Nearly six months had passed since we had been married, in a big Jewish ceremony that coincided, touchingly, with my grandparents' sixtieth wedding anniversary (I'd go into the whole getting-married-and-settling-down thing, but that's a story for another time. Suspend your disbelief.) Since the wedding, we had experienced the normal ups and downs of any two people who suddenly find themselves bound for life to an unbreakable contract: the panic, the resentment, the erratic bursts of wild, un-reasoned love. It occurred to me that this could be the first big crisis we would face together as husband and wife, our own little auxiliary unit within the larger family order. I wondered how we'd bear up.

"Something's happened to my grandmother," I said. "Just go back to sleep."

His genitals cupped comfortingly in hand, he was already snoring. I pressed the phone to my mouth tightly and walked into the living room.

"Is she going to be okay?" I asked again, furtively.

"You know, I think she is," said my mother. "The doctors seemed pretty optimistic. I mean, she's old, and things can go wrong, but I really don't think this is it. You know, *it*. She will probably have to go to the Blumkin Home, though, when she gets out of the hospital."

"Really?" My grandmother couldn't be in a nursing home. She *volunteered* at the nursing home. "You mean, forever?"

My mother laughed. "No, no, no! Probably just for a month or two, while she's recuperating. She'll need full-time care for a little while, that's all. Don't worry. She's going to be fine."

"Should I come home? I can book a flight—"

"Let's not worry about that for now," my mother interrupted lightly. "They don't want too many visitors in the burn unit. Too high a risk of infection. Why don't you plan on coming home when she's doing a little better, maybe in a few weeks?"

That was a relief. It wasn't a good week. I had things to do in New York—work, meetings, a cocktail party Ben didn't want to go to where I was looking forward to engaging in some of the pointless, slightly sweaty flirting that allows recently married women to feel that their life still holds possibility.

I waited until the next day to call my grandmother in the hospital, figuring she'd be a little stronger. When I got her on the phone she asked all the same questions she usually asked. How's Benjamin? How's the book coming? How's the apartment? What are you having for dinner? Don't you ever cook at home at all?

"No," I said. "I never do."

I don't remember now what else we talked about. You don't

catalogue these things at the time the way you should. I recall thinking it was strange that given all the painkillers she must have been on, Grandma seemed relatively Grandma-like, which indicated that she either had been senile for the past twenty years or was secretly shooting morphine from works she kept hidden in the kitchen in a giant canister of matzoh meal, like a Jewish Mary Tyrone. I mentioned this to my mother when I called her later.

"Senile," she replied. "I've been telling everyone that for years. Why do you think she didn't turn the hot water off when it was burning her? Because she couldn't remember what to do! I've always said they couldn't stay in that house much longer, that it wasn't safe for her anymore. But then I'm just the bitch daughter-in-law who never tells people what they want to hear. Why should anyone listen to me? I only test geriatric dementia levels in senior citizens for a fucking living—why should I know what I'm talking about?"

"I'm not casting aspersions on your professional reputation." These were old wounds, the kind that fester dully in families for years, rarely addressed and only resolved upon the eventual deaths of the aggrieved parties. The airing of them didn't help, only slit them back open to receive a fresh trickling of salt or lemon juice until the everyday business of life basted them up again. "All I said was that she sounded okay on the phone."

"Well, she was happy to hear from you." Her tone was still defensive, if softened somewhat. "But don't worry about calling too often—the doctor doesn't really want her on the phone. She can't really talk on the one in the room, with her bad hand, and they don't want people to bring their mobiles in, on account of the germs."

My grandfather, however, was eager to talk, brimming with plans. They would move out of their house into a brand-new apartment in a luxury retirement community. There would be a swimming pool and an activity center, and someone would do the shopping and cleaning and all of their friends would be jealous. They would have new furniture and new carpeting, and since Grandma wouldn't be driving for a while, he would trade in their two old cars for a brand-new one, with GPS and leather seats and a CD player to play her favorite music: *Your Hit Parade: 1942* and the cantorial stylings of Richard Tucker, as they drove through this new phase of their life together.

To which my grandmother replied dryly, "We'll see."

After several days of care, her burns showed no signs of improvement. Her sensitive skin, fragile and lacking elasticity under the best of circumstances, was simply too damaged to heal. The doctors put it to the family like this: they could perform a skin graft, a fairly risky proposition given her age and health concerns—high blood pressure, aortic stenosis, severely impaired kidney function; or they could do nothing as her flesh slowly became necrotic, killing her from the outside in.

How she felt going into surgery that day, knowing she might never wake up; that the last thing she might ever see was the gloved hand of the anesthesiologist putting the mask on her face, a spotlight hot against her skin as it faded into nothingness, I couldn't imagine. Or rather, I *could* imagine. I imagined little else. I imagined a prisoner walking to his execution, focusing on little details—a broken square of linoleum, a DANGER! HIGH VOLTAGE sign—the way I picked out faces from the crowd as I walked down the aisle at my wedding, knowing it would help me remember that feeling, that moment, for as long as I lived. But you remember nothing in death, and if Grandma noticed anything in her last ebb of consciousness—the pattern of the ugly peach wallpaper, the orderly with the long scar on his cheek and no eyebrows—it was a last-ditch effort, a vain attempt to keep a grasp on life, to the perception of experience that makes us ourselves and ends without warning. What a chilling thought that the mind, the only home you can never leave, will one day vanish. As long as death exists, none of us are safe.

"Okay," said my mother. "You really need to watch yourself."

"Watch myself do what?"

"I realize that Grandma is bringing up all of your *issues* with death, but all of us need you to hold it together right now."

"Issues with death?" I said, outraged. "Issues with death? Like it's weird? Everyone who's *alive* has issues with death."

"Yes," said my mother. "But other than patients I've had who are *actively* insane, I have never known anyone more afraid of it than you."

At any rate, my grandmother survived the three-hour surgery, to general jubilation and, in some quarters, surprise.

"She's still unconscious, possibly days away from opening her eyes, but she's alive and her blood pressure and heartbeat were stable," said my father; surely it could be only a matter of time before she breathed on her own, sat up, spoke, started knitting. Hugely relieved, we giddily turned our attention to the absurd gruesomeness of the procedure. Like something out of a horror movie, it was. They had cut away the dead, blistered skin from her stomach and replaced it with a swath of healthy skin from her back.

"That's so weird," said my mother. "What if you have a birthmark on your back and suddenly it's on your front? Wouldn't that be . . . *disorienting*?"

I agreed. "I mean, what if you didn't even know it was there, because it was on your back and you never saw it?"

"Or what if you had tattoos?" offered my sister. "I have a friend with, like, angel wings tattooed on her back. What if you suddenly had wings on your front?"

"Well," I said, "I guess then you could actually *see* the expression on people's faces when they realize what a douchebag you are."

Even odder, the deficit of skin left on Grandma's back was replaced with a piece from a donor, a twenty-seven-year-old male

Irish immigrant killed in a drunk-driving accident. This greatly amused my grandfather.

"Top o' the morning! That's what I say now when I go in to see her," he said, gleefully. "I said to the surgeon, I said, 'Well, if she wakes up and asks for a shot of whiskey, we'll know why!'"

If Dr. Reilly, the surgeon, found this as hilarious as he did, she offered no visible evidence.

"Oh boy!" he continued, rubbing his hands together with excitement. "We'll have a hell of a Saint Patrick's Day this year!"

For two weeks, every day was the same. My grandmother remained stable but didn't wake up, didn't speak. A battery of tests revealed no evidence of coma or stroke; rather, she was suspended in a kind of conscious unconsciousness, wakeful but unawake. The hypotheses for this odd state abounded; she was worn out, she was nocturnal, she was just enjoying some much deserved "me" time. My grandfather, lathered in disinfectant and swathed from head to toe in plastic, parked himself in the pink vinyl chair beside her bed as if it were his beloved La-Z-Boy at home and spoke incessantly about the exciting life the two of them would have when she got home, how they'd go back to Hawaii or Israel, or take a train trip through the Canadian Rockies like they'd always wanted. He'd talk to her about politics, lamenting the imbecility of the administration, the voters, people in general. He'd tell her how several people at the JCC had asked after her; how her friend Judy had been taking good care of him, leaving big pots of homemade stews and casseroles on the back porch for him every day; how in the parking lot he'd told someone with a BUSH/CHENEY '04 bumper sticker to go fuck themselves. He talked and talked and talked, and for his efforts he might get a slight flick of the hand, a slow waggle of the head. Once or twice his heart leapt in his chest when her legs raised several inches in the air, as though she was kicking in delight like a baby, and even a moment later when he realized that it was just the fancy automated hospital bed moving her lower body up and down to help circulation, he couldn't quite believe that it hadn't happened, that she wasn't about to throw off the bedclothes and shuffle down the hall to scold the nurses for not stocking more of his favorite soda in the pantry. It could only be a matter of time until she did. She wasn't getting better, but she wasn't getting worse. Surely if she was going to die, she would have died already. After all, you don't just survive surgery like that and then not live. That's impossible.

It was my father who called, so I knew there had to be something wrong. "It's time," he said. My father is strange sometimes. He misplaces his keys or the emollient he rubs in the crotch of his bike shorts, and you'd think the Gestapo was at the door. Faced with something more momentous, death or illness or the time, say, when one of his teenage daughters (I won't say which one, except that it wasn't my sister) was arrested at 2 A.M. for possession of marijuana on a stretch of interstate outside of Savannah, Missouri, and he can be surprisingly, at least outwardly, placid. His tone now, however, belied his struggle for calm: high, pinched, slightly electric.

I feigned ignorance. "Time for what?"

"Time to book a plane ticket home," he said, that strange voice breaking slightly. "Grandma . . . well, she's not going to make it."

She had developed some condition, he said, a condition he had never heard of before in all of his years of paranoid medical autodidacticism. It didn't seem to have a name, just initials, initials he couldn't remember for the life of him. I pictured him at the other end of the phone, thumping the side of his head with his palm like the bottom of a stubborn bottle of ketchup, as though the answer might tumble out with a little bit of force. Anyway, it didn't matter what the initials of this mystery ailment were; what mattered was that the initials were grinding my grandmother's circulatory system to an abrupt halt. Her blood pressure was dropping rapidly; it could be a day, an hour, even a matter of minutes until the blood ceased to reach her heart and Grandma would have left the building.

"Don't worry about the cost, we'll take care of it," my father said. "Just get here as soon as you can."

I had always hoped that when the day came that I would be called to the aid of my family, I would be brave, plunging myself headfirst into the reddish tide with a firm hand and a stiff lip. I imagined myself darting efficiently around the room, face lit from within with angelic determination, fetching a neat leather case and filling it with freshly laundered and folded linens, small glass vials of useful substances, a handgun and a bundle of crisp, new banknotes—sort of a cross between a courageous World War I field nurse and an unflappable mob wife. However, if you have read this book, you know that this sort of behavior is entirely incompatible with my personality.

"Calm down, baby," Ben pleaded, as he had done so many times before in our brief marriage. "Just calm down."

"I can't!" I shrieked. "This is something real! This is really happening!"

When the screaming, wailing, and thrashing had subsided to the point that Ben was satisfied I would break neither myself nor the furniture, he unpinned my arms and went online to check airfares while I packed a bag. I didn't have a neat leather case like in my rescue fantasy, nor did I have stacks of clean linen and unmarked bills. Instead, I had a large, unwieldy tote bag with a broken zipper and a missing wheel, its bottom lined with squashed tampons, wrapped and unwrapped; condom wrappers; and, although I have not smoked cigarettes in years, several unmatched socks covered in gritty bits of tobacco. To these things I added a single high-heeled shoe, a bottle of vodka, several pots of moisturizer, a biography of Walt Disney, a guidebook detailing the picturesque covered bridges of Vermont, four bras, and no underpants. A butter dish, a French textbook, a box of Hanukah candles, a carton of five hundred paper clips—it didn't matter what I threw in there, so long as it wasn't a black dress. No black dress. I wouldn't need it.

Meanwhile, back at the interweb, the ticketing situation was looking dire. A snowstorm earlier in the week had backed up hundreds of flights, and nothing was available for days. Finally, after over an hour of searching, we found a flight on an airline that I won't name except to say that it begins with an *N* and ends with *west,* scheduled to leave out of Newark in the early afternoon, strand me in Minneapolis for almost five hours, and land me in Omaha around midnight, all for the low, low price of $917.43. A flight to Omaha usually costs less than $300, but I was desperate. Hastily, I booked the seat, repacked my bag to contain wearable and hygienically oriented items (pausing only to pour a large quantity of the vodka down my throat), and began to systematically cancel my appointments for the week.

"You should really ask them about bereavement fares," said my friend Lauren, when I called her to say we couldn't have lunch the following day.

"I already booked the ticket on N—west," I said.

"Call them anyway," she advised. "They might at least sneak you on an earlier flight."

The reason I am bringing up this conversation is to make absolutely clear the fact that I spoke to a N—west ticketing agent that evening and tearfully relayed my situation, giving her my ID number, my confirmation number, my credit card number—every possible number pertaining to my flight. She was sympathetic, apologetic even, but explained that due to the inclement weather, the late date, and the generally disastrous nature of modern air travel, there was nothing available. In fact, she told me, I was lucky to have made the booking I did.

"I'll tell you what," she said. "It's late; there're no more flights tonight. Why don't you call back early tomorrow morning and see if we can squeeze you onto an earlier flight."

"Thank you," I said. "I really appreciate all your help."

"It's no problem. I'm so sorry to hear about your grand-mother," she said sincerely. "And thank you for flying N—-west!"

In the morning, another N—west ticketing agent (markedly less empathetic to my plight) said roughly the same thing. "You're lucky to have the flight you've got. Things are crazy out of New York this week." I thanked her for her time. "Thank you for fly-ing N—west!" she replied.

My cabdriver and I had a little altercation on the curb of the N—west terminal at Newark Liberty Airport. He had neglected to mention the fifteen-dollar surcharge for destinations outside the five boroughs, claiming it was clearly outlined on the Passen-ger's Bill of Rights sign posted in the back; I explained that the Passenger's Bill of Rights was obscured by a large footprint that appeared to have been made with dog shit, and that the Passen-ger's Bill of Rights also stated that it was my right to have "a cour-teous, English-speaking driver" who when asked to please turn down the muezzin's call to prayer on the stereo would not respond by increasing the volume as high as it would go. I hauled my own damn bag out of the trunk and sent him off without a tip. He re-sponded by carefully splattering my lower body with filthy slush from the street as he sped off.

The N—west check-in desk was empty, apart from a pair of befuddled Dutchmen connecting to Rotterdam and a woman with a crate containing a drugged Irish setter. I plugged my credit card into the computer to retrieve my reservation and re-ceived a screen picturing a 747 in flight over the words travelers of every nation dread with all their multicultural souls: *Assis-tance required. Please see an agent.* Unfortunately, the peculiar needs of the Irish setter seemed to be occupying all the mental resources of the single agent on duty, so I stood behind the Dutchmen, staring at my watch as I tried to listen in on their conversation—I had lived in the Netherlands for some time and was pleased to discover I could still pick out the Dutch words for "a," "the," and "iPod." Utterly stumped by the canine situation, the single ticketing agent disappeared, presumably to fetch a supervisor. I kept my eye on my watch and blinked back tears. Was Grandma dead already? Surely they would have called me if she was dead. Fifteen minutes passed, then thirty. The Dutchmen, shrugging, wandered off without a word, as though the airport was a shop they were browsing in with no intention to buy. More than forty minutes had passed when the agent finally returned, pulling a large dolly on which she intended to load the Irish setter for easy boarding. I was starting to run a little low on time.

"Excuse me," I said, stepping forward.

"Excuse *me,*" said the ticketing agent. "I am helping a customer." Do you know how some people just look like cunts? I mean, they actually, physically look like cunts, and by *cunt* I mean vagina?

"You've been helping the same damn customer for over a fucking hour," I said, emboldened by grief. "In the meantime, some of us are about to miss our flights."

A smug look crept across her cunt face. She had driven me to curse; now she had the upper hand. After two decades of traveling with my father, why had I not learned this simple lesson? Why? Why?

"There's absolutely no need for that kind of language," she said, smirking. "If you continue to be verbally abusive, I'll have no choice but to put you on the no-fly list." And here is where the terrorists have really won, my friends, by adding yet another layer of perversion to the airline customer service industry, already a brutal date rape of the social contract.

"She can go ahead of me, I don't mind," said the woman with the Irish setter.

"No," the agent replied sharply. "I'm helping you."

"Really," said the woman. "I've been taking up so much of your time, and this lady is going to miss her plane. Please, help her."

The ticketing agent ripped my driver's license out of my hand and wordlessly began to punch numbers into the machine with startling ferocity. Suddenly, she smiled. Something was clearly wrong.

"Well, I brought up your reservation, *ma'am,* and it seems you're booked on Continental." She kept smiling, her teeth gleaming brilliantly.

"That's impossible," I said. "I've spoken to two N—west customer-service people on the phone since I made the reservation. The confirmation number starts with *NW.* The e-mail I got said 'Your N—west Flight Itinerary' across the top, for fu— for Pete's sake."

Oh, but it was possible. Sometimes they pawned travelers off on partner airlines when things got busy. If I had examined the printout of my flight information more carefully, I would have noticed this information in tiny print at the bottom.

"Can't you just check me in here?" I asked desperately.

No. As the flight was operated by Continental, I would have to present myself at the Continental check-in.

"Is the Continental check-in in this terminal?"

Oh, no, no, no. This was terminal A. The Continental check-in was in terminal E. The shuttle train was just downstairs—it should arrive in fifteen minutes or so.

Despite pleading, begging, and shedding buckets of tears, the Continental check-in people refused to let me board the plane. I was too late. There would be no time to go through security or get my luggage on the aircraft.

"You don't understand," I said, sobbing. "My mother died."

I'm not quite sure why that came out. I certainly hadn't planned it. Perhaps I needed some way to explain my grief, something that seemed more proportionate. The death of a grandparent, no matter how sudden, can hardly come as a shock. Almost as soon as you're old enough to realize it, they start to kick off—heart attack, stomach cancer, emphysema; the list goes on—and once you hit your twenties, they start dropping like flies. Parents are another matter; generally, you might know someone in your grade who lost a parent early to a freak accident or an incurable illness, but those deaths seem remote, impossible, quite as unimaginable as your own. The death of a parent might reasonably induce in one the feeling that the world is crumbling into destruction, requiring the tearing of one's hair and the rending of one's garments; the death of a grandparent, no matter how beloved, is expected to a elicit a more moderate response. Unfortunately, there was no moderation in mine.

"My mother died!" I shrieked wildly, horrified with myself. A small girl with a knapsack at the next desk tightened her grip on her own mother's hand as she stared at me with a mixture of sympathy and disgust. I would have felt the same way at her age. How irresponsible to lose your parents. "Can't you let me on the fucking plane?"

They couldn't. However, they could put me on a flight to Omaha at the same time tomorrow for an additional cost of $396. Due to extenuating circumstances, my profanity was kindly left unmentioned.

"You didn't miss your flight because of a delay or cancellation," the not unsympathetic agent reminded me. "We'll have to issue you a new ticket, but due to your situation, we've been authorized to offer you a bereavement rate."

"Thank you," I said. "So, what is the bereavement rate?"

He looked at me like I was crazy. "Three hundred ninety-six dollars."

Back at the airport the next day on my second try, I had some time to kill, so I figured I'd go to the bookstore and pick up something to read on the plane. Nothing too heavy or difficult—a novel about a fat girl with a penchant for Gucci and a nagging mother finally ending up with the man of her dreams, something in pink with a purse on the cover that serves as a reminder of all that is troubling about women. I ended up with *The Year of Magical Thinking* by Joan Didion. The nation's leading literary critics trumpeted from the cover that it was precisely what I needed to read; one of them, from *The New York Review of Books,* went so far as to say that he "could not imagine dying without it." Whether he referred here to his own demise or to the concept of dying itself, as though without Joan Didion's expertise on the subject death would cease and we would be condemned to live eternally on a planet teeming with an ever more ancient population, holed up forever in their rent-controlled apartments with mountains of string and newspaper and causing fifty-car pile-ups on the freeway, I could not say, but I sat at the gate reading with increasing dread. Dread of what was to come for Joan Didion, dread of what was waiting for me when I finally got home, dread in the knowledge that when the time came, as it inevitably would, for me to write about my grief and loss, I would be utterly unable to do so with the lucidity, the force, and the indelibility of Joan Didion. In my own manner of magical thinking, it occurred to me that the reason for this was not the yawning discrepancy in our talent, skill, and experience, but that I did not have the right haircut. Prose on the level of Didion's seemed to require a precision bob, a sleek, short curtain of hair that swung into place as smoothly and neatly as the organization of her thoughts. I have tried many times to achieve a precision bob with the expectation that precision on the outside of my head will tame the tangled mess within, but I don't have precision-bob hair. It's too thick, too unruly, and each attempt to cut it short has left me with a series of irregular bumps

and ridges at various places, giving my head the look of a mushroom cloud or a battered phrenology bust. Nor could I imagine
myself cooking the sort of meal Joan Didion prepares just before
her husband falls dead at the table, which in my mind resembles
the photographs from the cookbooks my mother keeps from the
Berkeley days, casually, studiedly bohemian, a salad thrown together in a bowl hollowed out of an enormous nut, tastefully sized
steaks sizzling in a heavy grill pan enameled in the burnished Le
Creuset red-orange of the seventies intelligentsia. I do not have a
precision bob; the last thing I served my husband was a bag of
Skittles which I thoughtfully poured into a bowl decorated with
hula dancers; my breasts occasionally spill out the sides—not the
top but the sides!—of my bra in a way that is most vulgar; and far
from being a "cool customer," as Joan Didion refers to herself in
her wonderful book, I am a customer who flung my body against
the customer-service desk, sobbing and hysterical as a heavily
veiled witness to a suicide attack in Basra, wailing gut-wrenching
lies about my mother so they'd feel more sorry for me. Clearly, I
would be unable to grieve in a critically acclaimed way.

I felt a slight pain in the top of my thighs and reaching across
my lower back. I put away Joan Didion, reached for the ever-
present Mayo Clinic diagnostic manual in my carry-on, and helpfully diagnosed myself with ovarian cancer.

No matter what he actually looks like, my image of my father remains unchanged from my nursery school drawings: an enormous
striped tie obscuring most of his body, the scribbled pom-pom of
black hair, a wide mouth stretched into a smile. It was late when
he picked me up that night, so I'm sure he wasn't wearing a tie; the
black hair had long since turned to white, and he certainly wasn't
smiling with all that was going on, but in my memory a more ac-
curate image does not exist. We greeted each other, more or less in

silence. He hugged me fiercely at the baggage claim and I hugged him back, dreading the telltale tremble of his thin shoulders that would be the only sign that he was crying, silently, into my neck. I had felt it only a handful of times before—when they left me alone in my dorm at college, for example—but it never failed to send chills down my spine, the sudden, inescapable knowledge that my father was not a crayoned portrait fastened to the refrigerator with a magnet but a human being with feelings.

Thankfully, this time, the tremble did not come.

"She's actually stabilized," he said, looking away from me at a family in matching Huskers sweatshirts embracing in happy reunion. "It's quite something. Her numbers were dropping and dropping, and suddenly they started to go back up. I mean, when we called you at first we didn't think she'd make it through the night, but now . . ."

I heaved my bag off the carousel. "Do they think she might still make it?"

He shrugged. "I don't . . . well, she's stable anyway. We'll see."

My mother was waiting at home with my sister, who had flown in without mishap from Los Angeles the day before. She had moved to L.A. several months earlier after graduating from college, and it seemed that every time I had seen her since, her skin was tanner and her hair was blonder, giving her the look of my cherished Malibu Barbie—that is, before having all her hair shaved off during her tragic stint in a Barbie prisoner-of-war camp. We ate a desultory meal of warmed-over salmon with a few limp vegetables while my mother brought me up to speed on what had happened. Grandma was hanging on; it seemed the real trouble spots were the weekends, when A-team medical workers were off and the burn unit was staffed by an assortment of students, interns, and orderlies known to unplug a ventilator or two while mopping.

"The other night," my father said, shaking his head in wonderment, "my mother was *flatlining,* and this nineteen-year-old nursing student kind of wanders in, with her tongue hanging out"—here he cocked his head and made a gibbering noise with his lips, to indicate a total retard—"and just *stares* at the goddamn monitor like it's a time machine."

"Why a time machine?" my mother asked. "Was Christopher Lloyd there? Did it look like a DeLorian?"

We laughed, far more than the joke deserved.

The hospital did not allow visitors until 2 P.M. My sister had borrowed Grandma's car, so the two of us went to Target, had a sandwich, then drove around for a few hours, listening to Lil' Kim. Vestiges of our grandmother were all over; a print smock slung over her box of brushes and glazes for ceramics, uneaten candies melted in the sun and congealed over the drink holder like a thick volcanic crust, the wadded-up Kleenex that she would pick off of the floor and hand to us saying, "It's clean!"

"At least it hasn't been *that* drawn out," my sister was saying. "I mean, she hasn't had, like, cancer for fifteen years or anything. Maybe it's best this way."

"I don't know," I said. "If she was sick for years and years and then died, everyone would say, 'Oh, it's for the best, at least she's in a better place, out of her misery.' If it came out of nowhere, a heart attack or an aneurysm and she just dropped dead one day, we'd say, 'Well, at least it was sudden. She was active to the end. And at least she didn't suffer.' Whichever way their loved ones die, people will say that's the best way. But you're still dead, regardless."

We fell silent for a moment. Neither of us felt the need to point out the obvious—that Grandma was getting the worst of both worlds. Suffering and sudden.

"It's weird being in this car without her," I said. "It smells like her."

My sister wrinkled her nose. "I know," she said. "Musty. I can't believe all the shit she has in here. It's like one of those people who lives in their car with like, a bong and a really nasty dog."

We laughed. It felt good to make fun of Grandma, a time-honored tradition that seemed to keep the unthinkable at bay. You can't laugh at a dying person, therefore Grandma is not dying.

"It's weird," she contiued. "I always knew she'd die someday, but . . . I don't know. I can't believe it might be actually happening."

"I don't know. You kind of expect your grandparents to die," I repeated what had been my mantra through the past few days. *You are prepared for this. You are prepared.* "Poor Daddy. He must be so sad. I don't think you ever expect to your parents to die, no matter how old you are. I mean, when you're little, there's always that one kid whose parents died early and that's really weird, but it doesn't register as something that could happen to you."

My sister looked at me strangely.

"What?" I asked.

"You know," she said. "Mommy was that one kid."

My grandfather was already at the hospital when we arrived, sitting on a couch in the waiting room. CNN was playing, on a small TV tucked inside a wall unit, but he faced away from it, staring at the bank of elevators in the hallway.

"Nobody much comes up here," he explained. "There's only seven beds in the burn unit. Not too many visitors at all." His green sweatpants were hiked up, revealing his athletic socks and shins, rubbed smooth and hairless by eighty years of wearing pants, and his pale yellow T-shirt, a little too small, stretched firmly across his belly. GRANDMA'S HOUSE, it read, over an appliqué of a birdhouse covered in hearts, and below it, FREE KISSES, FREE HUGS, FREE BABYSITTING, FREE COOKIES.

"That's right," he said, catching me looking. "It's hers, and I'm gonna wear it."

"It looks nice," said my sister.

"I'll tell you something else." His voice grew softer, struggling to come out. "The day she sits up in the hospital bed, I'm gonna jump up to the ceiling and holler hallelujah."

Every year on my birthday, my grandma called early in the morning and told a variation of same story: "I was outside in the garden, planting my flowers, when I heard the phone ring. I rushed inside to answer it, and it was your father saying we had a beautiful little granddaughter. And when I told Grandpa the baby was a girl, he jumped so high in the air he hit his head on the ceiling!" As I was born quite late at night, it is doubtful my grandmother was gardening in the pitch dark, and my grandfather, even before he started shrinking, was neither tall nor athletic enough to even graze the ceiling with his fingers. But my grandmother was special in that regard, like Blanche DuBois without the Southern charm or the demons. She didn't tell you things the way they were, she told them the way they should have been, or more accurately, she told you what she thought you'd want to hear. Outside planting flowers at the moment my beautiful first grandchild was born is slightly more poetic than asleep in bed without my dentures in. This revisionism could be funny; once, when I asked her if her mother was born in Poland or Russia, she hesitated just a moment before replying: "Prussia."

Anyone could stand in the doorway of Grandma's room and wave to her bewilderedly, but due to her severely compromised immune system, only a few could actually go inside to see her. My grandfather had arranged for me to occupy the remaining spot on the list. I would be staying longer than my sister, and besides: "'You're a married woman now," he said gruffly. "I figure you can handle it."

I can handle this.

We scrubbed up in the small foyer in front of her room, slathered ourselves with antibacterial gel, and slipped our hands through plastic robes and latex gloves. Grandma lay motionless in the center of the room, surrounded by a wall of machines. Her arms and shoulders were bare above her torso, which was wrapped in white bandages, and her hair, colored a vivid orange in my childhood and softened to a pale strawberry blond over the years, lay flat and matted against the pillow, like the wig of a discarded doll.

"Hi, Grandma," I said.

"That's my oldest granddaughter," my grandfather was crowing to the young nurse. "The one that just got married in New York. Boy, Grandma loves her Rachel, don't you, Grandma?"

"Hi, Grandma," I said again.

"Did you hear that, honey?" my grandfather said. "Rachel's here!"

To say that her eyes flew open at that sounds corny or like a lie, but that's what they did. They opened, and her head jerked slightly in my direction, as far as it could go with the breathing tube in the way. I could hear her voice exclaim my name, except of course there was no sound.

"Can I touch her?" I asked the nurse.

"Sure you can touch her!" my grandfather boomed. "She won't break! Will you, honey?"

I reached for her hand and held the two knobby fingers that poked out under the dressing. The nails still shone with clear polish, and one of them was half missing. I remember when that happened years ago; while she was cutting a birthday cake the knife had slipped, severing a chunk of her fingernail. Not missing a beat, she sliced on; none of us even knew what had happened until my sister, playing under the table, noticed the blood seeping through the paper towel in Grandma's lap.

"There were still people who needed cake!" she protested. "I'm fine!"

"It's me, Grandma," I whispered. "I'm here. Ben sends his love. You're going to be just fine."

Her eyes had closed again, but tears trickled slowly from the corners and into her hair. I didn't know what else to say, so I just held her hand and stared at her, taking in the machines, the bandages, the yellow toenails poking out from the ends of her surgical stockings. Her breasts, I noticed, were nowhere to be found. Had they been damaged or removed or, horror of horrors, burned off like she was some sort of martyred virgin saint, tortured by the Romans before she was thrown to the lions? *Poor Grandma! What have they done with your boobs?*

She rasped for breath, the ventilator shaking her body, and I noticed something, some lump quiver slightly to the right of her hip. *There* they were.

"She was a little more responsive this morning," said the nurse. "But she's tired now. Why don't you come back tomorrow?"

I stayed a week; there didn't seem to be much point in staying any longer. She was still alive when I left, but each day was the same as the last, a kiddie roller-coaster of minor setbacks and meaningless improvement. She was stable; she wasn't stable. A dialysis session went fine; the next time, her blood coagulated in the tube, blocking the machine. One day she might open her eyes or lift her fingers; the next day, nothing. My grandfather sat at her bedside constantly, his voice breaking, asking the orderlies, the nurses, the technicians, if they thought she had a chance of making it out of there. He didn't care what kind of shape she was in, if she couldn't walk anymore, if she couldn't speak. He just needed to hear that she had a shot.

Their answers were diplomatic, purposefully vague. "She's a fighter, that's for sure." "I believe each of us has an angel looking out for us from heaven, and her angel's a pretty darn good one." "Well, Mr. Shukert, I'm not a gambling man, but if I was, I'd lay odds on it." And my grandfather, upon hearing these words of careful encouragement, would pump his arms in the air and clap his heavy hands together in delight. "That's all I needed to hear. Just a little bit of hope." The words came out of him in a rush, an exhale. He held his breath every time he asked the question, praying silently for the answer he wanted to hear. And in its judicious way, it always was. It would be impossible to tell my grandfather something he didn't want to hear. He simply wouldn't hear it.

"You hear that, baby?" he said, kissing the limp hand of my unconscious grandmother. "You're going to be just fine. They wouldn't say so if it wasn't true."

It was enough to break your heart, if it wasn't already breaking.

There are a few scribbles in my notebook from this time, providing me some clue to my mindset:

Homesickness is not missing home but missing life already lived. Therefore, mourning for the dead = grieving for a lost home, a lost time the dead people were a part of. Really, you could spend your whole life mourning if it wasn't for reality television . . .

Daddy, the noblest Roman of them all, says: *Dum spiro, spero*. While I breathe, I hope. Latin proverb, also state motto of South Carolina. Wonder if this has some significance, also wonder proportion of South Carolinians (Carolingians? Like Charlemagne?) who are familiar with this fun fact . . . personally, I hope Heaven is an enormous cruise ship, in which you are seated at all meals with very fascinating and attractive historical figures; conversely, Hell is an enormous Bar Mitzvah party in which you are seated with your family and forbidden from circulating . . .

N—west Airlines is going DOWN. Hope they declare bankruptcy again so I can dance on their grave; failing that, I will publish SCATHING critique of them in my book, to general glee of nation. $917.43 + $396 = RIDICULOUS. DIE FUCKERS DIE.

I'm grateful for these scraps of archival evidence. Vague and vengeful as they may be, I have only two other coherent memories from this period of constantly waiting for the phone to ring, of daily trolling the discount travel websites for flights to Omaha "just to see what's there," of sleepless nights and exhausted days. One is of a Saturday afternoon, shortly after I returned to New York. It was a beautiful day, the first that really felt like spring, and I decided to walk across Central Park from my apartment on the Upper East Side to the Museum of Natural History to see the new Hall of Human Origins that had recently opened to great fanfare. In some sense, I suppose, I was hoping the grandeur of the evolutionary march would help me cope, to see Grandma's inevitable passing as something more than the loss of a woman we loved but simply a small spoke in the unending, inescapable carousel of Life or some bullshit like that. Also, I'm a big fan of life-sized dioramas, particularly if they involve the Noble Savage.

The park was packed with New Yorkers eagerly emerging from their winter hibernation, full of bicycles, roller blades, and visible flesh in clothing the weather didn't quite call for yet. There's global warming, and then there's sunbathing on the Great Lawn in a bikini in March. It's weird enough to lie almost nude in the grass in August, when most people would gladly remove their skin if they could and display themselves in all their meaty, internal-organ-strewn glory like rotting sides of beef in a Third World marketplace, but when people around you are still wearing scarves, it's odd. Oh, well. If you've got it, flaunt it. You're only young once. Before you know it you'll be unconscious and slathered in disinfectant in an intensive care unit while your kidneys fail and your children fight over when they're going to let

Medicare pull the plug, because you have officially become an in-
excusable burden to the American taxpayer. Did I mention my
walk was supposed to cheer me up?

The park gave way to the majestic expanse of envy known as
Central Park West, a street that no matter how well I am dressed I
never feel quite good enough to walk on, as though the shoes from
Target that I bought on sale will leave slick streaks of poverty on
the pavement that will make the little girls dashing home from
ballet class slip and fall, requiring rescuing from their doormen,
who will shoot me a look both contemptuous and commiserating:
I'm wearing cheap shoes too, lady, but at least I work here. But today,
like Queen Victoria and Jackie Kennedy, I was ennobled by grief.

Two dressed-up little dark-haired girls scampered past me,
tearing ribbons from their hair, their sprigged skirts skimming the
sidewalk like soft bells. Close behind them, strolling at a more
leisurely pace, was a pair of Jewish daddies. Slim, dark, handsome,
dressed tastefully but not too fashionably in well-cut suits and ties
I was sure their wives had chosen, they were walking home from
synagogue, holding their tallis bags loosely by their sides, reaching
up periodically to check if their suede yarmulkes were still clipped
to their wiry hair.

The little girls were perilously close to a traffic light. "Leah,
careful!" cried one of the daddies, before falling back into conversation with his friend, which from experience I imagined to be a
mixture of baseball statistics, the week's Torah portion, and up-
dates from the world of business.

"Daddy!" screamed one of the little girls, now safely past the
intersection. "Look at this!" Laughing, she twirled around again
and again, so that the sides of her full skirt spun out like a parasol.

"Pretty!" said the daddy, with the practiced tone of a man who
has been invited to tea with the American Girls more than a few
times.

"Pretty!" said the little girl, spinning faster. She reached out her hands to touch the fabric softly as it swung around her. "Pretty, pretty, pretty, pretty!"

I was hit with a wave of homesickness so strong it nearly knocked me all the way back across the park. Sick for a life once lived. Sickened that it won't come back.

The other memory is a dream. I know it's as mercilessly boring to listen to someone else's dreams as it is fascinating to ponder your own, but I'll be brief. It was a typical dream for me. It's dark outside. We're on the train to Auschwitz; the floor of the boxcar is made from molten lava; and *Oklahoma!* is playing in the background, so loud as to drown out all other sound, but then I'm standing in front of the skill crane machine at the grocery store, trying to pick up a little stuffed lion with the metal claw, and President Clinton is standing next to me, only he's naked but he's also a paper doll. And suddenly my grandmother leans out a window and calls down to me. She is wrapped in bandages with her shoulders bare like when I last saw her, but her hair is combed and freshly colored, and she wears her glasses and the heavy gold necklace with the diamond pendant that would imprint the backward letter *D* into my forehead when she held me.

"It's okay," she calls down to me.

"What?" I call back.

"It's okay, sweetheart. I'm okay." She smiles and stretches out a knobby hand, although she can't reach me. "Don't be scared, dolly. Everything will turn out fine." She ducks her head back inside and shuts the window. I had never dreamed of her before; nor have I since.

She died on a Thursday, two days before Saint Patrick's Day, exhibiting the same Hibernian luck that had impelled the young man whose skin had slowly rotted on her back to his accidental death. I've often wondered at the accuracy of ascribing particular *mazel* to the Irish, a group whose long and tragic history seems only marginally more comfortable than that of my own hapless people; at any rate, the combination was too much for my grandmother. By all accounts, she slipped away peacefully. The morning nurses came in, saw her stats were dropping fast, and called my father, uncle, and grandfather to tell them that today was the day. They held court in the cafeteria, sipping soft drinks from paper cups with family and friends who stopped by to offer their respects, and when the end came they were there. Sitting at his mother's bedside, as her breath grew faint, then stopped, as the monitor flatlined, my father leaned over and whispered in her ear for the last time: "Mom. Real quick, tell me; what's it like?"

"You know what really got her, don't you?" My mother is a fan of the rhetorical question. "After the burns and the kidney failure and the blood pressure and everything, you know what she died from?" She paused dramatically. "A yeast infection."

I laughed out loud.

"A yeast infection," my mother repeated. "The bacteria spread into her blood and she turned septic. Can you imagine? I mean, how many yeast infections must she have had in her life? And that's what finally does it. Unbelievable."

"Is that what they're going to put down as cause of death?" I asked. "On the death certificate, I mean? Because that would be *hilarious*."

"I think they're just putting 'complications from accident' or something," said my mother. "But I agree, that would be funny."

"What do you do with the death certificate anyway?" I asked. "Can you frame it and hang it on the wall, like your diploma? So-and-so is officially graduated from life? Grandma loved having things framed. Maybe we could put it in one of those weird shadowboxes, like the creepy one she had made with Bubbe's hair? Like, we'd put the death certificate, and her hospital bracelet, and like, a piece of bandage or something in there, with a picture of her. It'd be like a reliquary, you know, like those things in the Vatican where it's all jeweled and everything and then, like, Saint Teresa's finger is sticking out the top like a candle on a cake? Do you know what I'm talking about?"

My mother was silent, deciding how to respond. "Buy yourself a plane ticket," she said finally, "and try to make it to the airport on time."

When the goyim[†] lose a loved one, they have so many decisions to make. Viewings must be arranged. Morticians must be hired, flowers ordered, a makeup design approved. The coffin must be considered—nothing too extravagant, but you don't want to look cheap—and, in a faintly Egyptian touch, mementos are chosen to

[†] Gentiles, it has been a while since our last meeting. However, as we are almost at the end of our journey together, I wanted to leave you with some parting thoughts. First of all, as I hope to have made clear, *goyim* is the plural form. Therefore, the next time you are attempting to proudly display your canny Yiddish know-how or "cosmopolitanism," as I have learned it was referred to in Soviet Russia, do not proclaim, "I am a goyim." You are not a goyim. You, as you have just made painfully obvious, are a goy. Furthermore, I would in general steer you away from using Yiddishisms in general. No one thinks it's cute to hear a former North Dakotan say *oy gevalt,* nor will misusing the term *farkakte* win you any brownie points with your significant other's Jewish parents, who are already trying very hard to like you as much as they can, under the circumstances, while hoping that the two of you will break up of your own accord before outside intervention is necessary. Other tips are obvious: don't order mayonnaise on a pastrami sandwich; if you find it difficult to make a guttural *ch* sound, substitute with a lazily neutral *h* sound instead of a hard *k*, which will make you sound like an illiterate; and should you find yourself for some reason in a Lactaid of Jews, as I like to call such a grouping, in the manner of a pride of lions or a coven of witches—a Bar Mitzvah, wedding, or other family occasion of said significant other—please do not think this is an appropriate time to commiserate with the plight of the Palestinians, or take it upon yourself to criticize Israeli military policy or the demarcation of American funds therein; after all, you're just pointing out the flaws of a government and that doesn't make you an anti-Semite. And I agree. A reasoned critique of Israeli policy on campus or in the pages of a left-wing newspaper is not inherently anti-Semitic; however, raising such an argument at the Leventhal family reunion in Palm Springs makes you a Nazi. Very well, Gentiles. That is all. Good luck, *l'chaim,* and may we live together in peace.

place inside it—family photographs, lucky charms, crucifixes, and such. Somebody is charged with the grim task of deciding what the deceased is to wear on her final journey. When I was very small and believed that flowers had feelings and a pot cried out in pain when you cooked in it, I thought there must be no worse fate for an item of clothing: elated to be brought home from the store, sure that it would accompany the wearer on all manner of happy occasions, only to spend all eternity moldering underground in a box of decomposing flesh; it seemed as unthinkable to me as the notion that my own body, which seemed so indestructible, inescapable, would one day rot along with the rest.

Jewish funerals are simple. To be buried as a Jew is to be buried exactly as has every Jew before you. The body is turned over to the Chevrah Kadisha, the burial society, a group of anonymous volunteers (often former doctors and nurses, who are unlikely to be squeamish), who prepare the body, wash it, and dress it in a simple white shroud. A male may also wear a yarmulke and prayer shawl. There is no embalming, no makeup, no flowers, no viewings. They take the body away and you never see it again, except at the front of the synagogue, where my grandmother was now, in a plain casket of unvarnished pine, its only decoration a Star of David carved on the closed lid. Ashes to ashes, dust to dust; the idea is to be buried in something as natural and biodegradable as possible, leaving little trace of having ever existed at all. We don't want to make too much trouble.

I sat beside my grandfather at the end of the pew, my arm resting protectively over the shoulder pads of his dark jacket. How he would hold up was anybody's guess. The past few days he had been understandably erratic, cracking jokes one minute, the next staring blankly at a wall and breaking into a wheezing sobs: "Why? Why? She didn't deserve to go like that, scalded like a chicken." He had proclaimed a newfound disbelief in God, a God that could let such a thing happen; we had also discovered, with some consternation, that despite reaching their mid-eighties in a city they had lived in for more than sixty years, my grandparents had never purchased a cemetery plot.

"I just thought if I never bought one, she would never die," my grandfather said, blinking. And if he died before her?

"She would have taken care of it. She always took care of me."

The pews of the synagogue were filling with family and friends, many of whom I had last seen at our wedding six months earlier. It was strange to see them now, dressed in somber black, many of them blinking back tears. "You must be so happy she lived to see you get married," they had said to me as we greeted each other in the lobby. "It meant so much to her; it must make you feel better."

No! I wanted to scream. *No, it doesn't! Fuck my wedding! I just want her back.*

"Oh yes," I said, smiling sadly. "Much better."

I had never heard the synagogue so quiet. The rabbi spoke for several minutes, and the cantor sang, before my father stood up, fingering the torn black ribbon the rabbi had blessed and pinned to his lapel before the service, to give the eulogy.

"How do you speak about your mother at her funeral? How do you eulogize someone who gave you life, raised you, offered you unconditional love and support for fifty-seven years?"

He went on to quote the Bible. "A woman of valor, who can find? Her price is far above that of rubies." He spoke of my grandmother's generosity, her compassion for those less fortunate, her incredible dexterity with a ball of yarn, and her willingness to invite lonely strangers into the house for a meal, a talk, a piece of advice. He spoke of her optimism, her love of family, of the way a few extra steaks or pounds of hamburger would find their way into the shopping bags of customers who needed them, of an early memory of her teaching him to ride a bike in their backyard, holding on to his waist reassuringly until he was ready to go on his own. When he'd finished there wasn't a dry eye in the house.

And then it was my grandfather's turn. I helped him up from the pew, and we watched with apprehension as he slowly shuffled his way to the bimah. The days leading up to the funeral were pregnant with hints of what was to come. He was angry, and he planned to let us know it. God was dead to him, and he didn't care, he was going to stand up there in front of the ark and the Torahs and his poor dead wife and say so. He'd gone to synagogue for eighty years, and it had failed to make Grandma immortal, therefore, we could all stop keeping kosher and donating money to the United Jewish Appeal because it was all a big plate of shit.

"What?" he said, looking at our faces. "Are you shocked? Haven't you ever heard someone talk like that about their religion before?"

"I have," I said, "but they're usually Catholics."

"Don't worry," he was saying now, addressing her coffin directly as though the rest of us had melted away, and it was just the two of them again, sitting in the cluttered TV room watching *Crossfire*, "I won't let them shut me up. I will always be a Democrat. I will always hate the Republicans and their damn presidents. I'll always say whatever is on my mind, and I don't care who hears me."

There was a strange gasping sound beside me. My mother was laughing, silently, hysterically, tears streaming down her face. "My God," she whispered to me, choking back her giggles. "My God. Has he no shame? Does the man have *no shame*?"

"Everything in the house, I pick it up," he continued. "Everything in the house"—the clowns and the cockatoos, the teapots and the bells, the commemorative spoons and the souvenir wind chimes, the Chinese vases and the Japanese fans and the dolls of many eras and the dolls of many lands, the Danbury Mint's Plates of the States and the Franklin Mint's Jacqueline

Kennedy Heirloom Bride Doll and the Great Buildings of the American Century porcelain collectible series—"I pick it up, and I kiss it, because she touched it."

My uncle shrugged, and spoke for the first time in days. "Well," he muttered grudgingly, "it could have been worse."

Cremation must be nice for the family. It happens out of sight, out of mind, and when it's done you are presented with a neat little urn of something bearing no relation to the person you knew, suitable for display on a mantelpiece or tasteful scattering over the windswept shore of somewhere attractive and seeped in WASPy mythology—Nantucket, the rocky coast of your ancestral Cornwall. Perhaps it lacks a certain finality, but at least you are spared the moment when the coffin is lowered into the ground and it all becomes terrifyingly, irrevocably real; you stand in line to scoop your shovelful of earth into the grave, each one covering a little more of the lid until only the raised Star of David is visible, poking out above the growing mound of earth, then gone forever. And the sounds, the sickening *thud* of dirt hitting wood, the dull sobs of the crowd, and above it all, my grandfather keening desperately, teetering back and forth on his chair at the side of the grave: "Good-bye, honey! Good-bye, honey!"

Again and again, "Good-bye, honey!" Terrified, like a small boy frantically waving to his parents when they drop him off for the first time at summer camp; as though if he keeps them in sight, keeps calling after them, they won't be gone at all. "Good-bye, honey!"

I bury my face in Ben's shoulder and cling to him, gripped with the terrible knowledge that someday, one of us will sit wailing in a folding chair at the grave while the other is lowered into the ground. "Good-bye, honey!" until the professional grave diggers, bearded types with visible prison tattoos, grow impatient with the wavering procession of mourning Jews and take over, grabbing the shovel from an elderly cousin's hands and making short work of the mound of dirt, filling in the gap between life and death in a matter of seconds. That's how the story ends. How everybody's story ends, how marriage ends—that is, if you're lucky.

"Darling." Ben strokes my back and murmurs into my ear. "Neither of us is going to die for a very long time." I look up at him, amazed as always at how he can read my mind.

"Really?" I whisper.

"Really. Remember, this is about your grandmother. And also," he added, "you're choking me."

My mother wobbles over, wiping tears from her eyes, her heels sinking into the soft lawn. "Come on," she says. "Let's get out of here. I have eleven noodle kugels to heat up."

And so it begins again.

My father drops me at the airport early. He has to get back to the office, so he kisses me good-bye at the check-in desk and I wander alone through the familiar terminal; the Omaha Steaks kiosk, the newsstand where I once asked for a copy of *The New Yorker* and was met with a blank stare: "Is that on the bestseller list?"

Even *I* am positive that the Omaha airport is not likely to contain terrorists; still, the security apparatus on the way to the gates is state-of-the-art. The DHS money had to go somewhere, I suppose. Steel and glass walls separate the passenger from the outside world as she strips herself of most of her clothing, unpacks her bag, submits herself to search by screeners who are not only out of their teens but seem genuinely knowledgeable and concerned about doing their jobs. As I pack my laptop back into its case, I notice an elderly woman who has been asked to move aside for further screening. She is of the generation that dressed up for travel, clad in a smart plum pantsuit and orthopedic shoes that look almost new. She is about my grandmother's age.

"I'm so sorry, ma'am," says the screener as he heaves her out of her wheelchair. "It's just a randomly selected check. Required by law, you know." She holds on to his shoulder for support as he begins to pat down her legs.

"Sorry?" she says. "I should be thanking you. A man hasn't touched me like this in thirty years!"

Wiping my nose with my sleeve, I walk to my gate. It's all so silly. There are no terrorists, not in Omaha. Just a half-empty terminal of football fans and steak lovers, tramping down the runway to somewhere.

Acknowledgments

I've been dreaming of writing this particular section my whole life, but now that I'm actually doing it, I find myself completely devoid of witty asides, self-deprecating bon mots, graceful segues, or profound ruminations on the act of book writing and how it takes a village. So I'll get to the point. There are a lot of people to thank.

First and foremost, for her support, encouragement, and almost pathological optimism, I would like to thank my incredible literary agent and friend, Rebecca Friedman. Able to talk a despairing writer off the ledge, build up your ego to dizzying heights, and pepper you with phone calls—"Are you playing Scrabble online instead of working? For how many hours now? It's okay, but you need to *Stop*"—she has few equals. My wonderful and highly skilled editor, Jill Schwartzman, navigated me through the tricky terrain of first-time authorhood with warmth, insight, and patience. Rebecca Shapiro taught me the proper use of a semicolon, among other things; for this, I remain in her debt. Incredible gratitude to my friend Dario Nucci for his design brilliance; also to Michelle Spear for understanding that booze makes the model. A huge thank-you to Adam Korn and Jane von Mehren, for believing in me from the start, to Kate Blum, my publicist, and to all the staff at Villard and Random House for their tireless efforts in making this book happen. Thank you as well to Michael Martin, Ada Calhoun, Josh Neuman, Shafer Hall, Derek Zasky, and Andy Horwitz for encouraging me to write and keep writing. Also to Jack Lechner, for his invaluable help.

I am eternally grateful to my friends Lauren Marks, Bj Lockhart, Stephen Brackett, Reginald Veneziano, Neal Medlyn, Julie Klausner, and Peter Cook, for their continued existence, hilarity, and support. Thank you to the people at the deli and the liquor store down the block, who never batted an eye or slipped me the number of a support group when I wandered into their establishments in my pajamas at all hours, wild-eyed and demanding beverages. Thank you to my cat, Angelica, for confining her sitting-on-the-computer-keyboard-while-licking-own-asshole activities to alternating Tuesdays and Thursdays.

My parents, Marty and Aveva Shukert, are the best sports in the world. They are also the best parents, always ready with an ear, a plane ticket, a diagnosis, or a piece of unsolicited advice. Consider renting them, if you can afford their day rate, which is unlikely as they are priceless. Thanks to my sister, Ariel Shukert, for being the only one who understands. Special thanks and love to my grandfather Nate Shukert, and my late grandmother Doris Garland Shukert, whom I miss every day. And to my husband, Ben Abramowitz, always and forever.

Most of all, thank you to the city of Omaha. It knows why.

About the Author

RACHEL SHUKERT was born and raised in Omaha, Nebraska. Her stories and poems have been published in *Nerve*, *Heeb*, and *McSweeney's*, and her plays have been performed extensively in New York City, as well as in Massachusetts and the Netherlands. *Have You No Shame?* is her first book. She lives in Manhattan with her husband, her cat, and her demons.